DEDICATED to all those around the world who are working in the spirit of divine love to help create a healthy, magnificent, universalistic human society.

cooking for consciousness

a handbook for the spiritually minded vegetarian

Recipe creation and testing: Joy McClure
Written by Kendall Layne, with some help
  from Jody Wright and Joy McClure
Illustrated by Andrea Waxler
Lay-out and production by Jody Wright

Ananda Marga Publications
854 Pearl Street
Denver, CO 80203
U.S.A.

second printing

Printed in the United States of America.

ISBN 0-88476-008-1

Library of Congress Catalog Card Number: 76-12831

Those interested in learning more about Ananda Marga, its service work or meditation teachings may contact Ananda Marga, 854 Pearl Street, Denver, Colorado 80203, U.S.A.

contents

OUR SAVIORS

We want to express our heartfelt appreciation of the many people who have helped bring this book into being. Special thanks to:

Anneshvari (Andrea Waxler), who used her creative talent to illustrate this book.

Jody Wright (Devi Nistha), our second wind, for super-human efforts, including taking responsibility for the layout and production;

(Laurie Ann Raspberry) S'yama, for the inspiration and the long hours at the layout table, which made it possible to meet our deadline;

Terry Twombly, who helped us with typing, recipe testing and moral support during the middle years of the project;

Michael Beeson, who prodded us along in the beginning and helped write a section or two;

our son Joshua, for being an angel and giving us space to finish this incredible undertaking;

Kate, for all the help with testing recipes;

The beautiful person who kept the only copy of the original manuscript for two months (after we lost it hitch-hiking) and finally figured out who we were and returned it to us;

Dr. Anthony Fink, Assistant Professor of Chemistry at UCSC, who read the second-to-the-last draft of the Nutrition section and pointed out some of the most glaring errors in it;

Kamala, who was supportive when we needed it most, and read and criticized the entire manuscript;

Jinaneshvar and Mahesh, who also read and commented on the manuscript;

Evelyn, who spent long hours typesetting;

Dianaji, who provided a crucial bit of last-minute inspiration;

Terry of Book People for his advice;

Prakash, Malati, Priya Devii, Gomati, Tapasvini, Larry Mills, Mike, Jayantha Kumar, Shakti Deva, Jane, and Arun, who all helped in their own ways.

Thanks also to everyone who helped test recipes, and to all our friends who, for four long years, believed in us (or at least didn't laugh too loudly at us) while we struggled to produce this book.

Lastly, but most important of all, our humble thanks to Shrii Shrii Anandamurtijii and his hard-working helpers, especially Acarya Yatiishvarananda Avadhutaji, Acarya Jagadevaji and Vimalanandaji for guiding us on the path of meditation, helping us learn to love unconditionally, and inspiring us to let our energies be utilized in the creation of this book.

Joy and Kendall

introduction

Preparing good tasting, nutritious natural food is easy and fun. All that's necessary are a few basic skills, the right ingredients, and a little bit of time. In order to help you discover your own unique way of cooking and living, we have gathered together some of the recipes and techniques which have evolved in our kitchens, and compiled information about food, nutrition, diet systems, herbs and many other topics.

Cooking for Consciousness is based on the practical experience of several natural food cooks. It is designed to introduce the beginning cook to the joy of natural food cookery as well as to provide the experienced cook with new and interesting approaches to the preparation of healthful, delicious foods.

An attempt has been made to present both the recipes and the general information in a form that encourages and assists exploration and experimentation, without ignoring more specific points on how to purchase and prepare natural food.

In the discussions of nutrition, digestion, cooking techniques and other subjects, we have tried to limit ourselves to providing information that can be used by each individual in his or her personal decisions about food. However, the general focus and tone of the book do reflect the attitudes and beliefs of the authors. Pure and simple natural foods, love, and nutritionally sound methods of preparation are emphasized throughout the book.

Here are some notes on the organization of the book:

• The recipes are organized into sections according to the main ingredients (**FRUITS, GRAINS AND CEREALS, MILK PRODUCTS**) or the type of recipe (**SALADS AND SALAD DRESSINGS, MAIN DISHES**, etc.).

• The arrangement of recipe sections tends to go from the simple and essential foods (**FRUITS** and **VEGETABLES**) to the more complex (**SAUCES AND GRAVIES** and **DESSERTS**), ending with **HERBS AND SPICES** and **CANNING AND PRESERVING**.

• A comprehensive **INDEX** is located in the very back of the book.

• Each section begins with a detailed **Table of Contents** to help make the finding of a favorite recipe as easy as possible. A separate **Recipe Index** following the comprehensive **Index** will also help you find these.

• Ingredients which are in **bold face** are the titles of recipes which can be found elsewhere in the book (example: **Citrus Cooler**). Check the **INDEX** for their location.

• Chapters on basic foods (**FRUITS, VEGE-TABLES, MILK PRODUCTS**, etc.) begin with mini-encyclopedias on the purchasing, storage, and preparation of foods in that category.

• All of the recipes in this book have been thoroughly tested. Many of the recipes include suggestions for substitutions or variations which the authors like but which have not been as thoroughly tested as the recipes themselves.

• **HERBS AND SPICES** section has many herb blend recipes that are called for throughout the book.

• The **KITCHEN WAYS** section discusses various aspects of establishing and working in a natural foods kitchen.

• **CONVERSIONS AND EQUIVALENTS** contains tables of equivalent measures and instructions for converting American measures to metrics and other systems of measurement.

All the good food in the world is not enough to make even a single person truly healthy and happy. Health and the sense of well-being which accompanies it is the result of attuning oneself to natural laws and living by the principles these laws make clear. This harmonizing of one's life is spiritual in nature. The goal of **Cooking for Consciousness** is to help us all to become more in tune with these natural precepts and begin to relate them to our eating habits. The information and recipes included here are intended as an aid to spiritual growth. They are a guide to the establishment of eating habits which will build a healthy body and create and strengthen the calm mental vibration needed for meditation.

In the pages that follow, you will find recipes for a wide assortment of dishes (some old favorites, and some new treats) which supply, in an appetising and easily digestible form, all the nutrients known to be beneficial.

When these nutrients are provided, together with adequate amounts of sunshine, fresh air, and pure water, the body can grow, do work, resist disease, repair itself, and carry on the multitude of activities necessary to provide a home for that mysterious thing we call consciousness. Physical health and emotional and mental well-being are the foundations of a satisfying and beautiful life. Spiritual growth and service to humanity are the culmination of that life, and the fullest expression of human potential.

All of us who worked on this book would like to extend our most heartfelt Namaskar to each of you. Namaskar means: I respect and love the divinity within you with all of my mind and all of my heart.

meditation

"There is in the living being
a thirst for limitlessness."
— Shrii Shrii Anandamurti

It is the inborn desire of all human beings
to seek an identity beyond our limited selves,
to try to find our place in the universe, and
to want to experience the harmonious unity
of creation. This search is basic to our
humanity, and although worldly activities
take up much of our time they can never
really satisfy our innermost desires.

Everyone has experienced the uncertainty
of this life, the loneliness and pain which are
part of not knowing where one is going. We
feel a certain restlessness inside of ourselves,
a kind of emptiness, if we do not know why
we are here on this earth.

A few years ago, under the direction of a
teacher trained in India by an organization
called Ananda Marga, the authors of this book
began to follow the systematic program of
spiritual practices developed by Shrii Shrii
Anandamurtijii. Through meditation and
supportive practices we have begun to realize
that the Infinite Divinity (which transcends
our limited selves) is to be found at the core
of our own beings. Making an effort, stretch-
ing and unfolding every part of our being and
striving to get in touch with that fountain of
love that is within us has been the most
wonderful and exhilarating experience of our
lives. This journey, despite all the conflicts it
has involved, has repaid us innumerable times
over for the trouble we took to establish a
regular pattern of twice-daily meditation in
our life. We have started to realize why we
have been born on this earth and our inner
longings are beginning to be filled.

Ananda Marga was founded by Shrii Shrii Anandamurti in 1955 for the purpose of spreading spiritual practices throughout the world. Ananda Marga local chapters offer free classes to anyone who wants to learn meditation. Advanced practices are taught by highly trained teachers whose intense dedication to serving humanity is an example for us all. Meditation and the other spiritual practices taught by Ananda Marga (Ananda Marga is a Sanskrit term meaning Path of Bliss) can help a person develop an improved ability to concentrate, increased energy and greater clarity of perception. Many people practicing these spiritual exercises have used this extra energy and their increased abilities to serve other people who have great needs. They have worked in prisons and rest homes to better conditions and inspire the residents. They have started schools and orphanages around the world, distributed food and clothing free of charge to those in need, and set up literacy programs in needy areas. They have set up relief teams which have instantly been able to go to the scenes of disasters, working in areas such as Bengladesh, Philippines, Nicaragua, and Guatemala. This work to improve the state of human life on this planet is an integral part of Ananda Marga spiritual practices.

If you are interested in finding out more about Ananda Marga or about meditation check the phone directory to see if one of the hundreds of chapters located around the world is in your area. Or, write to:

Ananda Marga
854 Pearl Street
Denver, Colorado 80203
U.S.A.

(303) 832 - 6465

food
and
consciousness

The effects of food on the body are fairly well understood. Current scientific theories hold that the physical molecules of the food are utilized by the body to supply energy and the substances necessary for the building, repairing, and regulating of the various tissues. Improper diet is well-known to have a negative effect on these processes.

The effects of food on the mind are, however, just beginning to be acknowledged here in the West. Fairly recent research indicates that the symptoms of schizophrenia, hyper-activity, and certain mental disorders can be alleviated by corrective diet therapy. Many people who have experimented with natural foods and vegetarianism have experienced themselves and the world around them in a different, more positive way as a result of changes in their diet. Although these pheno-mena are considered surprising, and difficult to explain to many Westerners, Eastern philosophy has a simple explanation for them which is quite logical and parallels some of the most far-reaching theorizing in Western science.

We have learned from Einstein's Theory of Relativity that the entire manifested universe is composed of vibrational energy. Matter can be understood as energy that is moving (or vibrating) slowly. Solids vibrate at the lowest (or slowest) frequencies, liquids and gases a little faster, and sound, light, thoughts and certain other energies vibrate at even higher frequencies. The higher frequencies can interpenetrate the lower frequencies. Light passes through water, sound travels through air, and in a similar way, the food we eat is permeated with its own subtle vibrations and those it has picked up from the people who have handled it. These subtle vibrations are incorporated into the mind of the person eating the food. Food that is grown, pre-pared, and eaten with love can uplift the mind as well as nourish the body.

Over the last few thousand years, spiritual teachers have based their eating habits on this knowledge. Certain foods affect consciousness in a positive way, sharpening and clearing the mind; these foods are called sentient (Sattvik in Sanskrit) and are the basis of the yogic diet. Foods which stimulate the body and mind are termed mutative (or Rajasik) and are eaten in moderation or not at all by those performing spiritual practices. Foods that are not normally beneficial to the mind or body are called static (or Tamasik) and are not normally part of the yogic diet.

We have listed below some common foods according to the way that they are classified by the preceptor of Ananda Marga, Shrii Shrii Anandamurti. These classifications may vary slightly according to the climate, and the age, health and activities of the individual.

FOOD CLASSIFICATIONS

SENTIENT FOODS:

fruits
most vegetables
most beans
grains
milk and milk products
moderate amounts of most herbs and spices

MUTATIVE FOODS:

caffinated beverages (coffee, regular tea, colas, etc.)
medicines prescribed by a doctor
excessive spices

STATIC FOODS:

meat and poultry
fish and shell fish
onions, garlic, green onions and chives
wine, beer and other alcoholic beverages
mushrooms or fungus
fermented soy sauce or tamari
drugs other than medicines
food that is fermented, stale or spoiled or been kept too long
eggs

It is clear that what we eat has a definite effect on our minds and bodies, particularly in relationship to spiritual practices. It is not surprising then that the reverse is also true: that the spiritual practices we do (along with the activities we do in our lives) also effect how food is absorbed by our bodies and how effectively it is used. Particularly, the practicing of asanas (yoga postures) are helpful to the digestive system and the general health of all the organs. A clean and healthy inner body allows food to be utilized most effectively. Asanas, like all spiritual practices, need to be part of a complete framework of practices involving physical, mental and spiritual growth. This is best learned under the instruction of teachers well-trained in the subtle aspects of these postures and in the teaching of meditation and related practices. With this proper guidance we can move towards a better understanding of the deeper truths of the universe.

For more information about vegetarianism, send $ .50 to:

Ananda Marga Publications
854 Pearl Street
Denver, Colorado 80203
U.S.A.

and ask for the booklet
What's Wrong With Eating Meat?

nourishment

NOURISHMENT

To nourish means "to support the growth of," so nourishment is that which supports growth. Meditation and other spiritual practices directly contribute to the growth of that Cosmic Consciousness which exists in seed form in every unit mind. The physical body is also nourished by meditation, but in the main we are reliant upon physical matter for the nourishment of the body. In this section, the ways and means of obtaining nourishment from food will be examined from three basic viewpoints.

First, the manner in which food is taken is considered in EATING HABITS. Then, information about various DIET SYSTEMS is presented. Lastly, the major nutrients are discussed in the sub-section on NUTRITION.

EATING HABITS

In recent times, scientific research (in the West) has not been too concerned with ascertaining the effects of eating habits on the health of the body and the mind. Quite a bit of attention has been paid to establishing and publicizing "minimum daily requirements" of protein, vitamins, and other nutritional factors, but little notice has been taken of the manner in which nourishment is obtained. Various guidelines for eating have been presented in books about natural foods and diet; however, since most of the authors lack scientific credentials, this potentially valuable source of information has not received a great deal of attention, and only in recent times has it begun to have much influence on popular opinion or behavior.

In the belief that how we eat may be as important as what we eat, we have listed here some of the most commonly offered advice about eating habits. Although no claims are made for their universal applicability, all of the practices suggested appear to the authors to be sensible and to contribute to proper digestion and an overall sense of well-being. If any of the suggestions sound reasonable to you, try following them for a while — a week, a month, or even intermittently — and see if the changes in how you feel are to your liking.

When making changes in your diet and eating habits, it is advisable to proceed gradually and carefully in the direction that you choose, paying close attention to signals from your body and avoiding drastic modification of your past habits. Rapid changes in the diet can cause considerable discomfort and may even lower the body's resistance to disease. Developing your intuition is probably the best way to learn what to eat: your body will let you know what it needs if you learn to listen to and interpret its messages.

One of the things which many people notice when they begin experimenting with new eating habits or diets is that they get impulses to revert to old habits, or to eat something they have eliminated from their diet. It is important to have firm discipline with oneself in these matters, but it is also important not to force oneself to ignore cravings, for they may indicate that the digestive system is not yet fully adjusted to the new eating habits or that a certain food is needed to provide a nutrient which is not available from the new diet. There is, however, a very fine line between being aware of and responsive to cravings and simply indulging desires, and the proper response to a craving is not always apparent. If you are convinced that an urge you feel is based on a genuine need of your system, try satisfying it — but remember to notice the effects on your mind and body, so that you can learn from the experience. In this way, one's awareness of the body's needs can develop into an accurate and reliable guide to behavior.

Learning to discipline oneself and consciously rearrange one's habits is perhaps the most difficult task there is, but it is also one of the most rewarding activities in which to engage oneself. In our striving to fulfill the divine purpose, we might easily get too attached to thinking or worrying about our diet, posture, and other concerns of the physical body, and this could distract our attention from meditation and other matters of importance. It is well to remember, though, that the body is a divine temple, and that a healthy body is a good foundation for a calm and peaceful awareness.

Here are the suggestions:

1) SEE ONLY GOD. Perhaps the most important part of taking food is the feeling of devotion which arises from realizing where the food comes from and the purpose for which it is being used. Food is a manifestation of Cosmic Consciousness. It is utilized to maintain the body, which is a necessity for doing spiritual practices.

2) EAT ONLY WHEN YOU ARE HUNGRY AND DO NOT OVEREAT. Americans have in the past enjoyed a material wealth which puts overeating within the means of almost all and overeating is indeed a common habit. Many times what people call "hunger pains" are in reality signs of indigestion, resulting from overeating at the previous meal.

In order to determine for yourself what real hunger feels like, you might want to try fasting for a day or two. If you find that you feel slightly nauseous during a fast, don't worry. Your body is cleansing itself of toxins, and you may experience some unpleasant sensations. Often the stomach is unable to cleanse itself because it is so overloaded with food all the time. When this happens, some people believe that toxins are stored. During a fast, these toxins are released into the bloodstream and eliminated. The nausea that accompanies this release of toxins is what is commonly misinterpreted as a signal to eat. After the nausea has passed, a wonderful, light, empty feeling comes, and after that, a genuine hunger — very different from what usually passes for hunger.

Fasting is often acclaimed as an aid to spiritual growth, which indeed it can be. However, it is not always beneficial, and in order to maximize the benefit of the fast, there are some pitfalls to avoid. Eating heavily right before a fast will reduce its cleansing effect, and breaking a fast with a heavy meal may be quite a shock to the system. If one is not accustomed to fasting, it may be wise to avoid strenuous activity during or immediately after the fast. Excessive fasting can be a strain on the body, and may lead to an overall decrease in health and vitality. There is more discussion of fasting under DIET SYSTEMS.

3) EAT SLOWLY AND CHEW THE FOOD THOROUGHLY. Hurried meals and the accompanying nervous tension are an invitation to indigestion. Food that is well chewed will practically swallow itself — an indication that it is ready to pass into the stomach. Thorough chewing reduces the size of food particles and mixes them with saliva, which greatly facilitates enzyme action in the stomach and small intestine during digestion. Careful chewing also reduces the likelihood of overeating; food that is bolted is usually not tasted, and the satisfaction of the taste buds is an important part of the meal. The desire for dessert often disappears when a meal is thoroughly chewed and enjoyed.

4) EAT A SUBSTANTIAL AMOUNT OF FRESH RAW FOODS, AND AVOID OVERCOOKED AND OVERPROCESSED FOODS. Fresh raw foods supply a subtle form of energy called "prana" or vital force. The yogic scriptures teach that all life is dependent on prana for its very existence, and that the foods we eat can be an important source of prana. Fresh raw foods, because they are closer to being alive than cooked or processed foods, are more able to give their life to us. Raw fruits and vegetables also ease the bowels, promoting the rapid elimination of waste products and rejuvenating intestinal walls made unhealthy by improper diet. They are also among the best dietary sources of many vitamins and trace minerals.

Sometimes cooking is an important aid to digestion — for example, it helps convert starches into the more easily assimilable sugars. However, many vitamins are heat sensitive and are destroyed during cooking. In addition, raw foods contain enzymes which aid digestion, and these too are often destroyed by heat. Proteins undergo certain changes in the presence of heat. Some of these changes render the protein harder to digest, while others make the protein easier to digest.

Processing of food, whether by the refining out of valuable nutrients or the addition of toxic chemicals, renders that food much less valuable to our bodies.

5) EAT ONLY WHEN CALM AND RELAXED. The physical body is influenced by the emotions, and digestion is generally hampered by tension, anger, and other negative states of mind. A few moments spent in silent appreciation of the perfection of the universe is one way to release tension and calm the mind before eating, and can help make meals a more enjoyable part of the day.

6) EAT REGULARLY. Biological organisms have rhythms that are attuned to cycles of day and night, spring and fall, et cetera, and regular meals are an important part of these rhythms. Some people advocate eating a large meal in the morning (perhaps including protein) to provide energy for the day. It is thought that the body can rest more fully if the stomach is not burdened with a large evening meal. Others maintain that eating in the morning occupies the body with digestion, when energy is needed for the day's tasks, and that digestion can proceed during sleep without harm. Still others take a large meal at midday. With some experimentation, you can probably find a rhythm that suits you and your lifestyle — but don't be afraid to vary it somewhat to adapt to changing conditions in your life.

7) ALLOW PLENTY OF TIME BETWEEN MEALS. Digestion is a complex process, and as each type of food digests most easily in a particular chemical environment, the addition of undigested food of the wrong kind to a partially digested meal can upset or interrupt the digestive processes. For example, a highly alkaline mass can interrupt protein digestion in the stomach, by altering the pH of the stomach contents. Eating two protein foods too close together may also reduce their digestibility, due to competition for digestive enzymes and absorption sites. Try waiting five or six hours between meals, until you are able to distinguish between wanting to eat again and being ready to eat again. A glass of warm water drunk twenty minutes to an hour before a meal will help clear away any food remaining in the stomach. This practice seems to help prevent indigestion.

8) BE GUIDED BY YOUR INTUITION. There is no rigid system of rules or guidelines that is appropriate at all times in all places. It is important to stay tuned to oneself, to feel what each new day has to offer and what you need to eat (if anything) to maximize your health and energy for the day. But be careful not to let your desires masquerade as intuition.

9) AVOID EATING VERY HOT OR VERY COLD FOODS. Hot and cold foods unnecessarily tax the digestive system. They interfere with the action of the digestive enzymes, many of which can function only within a limited range of temperature. In addition, hot foods may damage the mucous membranes which line the digestive tract.

10) DRINK PLENTY OF WATER. Water is the main constituent of the physical body. It is essential in innumerable ways to the maintenance of proper health. An adequate supply of water helps insure prompt elimination of waste products, helps regulate body temperature, and aids in digestion. However, some sources advise not drinking large quantities of liquids for half an hour before or an hour or so after a meal. The presence of too much liquid with a meal may cause the stomach to empty prematurely, resulting in incomplete digestion and absorption.

11) EAT SIMPLY. Although there is an abundant variety of food provided for our nourishment, not all of it is meant to be eaten at once. Observe young children who are allowed to choose their own food (and who haven't been overly conditioned by their surroundings). Often they will eat freely of one or two foods only at a meal, and then at the next meal they will eat something else. Of course it is important to eat a balanced diet — but it is not necessary to eat "a little of everything" at each meal.

DIET SYSTEMS

There are many theories about what constitutes an adequate, healthy diet, and a corresponding number of systems of diet based on these theories. Since lifestyle, genetic inheritance, metabolic processes and food preferences vary so widely from one individual to another, it might be possible for all these different theories to be at least somewhat "correct," even though they appear, on the surface, to be inconsistent with each other.

In this section, we have described and discussed a representative sampling of the currently popular systems of diet which are at home in a natural foods cookbook, trying in each case to relate the theory as well as the practice, and point out the shortcomings as well as the advantages of each system. There are whole books written on each of these diets. We have limited our comments, trying only to relate the general ideas of each system. Again, we suggest being open-minded but cautious in your dietary explorations.

We'll look first at what could be called a basic vegetarian "natural foods" diet. Although it more closely resembles the typical American diet than anything else we'll be considering, there are some important differences. Instead of relying primarily on flesh for a protein source, there is an emphasis on nuts and seeds, beans (especially soy), grains, and dairy products. Whole grains are eaten in preference to their refined counterparts (white rice, white flour, et cetera). They supply vitamins, minerals, and essential fatty acids, in addition to protein and carbohydrates.

Fresh fruits and vegetables, their juices, and unsulphured sun-dried fruit are excellent sources of vitamins and minerals, and these foods are important constituents of the basic natural foods diet.

In our experience, produce (and other foods) are generally better tasting and more nutritious when they are "organic," that is, planted in living soil which has been enriched without the use of chemical fertilizers, grown without the use of chemical sprays, and processed without the numerous additives, preservatives, and other adulterants commonly used by commercial operators. It's also a nice way to reduce one's involvement with practices which threaten the quality of our environment.

Pure unrefined vegetable oils are one of the most abundant sources of essential fatty acids, and are definitely preferable to highly refined oils. Vegetable oils, in their natural state, contain vitamin E and other anti-oxidants which are destroyed by the higher temperatures associated with most extraction processes. Apparently, from everything we've heard, sesame oil can be extracted at much lower temperatures than other oils. Unrefined virgin olive oil is excellent in salad dressing. Sesame and peanut oils have higher breaking points (i.e., can get hotter before they begin to smoke and undergo molecular breakdown) than most other oils. For this reason, they are good choices for frying. Peanuts, however, are typically subjected to much larger quantities of chlorinated hydrocarbons (including DDT) than other crops. "Cold pressed" safflower oil is (in our experience on the West Coast) often relatively inexpensive compared to oils of similar quality, and is suitable for salad dressing, baking, or sauteing at moderate temperatures. Safflower, peanut, soy, corn, sesame and sunflower oils are

apparently richer in essential fatty acids than most other oils, (Adelle Davis, **Let's Get Well**). Margarine is often made from cottonseed oil. Cotton is heavily poisoned, and these toxins may remain in the margarine. Also, there is some evidence that artificially hydrogenated fats (like margarine) may contain heavy metal residues. (Nickel is used as a catalyst in the process.)

Honey, date particles, molasses and pure maple syrup are used in preference to refined white sugar. Brown sugar and the so-called "raw" sugars are in reality (at least in California, under law) white sugar to which various quantities of molasses have been reintroduced. Some people believe that refined sugars overstimulate insulin production, causing a "let down" feeling, and also rob the body of protein and minerals. (Adelle Davis, **Let's Get Well.**) When purchasing honey, be aware that the words "raw" and "uncooked" are not synonymous, and that even when both are used to describe a given honey, it may have been heated to as much as 140°. (Heat is often destructive of enzymes and vitamins.) Darker honeys are said to contain more minerals than the lighter honeys. Color may also be an indicator of the amount of refining the honey has been through, though there is natural variation in the color of different kinds of honey.

Unrefined sea salt, which contains many trace minerals, is preferable to commercial salts, which usually contain dextrose and aluminum hydrochloride.

These foods are the basic ingredients of any natural foods diet. Many diet systems, however, emphasize or exclude certain of these foods, for various reasons. (Some also include other foods, such as flesh, eggs, etc.)

MACROBIOTICS, the "Oriental plan for total health" which has received so much public attention in Europe and North America, is perhaps the most criticized of all the various diet systems. Not being macrobiotics ourselves, we hesitantly include words which attempt to convey our understanding of the subject. Enshallah ("God willing," as the Arabs say), we will help alleviate confusion instead of creating more. Macrobiotics means "great techniques of rejuvenation." (Sakurazawa Nyoit, **You Are All Sanpaku**, p. 80.) The primary concern of this discipline, as it relates to food, is to balance the intake of "yin" foods and "yang" foods (the terms meaning respectively "expansive" and "contractive"), in order to rejuvenate the body and secure "physical well being, emotional happiness, sexual vigor and longevity." Grains, especially brown rice and buckwheat, are the heart of the macrobiotic diet; they are said to have the proper balance of sodium (yang) and potassium (yin).

Energy flows in the body seem to be related to the sodium-potassium balance in any given cell and in the organism as a whole, and from this standpoint, macrobiotics makes sense. Nutritionists and MD's, however, point out that the stricter macrobiotic regimens (there are ten different "levels" or diets) are not balanced diets. Raw fruits and vegetables, which are excellent sources of vitamins and minerals, are considered, in most cases, to be excessively yin, and although some macrobiotics eat animal products (primarily sea food and eggs), those who don't (if they follow the books by George Oshawa that we've read) may not get an adequate supply of complete protein.

Some vegetables are included in most macrobiotic diets, although tomatoes, potatoes and eggplant are regarded as overly yin. Sweet things and dairy products (except eggs) are shunned, and one is supposed to limit one's intake of fluids, drinking mostly small quantities of grain coffee and bancha tea. "Rice fasts" (eating only brown rice) and diet No. 7 (100% cereals and grains) are recommended for illness, and in general for yangizing out-of-balance systems. These recommendations do not make much sense if one believes the research which demonstrates the need in human nutrition for various vitamins (notably ascorbic acid and B-12) which are not provided in these diets.

According to our nutritional knowledge and beliefs, one could follow one of the macrobiotic diets which included a variety of foods including vegetables if they studied protein combining and made sure they were obtaining enough protein, and watched to make sure they got enough vitamins of all types.

Macrobiotics includes much more than just a change of diet. It includes a whole philosophy emphasizing living in harmony with the world. There are many books available, especially those by George Oshawa, that explain more about it.

Another system that is concerned with an abstract energy theory is the "Sattvic" or "yogic" diet (which is quite similar to, but not identical with, the "vegan" diet). The

Sattvic diet is discussed in the section on **Food and Consciousness**.

CLEANSING DIETS: There are a number of different cleansing diets, most of which emphasize raw foods. Some include only freshly extracted juices, others are limited to "mucusless" foods (fruits, vegetables, nuts and seeds), and still others define anything (except animal products) that is raw as "good" and anything cooked as "bad." These diets tend to be low protein, which many people regard as unhealthy. However, a belief commonly held by followers of these systems is that excessive protein intake is related to many maladies, and that a small amount of protein is sufficient for the body's needs if it is well digested. (People on excessively high protein diets end up using a lot of the protein as fuel — carbohydrates are a "cleaner" fuel.)

The general theory of cleansing diets is that cooked and processed foods are devitalized, and that they deplete the body instead of nourishing it. Some of these diets consider cultivated grains unhealthy because they are a product of civilization, not of nature. Others draw the line at cooked foods, and still others include some cooked vegetables in the ranks of "ok" food.

All of the diets we have (somewhat simple-mindedly) lumped together as "cleansing diets" can be tried for an occasional change of pace — some folks regularly vacillate between these diets and heavier food (such as grains, protein foods, etc.). One common practice is to prepare for a fast by eating only small amounts of raw foods, then to fast (perhaps taking water occasionally), and finally to break the fast with juices, gradually reintroducing heavier foods. This procedure can greatly enhance the benefits of fasting — it allows the body time to adjust itself to the changes instead of shocking the system by abruptly halting the food intake, and then shocking it again by reintroducing heavy foods immediately after the fast.

FASTING is, of course, a cleansing procedure and is employed as a purification technique in many cultures. One of the main reasons for fasting is to allow the body time to "catch up" on its housecleaning. For example, the stomach, when it is empty, can literally wash itself with its own secretions. However, if it is never allowed to become totally empty, this process apparently cannot take place, and unelimated toxins are then stored. During a fast, these toxins are eliminated, sometimes causing feelings of nausea or illness. Until fasting has become a familiar routine, it may be wise to plan your fast for a quiet day when you have no responsibilities, in order to allow the body and mind to concentrate on the cleansing process.

Shrii Shrii Anandamurti, the preceptor of Ananda Marga, recommends fasting on the 11th day after the full and new moons. These days seem to be ideal for cleansing the system and increasing mental and spiritual purity.

JUICE DIETS (which, according to some people, overtax the kidneys) are supposed to flush out the body's wastes. Juices are easily assimilable, and are excellent sources of many vitamins and minerals, but, as is typical of this kind of diet, supply only small amounts of protein. (See **JUICE** section.) Some folks regard juice diets somewhat negatively, due to the almost total dependency on technology (i.e., electric juicers) which is a necessary part of the regimen. However, hand-operated juicers are available. Other purists follow certain variations of the mucusless diet which is oriented toward reproducing man's "original diet" on the theory that this is the true key to health. Uncooked wild foods, fruits, vegetables, nuts, and seeds are the mainstays of this way of eating. There are numerous other diets which are based on raw foods and/or designed to cleanse the body, but in the interest of brevity, they will not be discussed here.

FOOD COMBINING: Yet another way of regarding diet remains to be examined: the art and science of food combining. Since, as was pointed out earlier in the text, each type of food digests most easily in a specific chemical environment, some people believe that it is important to combine at any given meal only those foods which can be easily and harmoniously digested together. A basic understanding of the process of digestion is an important foundation for wise food combining. Combining protein foods to increase their value to the body is discussed in the **NUTRITION** sub-section which follows this discussion. Here is an abbreviated explanation of what happens to the food we take into our bodies.

Digestion is a process of transformation. Complex food-stuffs are digested (literally "carried apart" from the Latin) into simpler substances that can pass into the bloodstream and be utilized or stored by the body. Most of the changes that occur during the process of digestion are chemical in nature. Certain protein molecules called enzymes act as catalysts (a catalyst is a substance that causes or speeds up a chemical reaction without itself undergoing any permanent chemical change) in the complex "breaking apart" (and reconstruction) of the molecules of foodstuffs into forms usable by the body. These enzymes are very specific, that is, each works only on a limited class of molecules. One enzyme, pepsin, is able to break long protein molecules into shorter molecules (called proteoses and peptones); others are required to separate these intermediary chains into amino acids, the form in which proteins may be assimilated. Still other enzymes are necessary for the digestion of sugars, fats, and other nutrients.

Enzymes and other digestive secretions are mixed with food in the mouth, stomach, and intestine. Carbohydrates, if they are thoroughly chewed, become mixed with pytalin, which is secreted in the saliva. They begin their digestion in the stomach, if the pH of the stomach contents is not too low. Other food-stuffs are broken into small particles by chewing and then mixed with secretions in the stomach and either begin to digest there, or else are emptied into the duodenum (upper small intestine) for digestion. Naturopaths speak about digestion as a process of controlled fermentation: if too much food, or the wrong combinations are eaten, the fermentation takes place spontaneously, out of control, resulting in toxic material which is useless and burdensome to the system. So, if this analogy is correct, it is important that food be digested before it rots. This is especially true of fruits.

Fruits move through the digestive tract relatively rapidly — unless they encounter obstacles, such as undigested food. (Generally, food is "layered" in the stomach and is digested roughly in the order in which it was ingested.) When fruits are left undigested, due to the presence of heavier food, they may rot fairly quickly, producing carbon dioxide gas, water, and alcohol. (This is speculation on the part of the authors. So far, biochemists have confirmed that this process is chemically possible, but no one we've talked to really knows what goes on in this situation.) For this reason, many people eat fruit alone, and only when they have a very empty stomach.

Proteins require an acid medium (optimal pH approximately 1 - 4) for the first stage of their digestion; carbohydrates require an alkaline medium (optimal pH approximately 5 - 7). Therefore, it is thought that proteins and starches do not combine well.

This belief is based on two ideas. The first is that carbohydrates can undergo a reasonable amount of digestion in the stomach, if the pH is not too low. Some studies have shown that the stomach is almost always too acidic for this to be possible. However, these results could be explained in terms of protein residue being more or less constantly present in the stomach, due to improper eating habits. (Meats, for example, can take an extraordinarily long time to digest). It is difficult to believe that our bodies are so inefficient that the stomach secretes hydrochloric acid even when that process is not necessary, i.e., when the stomach is truly empty. (This may seem like an overly complicated explanation, but it is the logical justification for not combining large amounts of starch and protein, and

therefore is of some importance) The second idea underlying beliefs about food combining is that it is desirable to digest food as efficiently as possible. Having carbohydrates waiting around for protein to "move on down the line" is seen as inefficient. In fact, experiments have shown that the presence of large quantities of carbohydrate will halt the action of pepsin completely, thereby disabling the body's protein digestion mechanism for a short period of time.

The main objection to this combination is that it increases the amount of time required for digestion. If you do not have trouble with combining proteins and starches you may not have to worry about this.

The presence of oil in the digestive tract triggers what is known as a "decrease in gastric motility" — which means it slows down the emptying of the stomach and increases the total time needed for digestion of whatever food it is mixed with during cooking or in the stomach. This functions to prevent overeating. A lack of fatty acids in the diet can result in obesity due to incessant hunger.

Although there are some differences of opinion in this matter, it is generally agreed by persons concerned with food combining that:

• non-starchy vegetables combine well with proteins;

• all vegetables (except tomatoes, which are an acid fruit) combine well with carbohydrates;

• milk products are best eaten alone or with vegetables or fruit (cheese can be combined with nuts, as both are high in oil — other proteins digest at different rates, and for this reason, it is better not to combine them with milk products);

• fruits are best eaten alone, on an empty stomach, although some people mix them with milk products or nuts, and claim that this doesn't cause them any problems;

• proteins do not combine well with carbohydrates.

These general rules will be more or less true for certain individuals, depending on what kind of shape the digestive system is in, various metabolic rates, et cetera. And, of course, many people seem quite content without following these suggestions at all.

Aside from the attempt to explain food combining in terms of optimizing biochemical processes, it is important to note that people generally get into following food combining rules for more practical reasons. Usually, a person gets turned on to the ideas, tries them out, and is impressed by the improvement in digestion, sense of well-being, et cetera. In short, most people who follow food combining rules do so because "it feels good."

NUTRITION

We owe it to the Divinity within us to provide our bodies with pure, healthful foods containing all the nutrients needed to maintain a state of glowing health. When the mind has been purified by meditation and the body has been purified by proper diet and practice of yoga postures (a'sanas), such perfect harmony can be established between mind and body that one knows intuitively what to eat, and the intellect is not needed to select the proper foods. For those (including ourselves) who still need to think about the foods they eat, we have collected some information about the needs of our bodies and how they can be met. The research we have done has led us to three general conclusions: (1) we all need certain substances, called nutrients, to establish and maintain our health. When any of these substances are not provided in the necessary amounts or combinations in the diet, health is imperfect. Although the resultant physical and psychological manifestations may not always appear to be related to diet, it is increasingly clear that many illnesses can be linked to improper diet. (2) The typical American diet is not the best diet that can be imagined. Many beneficial substances are processed out of our foods, and many strange manufactured things which might fairly be labelled garbage, are represented to the consumer as food. (3) The elimination of overprocessed, chemically treated foods from one's diet and the eating of primarily organically-grown, natural foods can result in a noticeable and remarkable improvement in health.

Health is more than just the ability to plod through the day and perform one's tasks: we understand the term to mean a sense of well being and satisfaction with life, as well as the absence of disease. In order to enjoy good health, we need to supply our systems with all the necessary nutrients, and from this standpoint, all are equally important. However, we begin our discussion of nutrition in a conventional way — by talking about protein.

PROTEIN

Protein is often referred to as the "building material" of the body. This is an accurate and literal description. Most of our body tissues are formed from protein. Proteins are also very important in enzyme systems, antibodies, and disease fighting white blood cells. Vegetarians obtain protein from milk products, soy and other beans, nuts, seeds, and grains primarily. Proteins are constructed from smaller molecules known as amino acids. When protein is ingested, it is broken down into its constituent amino acids, which are then utilized individually or re-assembled into the various types or protein the body needs. There are about 22 amino acids, of which all but eight so-called "essential amino acids" (EAAs) can normally be snythesized in the body. If one of these eight amino acids is missing, the others cannot be utilized; it is therefore advisable to eat all eight essential amino acids at the same meal, as the body apparently will not store the leftovers. The essential amino acids must also be present in certain pro-

portions to each other (eggs most closely approximate this proportion, and milk is next best). If the optimum portion of even one is not present, the excess of the other amino acids cannot be utilized. Foods or food combinations providing all the essential amino acids are said to contain complete protein. The more closely the composition of the protein resembles the optimum configuration of amino acids, the higher its biological value is said to be.

The Net Protein Utilization value (NPU) is arrived at by multiplying the biological value by the percentage of the protein which is digestible. Presumably, the digestibility of a protein is a function not only of its intrinsic properties, but also the circumstances under which it is eaten. There is significant variation in the efficiency of different people's digestive systems and even a given individual will sometimes be more or less able to digest a certain protein.

At this point, we want to lay to rest a common semantic misconception about the term "complete protein." Most proteins are complete, in that the 8 EAAs are all present. What varies is the percentage of the protein which is complete. It is a gross oversimplification to state, as many nutrition texts do, that. "Complete proteins . . . are of animal origin . . . incomplete proteins are those deficient in one or more of the EAAs. They are of plant origin . . . (**Nutrition & Diet Therapy**, Sue R. Williams, 1973). Protein quality varies across a whole spectrum, from those with low biological and/or NPU values to those with high values on those scales. Any rational comparison of protein quality, given our present knowledge, should at least begin by referring to biological or NPU values.

The other thing to consider in determining whether a food is a good protein source is the percentage of the food which is protein. For example, brown rice, with an NPU of 60-70 (depending on which protein standard it is compared to, data from USDA Home Economics Research Report No. 4, "Amino Acid Contents of Foods"), looks like a good protein source at first glance. However, since only 7.5% (**Composition of Foods**, USDA Handbook #8) of the brown rice is protein, one would have to eat quite a bit of it in order to obtain even the minimum recommended amount of protein (almost a pound and a half of dry rice to obtain 30 grams of complete protein!). Soybeans, on the other hand, have a somewhat lower NPU of 55-62 but contain a much greater percentage of protein (34%). Less than half a pound (6-7 ounces) of dry soybeans will provide 30 grams of complete protein. Other legumes and grains on which data is available are less valuable protein sources than soybeans or wheat,

respectively. Nuts and seeds generally supply more complete protein per given serving size than grains and legumes; however, nuts are generally not eaten in as large a quantity as grains or legumes. See the **NUTS AND SEEDS** section for a chart (p. 133) showing the grams of complete protein in these foods.

The quantity of protein which an individual needs to ingest each day depends on that person's age, activity level, metabolic condition, and other factors. One internationally accepted technique for figuring average protein requirements suggests that average normal adults need around 30 grams per day of average quality protein. This amount might vary by 20 to 50% depending on circumstances. We suggest trying 30 grams a day and making adjustments if you feel that they are necessary.

CARBOHYDRATES

Carbohydrates are one of the main dietary sources of fuel. Because of their natural abundance (and therefore realtively low cost), they form the major part (excepting water) of most human diets. Carbohydrates are a dietary essential. A minimum intake of approximately 100 grams of carbohydrate per day is advisable. The carbohydrate plays a vital role in a crucial set of metabolic reactions which produces energy from fats, carbohydrates, and proteins. If insufficient carbohydrate is present in the diet, this set of reactions (called the Krebs cycle) gets discombobulated, and the fats are converted into ketone bodies. The ketone bodies accumulate, creating a condition known as ketosis, which can lead to death.

The term carbohydrates covers all the various sugars available in food, as well as starch. Both the simple sugars and the more complex starch molecules are made from carbon, hydrogen and oxygen. Carbohydrates are "built" in green plants by a process called photosynthesis. Carbon dioxide and water are combined in the presence of chlorophyll, utilizing the energy of the sun. When carbohydrates are digested, releasing CO_2, H_2O, and energy, it is the energy from the sun that is liberated for use in the body.

Carbohydrates are classified on the basis of their molecular structure. The MONO (one) SACCHARIDES (sugars) are the basic unit.

GLUCOSE is the monosaccharide which is found in human blood. It is also referred to as dextrose because polarized light passed through the molecule rotates to the right. Some free glucose is found in grapes and in honey.

FRUCTOSE is also known as levulose, as it rotates polarized light to the left. Fruits, Jerusalem artichokes, and honey all contain fructose.

GALACTOSE has not been found alone in any foods yet. It occurs as part of a more complex sugar in milk.

These three monosaccharides are the most common and important basic sugars utilized by humans. Generally, they are ingested as part of larger molecules called DI (two) SACCHARIDES or POLY (multiple) SACCHARIDES. When two monosaccharides combine to form a disaccharide, one molecule of water is removed. Hence, during the digestion of disaccharides, some water is used to restore the molecules to their original form. (This process is called hydrolyzing.)

The three disaccharides involved in human nutrition are SUCROSE, LACTOSE, and MALTOSE. Sucrose is by far the most common, occuring in table sugar, fruits, and vegetables. Sucrose is formed from one molecule of glucose and one molecule of fructose. Lactose is formed from one molecule of glucose and one of galactose. Lactose is commonly called milk sugar, since milk is the only food in which it is found. Lactose which is not absorbed is converted to lactic acid in the intestine. Maltose, a double glucose molecule, occurs in germinating grains, as a result of the breakdown of the starch molecules. This process helps make sprouted grains very easy to digest. Maltose is also the building block of starch molecules.

Glucose is absorbed by active transport into the blood stream, and it provides "quick energy." However, if it is introduced in excessive quantities, the pancreas is stimulated to release insulin, which causes the glucose to be stored in the liver and muscles as glycogen. In hypoglycemia, the insulin reacion is an "over-reaction," and the result is blood sugar levels below the approximately 100 mg./ 100 ml. of blood necessary to maintain normal metabolism. Hyperglycemia (diabetes) is the failure of the insulin reaction to hold blood sugar levels below approximately 100 mg./100 ml.

Glucose and galactose are absorbed at roughly equal rates. Fructose is absorbed by passive diffusion, at less than one-third the rate of glucose and galactose. This means that fructose is less likely to trigger an insulin reaction, because the sugar will tend to be absorbed only as it is needed; therefore the blood sugar level will not rise past the "insulin-trigger" point. Also, fructose has over twice the sweetening power of glucose, and therefore satisfies a given level of "sweetness desire" with far fewer calories than glucose or galactose. Some people feel that this boils down to a logical reason to choose honey over refined sugar, because the proportion of fructose/glucose is higher in honey than it is in refined sugar. However, it's not that simple. Sucrose (table sugar) is absorbed at a rate in between that of glucose and fructose (the constituents of honey). The experience of many people is that white sugar gives a "rush and a "letdown." Whether this is likely for bio-chemical reasons has not been completely established, as far as we know. There are many other arguments against the use of white sugar (and even some against the use of honey). Just to mention a few (and reveal our bias):

1) Refined sugar is sometimes filtered through charred beef bones (all sugar cane products sold in California, and possibly other states, must by law be made with refined sugar. Brown sugar is refined sugar plus molasses.)

2) Honey contains some trace minerals, vitamins and enzymes — sugar does not. Generally, sugar is an agribusiness product and honey is produced locally by bee keepers.

Recipes in this book call for honey, barley malt syrup (made from sprouted barley and sometimes corn), date particles or date sugar (more refined than date particles), and occasionally molasses. Molasses does contain trace minerals (unlike refined sugar), and although the method of its production is somewhat less acceptable than that of honey, molasses does impart a distinctive flavor which is desirable in some dishes.

POLYSACCHARIDES are long chains of mono-saccharide molecules. Their digestion is somewhat more complex than the digestion of simple sugars.

DEXTRIN is a slightly soluble intermediate-length carbohydrate molecule which is produced from starch during digestion or by dry heat (toasting bread, browning flour or whole grains, etc.). Dextrin is sweeter and easier to digest than the more complex starches from which it is made.

CELLULOSE, the most common poly-saccharide on the planet, is not digestible by humans. It provides the fibrous bulk which is essential for proper elimination of solid waste.

VITAMINS

Vitamins are important substances which are necessary for the body's proper functioning. They are used in minute quantities and do not provide energy or serve as building units per se, but rather act in the regulation of metabolic processes. For example they may function as co-enzymes or hormones, which catalyze and direct the chemical processes which underlie the functioning of our body.

VITAMIN C is contained in almost all raw, fresh fruits and vegetables, especially citrus fruits, bell peppers, fresh tomato juice, raw cabbage, broccoli, rosehips, sprouts and fresh strawberries. Ascorbic acid (vitamin C) is highly soluble in water and easily destroyed by heat, oxygen, light, and alkaline substances.

The connective tissue which holds cells together and forms the ligaments, cartilage, and the walls of blood vessels cannot be formed without vitamin C. In children, teeth formed during a deficiency of vitamin C decay easily. Vitamin C concentrates in the lens of the eye and plays a role in vision which is not yet completely understood. Ascorbic acid apparently facilitates the absorption and utilization of other nutrients, particularly calcium, iron, and some B vitamins. It aids in the healing of wounds and may help keep blood cholesteral levels low. Perhaps the most important role of vitamin C is as a detoxifier in the blood stream — it participates in (and is destroyed by) reactions eliminating foreign substances from the blood. These foreign substances may be disease-producing agents, toxic wastes from improper digestion, or the end products of sugar metabolism (especially lactic acid), which cause fatigue.

An adequate supply of vitamin C may be obtained from a proper diet, but there are a growing number of people who advocate supplemental vitamin C (in tablet or powder form) as a regular part of the diet. Some people believe that natural vitamin C (derived from rosehips or similar sources) is somehow more valuable than synthetic ascorbic acid. There is no hard experimental evidence to support this belief. Bioflavinoids and other substances which are generally associated with naturally occuring vitamin C may have as-yet-unproven value. However, the percentage of vitamin C in rosehips is low enough that probably even "natural vitamin C" tablets contain synthetic ascorbic acid to supplement the rosehips. Usually, the most economical way to purchase ascorbic acid is in crystalline granules. Also, since this form does not include buffers, there is less danger of adverse reactions from high doses. Currently, there is a controversy in scientific circles as to whether high doses of vitamin C can cause trouble in the body.

The B VITAMINS are closely-related compounds that are often found together in foods. The best vegetarian sources are leafy green vegetables, whole grains, nutritional yeast, wheat germ, rice polish, and sprouts. Most Americans eat sparingly, if at all, of most of these foods, and thanks in part to modern methods of processing wheat and rice, vitamin B deficiency is perhaps more common than it should be. We have not taken the space to discuss the B vitamins separately, as they function together and are usually obtained together as well. The B complex is involved in dozens of vital body functions, including growth, energy metabolisms, the formation of the sheath of nerve cells, proper kidney functioning, and the production of nucleic acids. The most common symptoms of deficiency include irritability, inefficiency, depression, mental sluggishness, fatigue, apprehension, confusion, worry, instability, moodiness, bad breath, canker sores and "trench mouth." If you are never inappropriately tired, or irritable, if your tongue is not swollen, is an even pink in color, and shows no grooves, fissures, indentations, etc., then you are probably getting enough B vitamins.

Pregnant women usually benefit from moderate B-6 supplementation (as well as more protein and all other nutrients). People who do not take milk products or eat eggs or flesh very definitely need to take supplemental B-12, as it occurs only in animal products. Vitamin B-12 is known to be extremely important in the prevention of pernicious anemia, a disease which may reach a dangerous point before being noticed. If you decide to take vitamin B tablets, be aware that the B vitamins work "synergistically"; that is, increasing the supply of one generally increases the need for the others. Therefore it is probably important to take all the B vitamins in the proper proportions if you take any.

Brewer's yeast (or nutritional yeast) contains a balance of B vitamins which comes close to the proportions found in the human body. It may be taken as a B vitamin supplement when needed to restore health. Many people find that mixing a tablespoon or two into orange juice or milk is the easiest way to take the yeast. Thre is at least one brand which actually disperses fairly well in the liquid and tastes reasonably good. Most B vitamins are water soluble and must be taken each day for effective supplementation. Some B vitamins are destroyed by heat, light, or oxygen, while others are relatively stable.

Even if you are not eating many B vitamins, your intestinal bacteria are (hopefully) synthesizing them for you. Eating cultured milk products such as yogurt, buttermilk, or kefir will help you maintain a population of these beneficial bacteria. If for some reason one must take antibiotics, afterwards one can eat yogurt to help re-establish the intestinal bacteria, or perhaps take a vitamin B supplement for a while.

VITAMIN A is made in the body from carotenoid compounds, which are found in (among other things) fresh and dried apricots, whole milk, sweet potatoes, carrots, broccoli, mangoes, and all green vegetables (the quantity increasing with the intensity of the yellow or green color). Vitamin A is involved in the formation of "visual purple" which is broken down in the process of vision. A deficiency of vitamin A manifests itself in poor night vision (day vision has an additional mechanism not dependent on vitamin A). Test yourself by seeing how rapidly you recover normal vision after being blinded by oncoming headlights at night. Other symptoms of a deficiency are acne or roughness of skin (especially on elbows and knees). Whiteheads and blackheads may occur as a result of cells dying and clogging the pores. The same process takes place internally, and the mucous that covers and protects the internal organs may become clogged with dead cells, reducing one's resistance to infection.

From raw carrots, the body apparently absorbs only one percent of the carotene; from cooked carrots, about 20%; and from carrot juice, almost all of the carotene — provided the juice is drunk immediately after juicing, before the carotene is oxidized.

VITAMIN A is fairly stable, except that it is easily oxidized. It is fat soluble rather than water soluble. Vitamin A is stored in the liver. In the average American diet, roughly one-fourth of the vitamin A is supplied by flesh and eggs. Presumably the increased consumption of dairy products, fruits and vegetables by vegetarians compensates for this reduction in vitamin A intake. There is evidence that the nitrates in chemical fertilizers destroy carotenoid compounds. Excessive A can be toxic. Symptoms of vitamin A toxicity (which generally manifest three to fifteen months after the beginning of high doses) include loss of hair, weight loss (in infants), cessation of menstruation, and rapid resorbtion of bone. Toxicity is produced only by preformed vitamin A derived from animal products (most supplements). Symptoms usually disappear soon after the high doses (50,000

I.U. or more a day) are discontinued.

VITAMIN D is involved in the absorption of caclium, and is therefore an important factor in bone formation and the maintenance of the blood calcium level.

Vitamin D can be formed on the skin during certain periods of clear days, when ultraviolet ray penetration is at its maximum level. Window glass, smoke, clothing and skin pigmentation all screen out ultraviolet light, thereby inhibiting vitamin D formation. Because it is difficult to obtain much vitamin D through natural irradiation, milk and other foods are commonly fortified with vitamin D. This has helped reduce incidences of rickets. However, evidence is accumulating that vitamin D favors calcium absorption over magnesium absorption, and that magnesium deficiency may be related to heart disease.

VITAMIN E is found in the oils of grains, nuts, and seeds. Generally the vitamin E content of food is proportional to the amount of polyunsaturated fats. Vitamin E is stable to heat but oxidizes very rapidly. Its functions include the prevention of the oxidation of unsaturated fatty acids, vitamin A and certain hormones. If there is adequate vitamin E, it concentrates in the pituitary gland, and is necessary for the proper functioning of that organ. Before the introduction of modern milling methods, we used to get about 150 mg of vitamin E per day. Now most Americans get 8 mg a day. Vitamin E may also help the liver detoxify harmful substances such as preservatives, bleaches used in flour, pesticide residues, nitrates and nitrites from fertilizers, etc.

VITAMIN K is important in blood clotting. It is produced by intestinal bacteria.

Natural vegetable oils, in addition to supplying vitamin E, are an excellent source of ESSENTIAL FATTY ACIDS. The symptoms of a deficiency of essential fatty acids include dry hair, dry scaly skin, and tendency to be overweight due to excessive retention of water. In fact, eating too little fat is a common cause of overweight, both because of water retention and because the body changes sugar to fat rapidly to try to supply the missing nutrients — this lowers the blood sugar and produces hunger. Fats are necessary for the proper functioning of the gall bladder, and this organ must function properly to absorb vitamins — so a fat deficiency can produce vitamin deficiencies.

Many nutritionists advise that some natural, unrefined, cold-pressed vegetable oil be eaten every day. The recommended tablespoon or two per day can easily be obtained by eating salad dressing or using **Butter-oil Spread** in place of butter.

LIPIDS (fats and oils) are important in the diet for several reasons. First, they provide a lot of calories and energy, even when taken in small portions. This is especially important in cold climates and for people doing heavy physical work. Secondly, since the fats leave the stomach slowly, they contribute to a feeling of satisfaction after a meal, and prolong the interval before hunger is felt again. This is particularly important for people who are overweight, in controlling overeating. Fats aid in the assimilation of the fat soluble vitamins A, D, E, and K. Most importantly, lipids provide linoleic acid, an essential fatty acid. The best sources of linoleic acid are unrefined vegetable oils, especially those derived from corn, soybeans, and safflower seed.

Lipids may be divided into two groups — those which contain mostly unsaturated fatty acids, and those which contain mostly fatty acids whose available bonding sites are saturated with hydrogen molecules. Saturated fats tend to be solid at room temperature, and unsaturated fats tend to be liquid at room temperature. Unsaturated fatty acids are more soluble and more digestible than saturated fatty acids. In America, there is a high correlation between diets which contain a lot of saturated fat and high blood cholesterol levels, which increases the likelihood of atherosclerosis (hardening and narrowing of the arteries). If you don't feel like giving up butter, we suggest that you switch to **Butter-oil Spread**, which contains many more nutrients than plain butter.

MINERALS

MINERALS perform many important functions in the body. They help maintain the internal pH balance, serve as catalysts in many different bio-chemical reactions, maintain water balance in various tissues, participate in the transmission of nerve impulses, and play a part in building certain tissues.

CALCIUM is needed to form the bones and connective tissues. Persons with low blood calcium levels may be irritable. Radical deficiencies can result in rickets, osteoporosis, or osteomalacia. Normally, the blood calcium level will be maintained at the expense of body tissues, so the whole body is affected in cases of deficiency.

Calcium is involved in many biological reactions, including muscle contraction and absorption of B-12. The person who does not eat milk products needs to be very careful to obtain enough calcium. Common vegetarian sources of calcium include milk products, almonds, collard and turnip greens, beans, sunflower seeds, dried figs and broccoli. Americans consume more calcium than the world average. Although there may be negative results from this habit, high calcium intake tends to limit absorption and storage of radioactive strontium 90, a deadly poison.

PHOSPHORUS is used in ATP and ADP, two chemicals which form the basis of energy storage and release in the human body, and in the metabolism of calcium. It is found in milk products, brewer's yeast, wheat bran and germ, rice bran and polish, legumes, nuts and seeds.

MAGNESIUM is needed in proportion to the amount of calcium eaten. A deficiency is thought to increase one's susceptibility to cardio-vascular diseases. Good sources of magnesium include nuts, soybeans, whole grains and leafy vegetables.

POTASSIUM is concentrated inside the cells of the body. In conjunction with the sodium in the extra-cellular fluids, it is a major factor in maintaining the fluid balance in the body. Potassium and calcium are both involved in muscle relaxation. Potassium occurs in most foods, so usually deficiency is related to excessive salt intake: "Because of the antagonistic relationship between sodium and potassium an excessive intake of sodium may have the same effect as a sub-optimal level of potassium." (Introductory Nutrition, by Helen Guthrie, 1967). In other words, the large amount of sodium chloride (table salt) which many people consume may directly contribute to increased muscle tension. Potassium is highly soluble, so care should be taken to use all cooking water.

SODIUM and potassium (to a lesser extent) help maintain pH balance in the body by neutralizing excess acid. Sodium is also in-volved in the transmission of nerve impulses and the absorption of glucose. Although excess sodium intake should be avoided (see potassium), pregnant women apparently have a greater need for sodium than other people. "Clinical studies on humans indicate that high sodium rather than low sodium diets are effective in preventing or relieving toxemia . . . (in pregnancy)". (Op. cit.)

Sodium chloride is also one of the best sources of CHLORINE, which is a constituent of the cerebrospinal fluid, and part of the hydrochloric acid which is so important in protein digestion. Tomatoes, celery, cabbage, iceburg lettuce, spinach, and parsnips are all chlorine-rich foods.

SULFUR is obtained from the amino acids cystine and methionine. Inorganic sulfur as sulfate is not useful to the body. Sulfur is present in certain body proteins (such as hair, skin, nails) much more than in other tissues. It is involved in blood clotting, energy transfer, and detoxification of waste products.

MICRONUTRIENT or trace minerals are now thought to be fairly important in human nutrition. Unfortunately, traditional agricul-tural practices make no particular attempt to replenish the supply of trace minerals in the soil. As a result, our food now contains fewer trace minerals than it once did.

Of the micronutrient minerals, IRON is present in the largest quantities. Iron plays several important roles in the blood. It is incorporated into the hemoglobin which is responsible for transporting oxygen from the lungs to the various parts of the body and carrying carbon dioxide from the tissues back to the lungs for elimination. Prune juice dried apricots, other dried fruit, legumes, green vegetables and molasses all provide reasonably large amounts of iron. Oats (and to a lesser extent, other whole grains) contain phytic acid, which combines with iron to make an insoluble compound which is useless to the body. Therefore steady use of oats in the diet is not recommended for those especially needing iron. Iron is water soluble, so it is lost if the cooking water is not eaten. Iron deficiency anemia is a common problem among young children, adolescents and women. A constant supply of iron is needed to produce new hemoglobin cells. Menstru-ation causes the loss of iron, which is why women have a higher need for iron than adult men, and have a much higher incidence of anemia. Women and growing children should be very careful to obtain enough iron. Symp-toms of iron deficiency include tiredness, headaches, tendency to run out of breath easily, and the like. A simple blood test can be used to check for deficiency.

IODINE is crucial for the proper function-ing of the thyroid gland. It is obtained from unrefined salt, iodized refined salt (which usually also contains aluminum silicate to prevent lumping), seaweed, and to a lesser extent from dairy products and vegetables. Rutabagas, turnips, cabbage and nuts all contain substances which interfere with iodine utilization. A high calcium diet may also interfere with iodine absorption.

ZINC is related to insulin production or storage and is necessary for tissue respiration. Zinc is concentrated in the retina of the eye, but its role in vision is not clearly understood. Parsley, peas, whole wheat cereals, oatmeal, corn, peanut butter and milk all supply zinc.

SELENIUM can replace vitamin E in some processes and helps promote normal growth and fertility. The bran and germ of cereal grains are relatively rich in selenium, if it was present in its growing soil.

MANGANESE is a catalyst to many enzymes and appears to be involved in bone development. Nuts, whole grain cereals and legumes are good sources of manganese.

COPPER is involved in prolonging the life of red blood cells and in maintaining healthy nerve fibers. Good sources include nuts, legumes and whole grains.

Now that you have read this very basic information on nutrients, you are probably beginning to realize that nutrition is a complicated science. If you want to learn more, we suggest looking carefully at a college-level nutrition text.

We have one very simple suggestion which we feel summarizes the nutritional information presented in this subsection. Eat a balanced diet which includes fresh fruit and vegetables (both yellow and green), high quality protein (from milk products, soy products, and nuts and seeds), essential fatty acids, and, if necessary to supplement caloric intake, additional carbohydrates (fruits supply some). If you have the time and energy to analyze your diet and tabulate exact amounts of specific nutrients, you can go about it by recording your food intake for a week or more, and then using a Table of Food Composition to figure out how much of each nutrient you are getting. Then compare these amounts to the Recommended Daily Allowances (see most popular nutrition books). This is really quite a chore but can point out deficiencies that can be remedied by a better diet or a short period of supplementation. In general, we do not recommend the use of pills except for short periods of time for those who really need it (pregnant and lactating women, those with definite deficiencies, etc.). Our feeling is that a wholesome, balanced diet of natural foods is the best possible foundation for proper nutrition.

kitchen
ways

KITCHEN WAYS

OBTAINING FOOD

Kitchens without food are like bodies without souls: the main ingredient is missing. So, in contemplation of kitchen ways, we begin by examining some different methods of obtaining food.

GROW YOUR OWN (and some for friends, too). This path involves a certain amount of dedication to the earth, and is uplifting in proportion to the love with which it is approached. Working in home or community gardens is an excellent way to get back in touch with the experience of the universe as a connected whole. It is nice to eat home grown food, too. Garden fresh vegetables and tree-ripened fruit taste as wonderful and sweet as the love they were grown with.

As well as sharing what your efforts produce, you can USE WHAT WOULD OTHERWISE BE WASTED.

Many folks have orchards that they don't pick, or which produce more than they can use, but not enough to bother marketing. Quite often we have found these people willing to share. They are grateful for the opportunity to be of service to someone and pleased that the food will not go to waste. (It might be appropriate to offer to help clean up the fruit which has already fallen and is beginning to rot. Although it is good fertilizer, it sometimes attracts a lot of yellow jackets.)

People who grow gardens often end up with surplus lettuce, chard, tomatoes, summer squash, and other crops, and are happy to share their abundance with those in need.

Supermarkets also waste food — especially produce. In some cases, produce workers will help people salvage this food — in other instances it is possible to learn the routine at a given store, and recover clean cardboard boxes full of food from the trash container minutes after it is discarded. Although this food may be slightly funky, there is almost always something worth eating. For example, heads of lettuce and celery are trimmed before being displayed, and unsightly pieces, (which may or may not be spoiled) are thrown away. Fruit with bad spots meets the same fate, and a paring knife and some running water can restore it to the roster of edibles in very short order.

It is also possible to GATHER WILD FOODS. A significant portion of the wild plant life of any particular region is not only edible, but tasty and nutritious as well. Local libraries and book stores are good places to check for books to help identify local wild foods.

Fortunately for those of us who are unable or unwilling to obtain food in the aforementioned ways, we can BUY FROM GROWERS AND FARM MARKETS. Roadside stands and farmers' markets sell in small quantities, or it may be possible to buy large quantities from these sources at substantial savings, if you are able to store or distribute what you can't use right away. On an even larger scale, you might want to START (or join) A CO-OP — anything from a small group of people who purchase food together (a buying club) to a retail store which sells food to members of the co-op (or the public) at a discount.

All of these alternatives are viable ways to disentangle one's self from the supermarket

habit, a habit which we encourage everyone to kick. Since fresh, wholesome foods deteriorate unless they are properly stored, it is important to learn a little about food storage procedures as we move away from the supermarket and into the garden, so to speak.

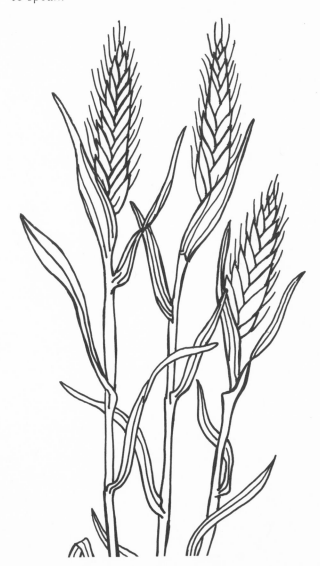

STORAGE

First of all, a word about containers. Glass jars, plastic containers, and metal honey or coffee cans can be used to store almost anything in. Remember that wide mouth containers are easier to clean than others, and airtight lids keep food fresh longer. Labels can be made with ball point pen and masking tape, or with grease pencil directly on the container. Note: metal cans may react with acid foods. We suggest avoiding this possibility by using some other type of container for acid foods.

Plastic wrap and aluminum foil are fairly difficult to re-use, and they are not especially biodegradable. Leftover food can be covered with the lid of the pan it was cooked in (place the lid upside down to save space) or a plate can be used to cover the food in bowls. Other things (hunks of cheese, apple halves, etc.) are easily stored in **plastic bags,** which can be reused. We usually **select heavy** duty bags (which don't tear as easily as the cheap ones), and in between uses, we turn them inside out and rinse them (or wash with soap and water). They can be dried in various places around the house, or on a special little clothes line. It's necessary to make sure the sides don't stick together (otherwise they won't dry inside) and also to turn the bags right side out again after the one side has thoroughly dried. Be careful about letting the plastic bags get too close to hot things, as they will melt and/or burn.

Paper bags are okay for some things, but when they are put into a refrigerator, they often end up getting wet and making a huge mess. Also, they aren't very suitable for long term dry storage as they don't deter moths, mice, rats and the like.

Here's how we generally store different foods:

FRESH VEGETABLES: In tightly sealed plastic bags in the refrigerator. The idea is to keep the moisture content stable and to prevent oxidation (and vitamin loss) by excluding air and storing at low temperatures.

Exceptions: Potatoes and winter squash should be stored in a cool, dark, dry place where air can circulate around them. Store unripe tomatoes stem down one layer deep, not touching each other, in a cool, dark, dry place. Unripe eggplant can be stored on a counter or shelf out of direct sunlight.

Of course, vegetables may be frozen, canned, or stored in root cellars. These methods of long term storage are discussed in the **CANNING AND PRESERVING** section.

FRESH FRUIT: Ripe: in sealed plastic bags in the refrigerator, or, unless it's really hot, in bowls or on a counter out of direct sun. Stack as for unripe. Unripe: at room temperature stacked so that air can circulate through the stack, and with the soft fruits, so that they won't be bruised by their own weight. Keep a sharp eye out for fruit flies — they are mainly attracted to really ripe or damaged fruit.

Exceptions: Bananas produce a gas as part of their ripening process — paper or plastic bags help retain this gas, which speeds ripening. Also, bananas are extremely sensitive to temperature changes. Like most fruits, they ripen faster at warm temperatures, and much slower when they are cold. Refrigeration seems to disagree with bananas — it turns their skins black, and may permanently interfere with ripening — but when they're ripe they can be frozen, unpeeled or peeled and mashed in containers. See **Banana Ice Cream** recipe.

DRIED FRUIT, BEANS, WHOLE GRAINS, and FLOURS are all subject to infestation by various insects and rodents. Storage in strong airtight containers will keep the pests out and help reduce oxidation.

Plastic bags tend to develop holes, and aren't very rodent proof; so for long term storage, we don't use them, except sometimes as liners for other containers. Most things keep better in the refrigerator. Freshly ground flours definitely belong there (in moisture and airtight containers), as many nutrients are lost through oxidation at room temperature. Dried fruit also keeps longer when it is refrigerated, but only rarely have we ever had the space or felt the need to refrigerate it, or our grains and beans. (Very moist dried fruit will ferment unless it is refrigerated.)

UNREFINED OILS should be kept refrigerated, or at least cool. Oils that have not been over-processed do eventually turn rancid, and heat accelerates the deterioration.

FRESH JUICES, MILK, CHEESE, TOFU, sprouts that are ready to eat, leftovers, et cetera, should of course be kept cold. The new generation of refrigerators have de-humidifers which dry out food that is not in airtight containers, cheese and leftovers being especially vulnerable. It's a good idea to keep leftovers all in one easily noticed place so that they get eaten before they spoil.

HONEY and MOLASSES can be protected from ants by standing the covered containers in a pie pan or bowl filled with enough water to create a moat 1/2 - 1 inch deep. Remember to replenish the moat as it evaporates.

HERBS and SPICES retain their flavor much longer when they are stored in airtight containers in a cool dark place (i.e. NOT above the stove or in front of a window). If these criteria seem to eliminate all possible places in your kitchen, don't worry. Pottery containers or thick dark glass bottles with tight lids will work well almost anywhere.

RECYCLING

Hopefully the utilization of these storage methods will reduce the amount of food which is lost through spoilage, but even spoiled food need not be wasted. All spoiled food, as well as food scraps (nut shells, fruit and vegetable peels, etc.) can be returned to the earth for reprocessing into life again. There are basically two ways to do this. One can start a formal compost heap (in which case finding a good composting book is suggested), or the compost can simply be buried in the garden or backyard. Ideally, there should be enough dirt covering the food to keep dogs and other animals from digging it up — 6" to 1' is usually adequate. To keep the smell down in the kitchen, we keep a small container with a lid inside, and a larger (3 - 5 gallon) receptacle outside. It's easier to dig a few big holes every once in a while than it is to dig a lot of little holes all the time. If you have extra freezer space and not much compost, a plastic bag or milk carton in the freezer works well. (The freezer practically halts decomposition, thereby keeping unpleasant smells to a minimum.)

KEEPING IT TOGETHER

One thing that we've found to be a great help in keeping the kitchen vibration high is to think ahead (at least a little) so that the oven gets turned on in time to heat up, the baked potatoes get started before the steamed spinach so both are ready at the same time, the sink isn't full of dirty dishes when we need to wash some food, we don't find ourselves missing some ingredient halfway through a complicated recipe . . .

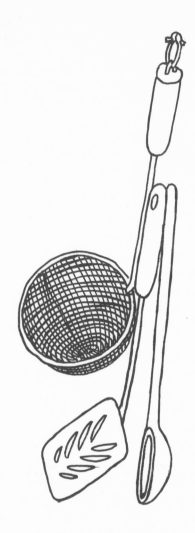

There are certain procedures and materials which facilitate creative expression in the kitchen, but they are only a foundation, a place to touch down when necessary. On the whole, good cooking results from the interplay of experience and intuition, with rules playing only a minor role. However, for the benefit of those who haven't had much experience in the kitchen, or who would like to see how someone else goes about things, here are some thoughts or guidelines about preparing food, which are based on our experience. Perhaps you can learn from our mistakes and successes.

WASHING: Garden fresh vegetables tend to need cleaning before they are eaten. Really muddy root vegetables, lettuce and other goodies from the garden can be rinsed outside before they are brought into the kitchen. Fiber brushes work very well for scrubbing squash, celery, potatoes, and similar vegetables. This eliminates the need for the common but unwise practice of peeling away the skins, which contain or protect a substantial portion of the nutrients. Lettuce can be washed either by dipping each leaf under running water (or in a pan of water), or by cutting off the stem and holding head right side up (most of the dirt is towards the bottom) under running water. The leaves can be dried by placing them on towels or whirling them in a mesh basket (or pillow case). Vegetables keep better if they aren't too wet when they are put away.

Fruits can usually just be rinsed in cold water, but in order to remove the wax which coats most commercially packed apples (and bell peppers and cucumbers) it may be necessary to scrub the fruit with a plastic mesh ball in very hot water or peel the fruit. ˙

Grains and dried beans can be rinsed clean by putting them into a large pan, swirling a lot of water around them, and carefully pouring off the water (repeat until water is clear). Alternately, rinse them in a colander.

CUTTING: There are as many ways of cutting fruits and vegetables as there are cooks, but there are certain basic considerations which we will explore here. Aside from confining the chopping to the food (i.e. watching out for the fingers) it is possible to arrange things so that the doing gets done with a minimum of effort, and the pieces end up the right size. For instance, we've found that it is easiest to cube a potato or similarly shaped vegetable in the following way: first slice lengthwise into oval "sheets," then divide the sheets into two piles, place cut face down and slice into slivers, then crosswise — voilá, the cubes. Whether or not you slice them this way doesn't really matter — we just wanted to point out that efficient ways of cutting do exist for those times when there is a huge pile of food to prepare. Attractive slices can be made from zucchini and cucumbers by making lengthwise grooves with the tines of a fork before slicing. Carrots, celery and other vegetables can be sliced on the diagonal ("nituke" style) for an interesting shape. This also cuts open more cell walls, rendering the vitamins inside more available for assimilation. Mechanical choppers and shredders of various degrees of complexity are available, and they can be fun work savers. However, working with a knife is a beautiful meditation, a simpler rhythm.

Once fruits and vegetables have been cut up, the vitamin content begins to decrease, due to losses from oxidation and exposure to light. For this reason, we suggest that salads be made

fresh right before they are eaten. In some cases, chopping foods after they are cooked may reduce vitamin losses.

RAW FOODS. Many times a simple meal of raw foods is an acceptable alternative to the usual habit of "cooking" a meal. A platter of raw fruit or vegetables takes much less time to prepare than a salad or a cooked dish, and it can be served as a meal all by itself or with milk, cheese, or bread, when a meal is required unexpectedly. Raw foods contain many valuable vitamins and enzymes which may be destroyed by cooking, and should be included in the diet unless there is a medical problem of some sort.

COOKING. Ever since humankind discovered that food dropped into the fire or left in the sun tasted different from (and sometimes better than) raw foods, the diet of the human race has generally been evolving (or degenerating, depending on the point of view) in the direction of cooked food. Cooking has two basic functions: it changes the taste, and it changes the digestibility of the food. Sometimes the changes are desirable — herb teas made in cold water just aren't as flavorful or useful as those made with hot water. Conversely, sometimes the changes are of questionable benefit: protein is in some instances harder to digest after cooking, and some foods (primarily fruits and vegetables) suffer great losses of vitamins, enzymes and even taste when they are cooked. Overcooking any food increases the likelihood that it will change for the worse.

Different cultures have developed cooking methods which are suited to the food which is available, the environmental conditions, and the lifestyle of the people. Natural food cookery draws from different national styles, but it is characterized by certain approaches which transcend cultural borders. The basic concern of natural food cooking, as we see it, is to prepare food in such a way that the natural nutritive values and good tastes are preserved and enhanced, rather than lost or covered up with other flavors. Cooking methods for particular foods which are consistent with this principle are discussed in detail in the appropriate sections (beans are hiding in the **MAIN DISH** section).

PREPARING FOOD

Here are some general thoughts:

• Enjoy yourself. If you feel tense or upset, sit quietly for a few minutes and establish a calm vibration before beginning to cook. Food that is prepared and served in a calm, loving manner will nourish more than just the physical body.

• Use your energy wisely. Try getting everything that is needed for a recipe in one place before beginning to mix anything. This saves walking back and forth between the cupboard and the counter eighteen times in the course of as many minutes. (Floors won't wear out as fast either.) Clean up as you go — it's a lot easier to rinse a bowl or spoon right away than it is to scrub it later, after the food has dried.

• Be here now. There's an old saying that "you can't cook in the living room." It took quite a few burned or boiled-over pans, ruined cookies and similar messes to convince us of the truth of this.

• Keep it clean. Wash your hands before beginning to cook and frequently enough to avoid getting sticky stuff on the outside of spice jars, refrigerator handles, and other places that like to be clean. Rinse graters, blenders, and other one-in-the-kitchen items right away, so that they will be clean when they are needed next. (Especially if someone else is cooking at the same time.)

• Keep it simple. Especially when first learning to cook, don't overextend yourself by trying to cook a lot of fancy dishes at once. There are many recipes in this book that need only the addition of a salad or some bread and a beverage to make a complete meal.

• Use the right tool. Chopping raw carrots with a paring knife just isn't proper utilization of time or energy. A sharp knife that's the right type and size for the job is a blessing (we keep a sharpening stone handy). Dishtowels used as potholders have a habit of catching fire. While we are on the subject . . .

• Fire is a reality. Please don't endanger your life (or even your peace of mind) by putting cloth or paper towels on the stove or hanging near a burner. Don't leave hot grease unattended. By the way, plastic melts, so keep plastic bags, spoons, measuring cups and bowls away from heat.

• Baking soda is wonderful. Besides smothering fires (salt works too) it helps keep refrigerators clean. Smelly sponges can be soaked in a solution of soda and warm water. (Alternately, wash the sponge with the clothes.) Soda helps clean burned pans, too. Boil a strong solution in the pan for a while to loosen burned stuff. We have mixed feelings about actually using the stuff in food, though.

• Plan ahead, at least enough so that you won't find yourself out of food with unexpected (and hungry) guests. Many foods freeze well — see the **CANNING AND PRESERVING** section. Those who cook for others, especially young children, need to take care that meals are nutritionally balanced, appealing (color, taste and texture are all important), and varied enough to suit different situations and hold people's interest. It is also good to establish some kind of rhythmic schedule so that cooking and eating are part of the day's flow, rather than an interruption. People who work and don't have time to cook during the week, take note: if you can cook one day a week, and freeze stuff, after a few weeks, with some careful planning, you'll be able to serve a great variety of things with very little effort. Cook large quantities and freeze in easily defrostable, meal-size containers. Choose things like **Spaghetti Sauce**, which are the basis for many different dishes (**Eggplant Parmesan, Pizza, Lasagna**, etc.). Teach the family how to cook — it's fun, and they can be great help.

NOTES TO THE NOVICE:

• The top shelf of the oven is hotter, but stuff is more likely to burn on the bottom shelf, if it gets too close to the heat source.

• Aluminum foil can be used to line the bottom of the oven (but don't let it touch the heating element), and placed under burners to catch spills and drippings.

- Don't put a pan on a hot burner without putting food, water or oil in it first.

- Keep hair tied back so it stays out of the food and out of the fire.

- Food generally cooks faster with a lid. (Saves energy.)

- To reheat food it is usually necessary to add liquid and simmer in a covered pan. Stir well and frequently.

- Stirring distributes heat and keeps the food from burning or sticking. Stir so that the food is mixed up and down as well as around.

- Oil, turmeric, berry juice and many other goodies stain clothing. Wearing an apron helps keep your clothes clean.

TOOLS

The simpler your life is, the fewer you'll need. A friendly knife, and perhaps a bowl, a spoon, and a cooking pot, will do for those who love to wander. The path of the householder, however is strewn with attachments, and the kitchen is no exception. May we suggest giving away what you don't use or need to someone who will worship it by utilizing its potential? If there are things you need, ask your friends first before you add your dollars to the bonfire of consumerism.

Earth's precious resources are provided for the collective welfare, and need to be used wisely.

If we were setting up a minimal kitchen from scratch, here's what we'd get:

FOR EATING:

- mugs or glasses

- eating bowls and plates

- silverware or woodenware for eating with (we have an aversion to plastic, and would be inclined towards ceramics and wood.)

FOR PREPARATION:

- two knives: one small and one large (these are essential and should be good quality. A paring knife and a French chef's knife would be a good combination.)

- cutting board — a scrap piece of wood about 2" X 12" X however long, or bigger (Moderately hard woods are best, but even plywood will do).

- a compost container

FOR CLEANING:

- a sink

- a brush to clean vegetables

- one small and one large saucepan with tight fitting lids (please see the discussion of various types of pans which follows)

- a cast iron or other heavy frying pan

- a wooden spoon

- a pyrex or metal baking pan (8" X 12" X 2")

- a plastic scrubby to get the pans clean

- hot pads

Optional Items:

- measuring spoons and cups

- small and large mixing bowls (if they have lids you can store leftovers in them)

- plastic bags and other storage containers

- a rubber spatula

- a pancake turner

- a dish cloth or sponge

- a dish drainer

For those whose diets include cooked food:

Main Things:

- a stove

- an oven mit

- a bread knife

- a timer (for those who are serious about cooking)

These Things Are Really Nice:

- a sharpening stone for the knives

- a grater

- a sprout jar

- a steaming rack

- a colander

- a soup ladle

- a rice paddle

- a slotted spoon

- another frying pan or a wok

- more of most of the essentials in different sizes

- cookie sheets

- a tea strainer

- a vegetable peeler (for waxed apples and carrots with bitter skins)

- a wire whip

- herb and spice containers

- a salad bowl

- a hand citrus juicer (glass or plastic)

To Live In Luxury One Could Add:

- a toaster

- a blender

- a double boiler

- a food mill

- a grain mill

- a suribachi or mortar and pestle

- and whatever else the heart desires that can be provided without detriment to the collective welfare

NOTES ABOUT COOKING UTENSILS

We had hoped to find out if any really convincing research has been done regarding the effects of using cooking utensils made from various materials. Although we did not find time for this task, we would like to pass along the information (and opinions) which we have collected.

GLASS is very stable under the conditions normally encountered in the kitchen. It is difficult to imagine any problem with contamination from the use of glass cooking utensils. CARE: Avoid rapid temperature changes and physical shocks to prevent breakage. IDEAL FOR: Bread and cake pans, casseroles, citrus juicers.

CAST IRON is the height of luxury for the old-fashioned cook. It holds heat well, and in normal use is not a health hazard. In fact, if iron does enter the food, it can be utilized just as other forms of dietary iron are. However, exclusive use of iron cookware in conjunction with a diet low in phosphates (which are needed to eliminate excess iron) may result in an accumulation of iron in the liver and subsequent liver damage. The only group for which this has proven to be a problem are the Bantu people of Africa. (See **Nutrition and Diet Therapy**, Sue Rodwell Williams 1973, p. 143.) CARE: Cast iron ware is traditionally "seasoned" in the following manner. If the pan is old and has meat grease in it or a "blotchy" old seasoning, the first step is literally to burn out the old seasoning by heating the pan until it quits smoking. The actual seasoning involves coating the iron (while it is quite warm) with a vegetable oil (preferably sesame oil). This is the down home version of the non-stick cooking surface, and it doesn't make the food taste funny. (Unlike some techno-

logical solutions to the same problem.) To preserve the seasoning in a cast iron pan, avoid using anything except wooden spoons, plastic spatulas, or non-metallic pot scrubbers on the cooking surface. Soap will remove the seasoning and is generally not needed — the well seasoned pan is easy to clean. After rinsing the pan, dry over a low heat on the stove (to prevent rusting). Avoid rapid changes in temperature and physical shocks — cast iron is breakable. Cast iron is a good choice for frying pans and for big covered kettles (Dutch ovens) to braise vegetables in, for stews, and for other long, slow cooking.

ENAMELWARE is generally either very expensive or else very short-lived. The enamel coating on the cheap pans has a greater tendency to chip off. Enamelware made in the proper way (especially, without lead glazes) is probably non-toxic and non-reactive with food, as long as the enamel is not chipped or cracked. There is a good possibility that fairly toxic heavy metals used in the glazes are released into the food once the ceramic surface is chipped or cracked. CARE: Avoid rapid temperature changes and physical shocks. Do not use anything on the pan which might chip or crack the enamel. Do not overheat — an enamel pan left unattended and empty on a hot burner can be ruined. It probably should be discarded or used to catch rain drips once the enamel is damaged. RECOMMENDED only for careful, well-to-do cooks.

STAINLESS STEEL is often touted by natural food enthusiasts. Some people believe that toxic heavy metals can be released into the food once the surface layer (which gives the "stainless" quality) is scratched. This is one of the questions we were not able to resolve. Stainless steel does not distribute heat well, so it is often combined with a copper, aluminum, or iron "core" or plating. These hybrid pans are easier to cook with than straight stainless steel, but are also more expensive. CARE: very rugged. Do not overheat or smash, as lids may not fit afterwards. Wash with soap and water. It is probably best to avoid scratching the cooking surface by not using metal spoons or pot scrubbers on the pan. RECOMMENDED for general use, especially in situations where cast iron or glass is inappropriate. (For instance, steaming vegetables on the stove. Most glass pans are not "burner-proof," and cast iron would tend to rust if the pan wasn't cleaned out fairly promptly.)

ALUMINUM pans are not popular with most natural food cooks. Many people believe that aluminum salts (which end up in food cooked in aluminum) are toxic and cause all sorts of health problems. The classic response to this belief is that aluminum salts are water soluble, and therefore are not a problem, because they leave the body fairly rapidly. All this response really implies is that aluminum salts probably do not accumulate in the body. Even this claim is open to question because there is probably some substance which is used up in the detoxification and elimination of aluminum salts. If that substance is in short supply (recall the situation of the Bantu described under CAST IRON) or the body reserves are used up over a period of time, the aluminum compounds might be stored in the body. Even if they aren't stored, we are still left wondering exactly what they

do while they are in our bodies, however briefly. How often would one have to eat food cooked in an aluminum pot in order to insure the constant presence of aluminum salts in one's body? Once a day? Twice? The lack of definitive empirical evidence demonstrating the safety of cooking in aluminum, the relative ease with which aluminum salts are produced during cooking, and the numerous testimonials suggesting that aluminum is dangerous lead us to avoid eating food cooked in aluminum. It is NOT RECOMMENDED for any use. Regardless of whether one fears the potential toxicity of the aluminum salts, it is important to note that aluminum cookware discolors some foods and (in our experience) imparts an unpleasant flavor to almost anything that is cooked in it. Although it heats up quite rapidly, aluminum cookware is difficult to use. It loses heat rapidly, is very prone to bending and denting, and tends to increase the possibility of burning the food. (Once it gets scratched, things stick to it very easily.)

Cookware made with NON-STICK finishes pushes our "plastic paranoia" button. We prefer to avoid having anything to do with it, on the theory that it might well be a health hazard. Properly maintained pans made from cast iron, glass and stainless steel have excellent anti-stick properties.

Note: Wooden bowls, spoons and other tools may crack and split if they are left soaking too long. Sharp knives will lose their edge if they are allowed to bang around with other tools. We suggest a knife rack or some other protected location for storing these essential tools. Stainless steel does not hold an edge as well as regular steel. However, regular steel knives need to be dried after they are washed, in order to prevent rusting. Take your choice.

58

FRUIT DESCRIPTIONS

Fresh ripe fruits are simply delicious, and the easily digestible sugars they contain are among the best sources of "quick energy." Their clear and delicate flavors are more like the legendary food of the gods than anything on earth.

Fruits, which take their name from a word which means "to enjoy," are nature's cleansers and purifiers. The light, wonderful feeling that can suffuse one's whole being after eating only fruit for a while is adequate testimony to the appropriateness of the name. The flavor and nutritive value of fruit varies widely, depending on the type of fruit, where and how it was grown, and also how ripe it is. In general ripe fruit is sweeter and easier to digest. Most raw fruits are good sources of vitamins and minerals, and extremely poor (quantity-wise) sources of protein.

In order to help you enjoy the maximum benefit from the fruit you eat, we have pre-faced the recipes in this section with a guide to the purchasing and preparation of the most common fruits. General comments are followed by more specific discussions of the individual fruits which are listed alphabetically within classes or groups. The classes, which are based on characteristics of the fruit, are as follows:

• MELONS form a class of their own due to the extremely high percentage of water which they contain and their reputation of being best eaten alone.

• ACID FRUITS include grapes, some sour berries, the citrus fruits, and pineapple. The acid taste of these fruits is a clue to their special digestive requirements. (The pH of the digestive secretions varies according to, among other things, the pH of the food which is eaten.)

• SWEET FRUITS such as apples, apricots, bananas, most berries, coconut, fresh figs, nectarines, papayas, peaches, and pears tend to contain more carbohydrates (by weight) than the acid fruits. Because of their similarity to the sweet fruits, we have included fruits normally classed as "sub-acid" (apricots, nectarines, etc.) in this class.

• DRIED FRUITS are a concentrated source of readily available energy. Sun dried fruits of all kinds, when they are processed without the use of chemicals, are an excellent substitute for candy. (Please see the section on **CANNING AND PRESERVING** for information on drying your own fruit.)

GENERAL COMMENTS

Fruits are like delicate flowers: if they are picked too early, they won't ever develop their full beauty. With few exceptions, tree ripened fruit is so exquisitely good that it is impossible to compare it with fruit that has been picked green. Fruits draw nourishment from the plants on which they grow; if they are picked too soon, they will ripen after a fashion, but the sugar content will rarely reach the level that it would were the fruit allowed to ripen naturally on the plant.

In order to maximize the cash return on a crop, most commercial growers pick their orchards when most of the fruit is at the

critical point between being too green to ever ripen and too ripe to ship. Unfortunately, with soft, easily bruised fruit, the critical point is reached long before the fruit is at its peak. In many places, it is possible to get tree-ripened fruit, either by picking it yourself, or by dealing with markets or local growers who understand the advantages of tree-ripened fruit.

If you have never had fruit that tasted like sweet sunshine, look a little harder for the natural tree-ripened item: you're in for a pleasant surprise. Out of season fruits are more expensive and usually of lower quality than in season food.

Fruits are very perishable. Buy only what will be used before it spoils. (See the **KITCHEN WAYS** section on STORAGE.)

Most fruits bruise easily. Love 'em, smell 'em, look at 'em, but easy on the squeezin'. The cost of food damaged by shoppers is reflected in the price we pay. "Waste not, want not."

Most store-bought fruit will need to finish ripening at home. Really ripe fruit usually can't survive the amount of handling it would get at a market, so usually the fruit that is sold is not quite ripe. (Sometimes the ripest, tastiest fruit gets given away because it is considered unsaleable!)

MELONS

Melons are subjected to more unproductive thumping, smelling, hefting, and general going-over than any other food that comes to mind.

Choosing a good tasting melon can be difficult, but knowing what to look for takes a lot of the guesswork out of the process.

CANTALOUPES smell good when they are ripe — a rich, definite "cantaloupey" odor. They get soft (especially at the blossom end) as they ripen and even softer as they get over-ripe. (This is true of all melons except watermelons). Immature fruit (which was picked too soon) will never ripen completely — so check for these indicators of maturity: Skin color — light yellow, possibly with a grey or buff cast. Stem end — should be a smooth, evenly shaped hollow. Surface texture — veining or netting which is well developed, thick and rough to touch. AVOID: very green melons, those with irregularly broken stems, and over-ripe melons, identifiable by mold, large bruises, or general mushy feeling accompanied by a bright yellow color.

CASABAS look a little like yellow pumpkins. The skin may have a greenish tint, and the blossom end may be slightly pointed. Their skin is thicker than that of a cantaloupe, and the stem remains attached after harvesting. They turn golden colored and get slightly soft as they ripen. As with all melons, wet brown depressions indicate decay.

CRENSHAWS are generally large, and colored like casabas, though often the skin is much greener. They have a fairly smooth skin with small lengthwise ridges (like an acorn squash). As with most other melons, look for a slight to moderate softening and a nice aroma.

HONEYDEWS are also large. They have a smooth skin which is greenish white, tending towards yellow as the melon ripens. Mature melons feel soft when stroked — hard, shiny

feeling skin indicates a melon that probably won't get ripe.

PERSIANS are very similar to cantaloupes (although much tastier and more expensive). They are selected by the same criteria, except that their netting is finer than that of a cantaloupe.

WATERMELONS are often sold in cut sections. Look for a deep red color (although striped-skin varieties have lighter insides) and dark colored seeds. White seeds indicate an immature melon. Melons that are past their prime will be dry and mealy or stringy.

We're told that an uncut watermelon can be judged by balancing a broomstraw cross-wise on the melon in a draft free room. Supposedly, on a ripe melon, the straw will move like a compass needle until it is lined up with the length of the melon.

If you don't have a broomstraw or a draft free room, look for a slightly dull skin and well-rounded ends. Thumping is somewhat unreliable, but a dull thud is indicative of an under-ripe melon, and a resounding boom is a sign that the melon is ripe.

ACID FRUITS

ACID FRUITS tend to contain more citric, oxalic, and ascorbic acid than other fruits (although their malic acid content is slightly below average.) They all have a distinct sharp or tart taste, which may disappear as the fruit becomes perfectly ripe.

CRANBERRIES aren't very palatable raw. They are grown primarily in Washington and Maine, along the sea coast, and are used in puddings, sauces, cakes, and sweet breads. See recipe for **Cranberry Pudding**.

CURRANTS are little sour fruits mostly used in cooking (jelly). Currants are very sweet when dried — they look like baby raisins. Some varieties are red, some are black.

GOOSE BERRIES are green waxy looking berries which grow wild in many mountainous regions. Great in pies and jams — require a lot of sweetening. See **Basic Pie Recipes**.

GRAPES can conveniently be divided into green and red-to-purple varieties. Thompson Seedless, Muscat, and other green grapes actually turn slightly yellow-brown and translucent when they are ripe. Concord, Cardinal, Emperor and other red-purple grapes are ripest when the color is very deep and dark and the fruit is slightly soft. The bitter taste of some grapes may be due to chemical residues; however, some varieties do have bitter skins naturally. Organically grown grapes are quite sweet, and may be smaller than chemically fertilized fruit.

GRAPEFRUIT. There are many varieties of grapefruit which are grown commercially in Florida and the hot South-West. Ruby Red, one of the most popular types, is identified by the red blush which shows through a small circular section of thin skin. Both ruby red and pink grapefruit have a reddish cast to their skins. White grapefruit tastes somewhat different from the red varieties, and its skin has a greenish cast. Ripe grapefruits are sometimes sweet enough to be enjoyed like oranges. (The bitter taste is from the quinine

in the thick membranes.) Grapefruit juice is very cleansing and may be mixed with other citrus juices. See **Broiled Grapefruit**.

61

LEMON trees are very beautiful and sweet scented and are often planted as ornamentals. Although some people eat lemons alone, most often they are juiced for salad dressing, lemon water, or lemonade. Lemon wedges may be used as a garnish. Lemon juice added to a dish right before serving will heighten and accent the flavors of the dish. Meyer's lemon is a sweet lemon which is occasionally available.

LIMES are similar in size and shape to lemons, but their skin is green and their juice more sharp and delicately flavored. May be used like lemons.

ORANGES are very cleansing, due in part to their high vitamin C content. The two varieties which are most popular in this country are Valencias (a natural strain) and the hybridized, winter-ripening navels (so-called because of the depression left when the "baby-orange" is removed). Both can be of high quality if bought in season. Ripe valencias may not always be orange. At certain times, the tree produces a lot of chlorophyll while in fruit, and the skin of the oranges may "re-green." Ripe oranges are slightly soft all over. Juicy oranges (and other citrus) are heavy for their size (an important clue to good fruit during a dry spell.) Citrus which is held for extended periods in cold storage or shipped cross-country is generally treated with chemicals to "prevent spoilage in transit." These chemicals don't taste too good, and may well not be too appropriate to include in one's diet. Fresh squeezed orange juice is delicious by itself, or as the base for any number of drinks. Try it mixed with yogurt or berries. See **Citrus Cooler**.

PINEAPPLES which are ripe will give slightly when pushed at the stem end, and the center leaves will detach with a gentle pull. Normally, the skin is green-brown when un-ripe, yellow when almost ready to eat, and tinged with red and orange when fully ripe. The "pineapple smell" will get stronger and stronger as the fruit ripens. Mold on the bottom end indicates that the fruit has probably passed its prime. Removing the touch outer skin and core needn't be difficult. We've found that these two ways work fine:

Method 1: Hold the fruit by the leaves at the top and slice the skin from the sides with vertical passes of a sharp, preferably wide-bladed knife. (Since the fruit is round, and the knife is not, this method involves some waste, but not much.) Next, slice the peel from the bottom and cut off the top. Stand the fruit up on one of the flat ends and slice the soft portion away from the tough central core in four to six sections. One needn't be too precise — any soft fruit left on the core can be gnawed off, like corn from the cob.

Method 2: Slice the fruit into rings and core each one individually, removing the skin by tracing around the edge with a paring knife.

Pineapple is often used in fruit curries — it can also be mixed with Papayas, Mangoes, and Bananas for a tropical salad. (Coconut tastes good in that salad also, but may cut your tongue just enough to allow the pineapple juice to sting unmercifully.) For a simple salad try mixing sliced pineapple, halved orange sections, and avocado or yogurt and honey.

TANGELOS, TANGERINES, TEMPLE ORANGES, and MANDARIN ORANGES are all small orange-like fruits. Depending on where and how they were grown, they may or may not be sweeter than regular oranges. Each one has a distinct and interesting flavor, and they are all good to eat as they are, juiced, in a smoothie, or in a fruit salad. Tangerines and Temple oranges are related to Mandarin oranges. Tangelos are a cross between a grapefruit and a tangerine.

SWEET FRUITS

APPLES are one of the most popular fruits in the U.S. They can be used in many ways, are available throughout the year, and are relatively inexpensive. There are many different kinds of apples growing in different parts of the country. Here's a list of some of the most common varieties and a little information about each one.

• RED DELICIOUS are produced in large quantities for the commercial market. An attractive apple with a snow white inside and deep red (or red and green or yellow) skin, delicious apples are crisp and have a high sugar content which justifies their name. Best for eating fresh because they don't store as well as some other types. Delicious apples can be identified by their conical shape and the five bumps on the blossom end. They shouldn't have too much green in the skin or immediately under it when they are ripe.

• GOLDEN OR YELLOW DELICIOUS are very similar to red delicious, but have a some-what more delicate flavor than their dark-skinned cousins. They seem to survive storage a little better than red delicious.

• JONATHANS are tender, tart, and have a bright red skin which may be flecked with green. Good for eating or cooking.

• WINESAP is one of the oldest American varieties. Typically small and somewhat rounded, the fruit is firm and tart, and has a deep red skin. A good all purpose apple which may be eaten fresh, cooked, baked, or juiced.

• MCINTOSH have a rich, spicy taste. The tender fruit comes in a two tone red and green skin. An all purpose apple which stores fairly well.

• ROME BEAUTIES are big and round and have green stripes or specks in the predominantly red skin. Their firm texture and mild flavor make them ideal for cooking or baking. A little tart, but some folks like to eat them raw. They store well.

• NORTHERN SPY is a large, fine textured apple with a waxy, bright-red skin and a pleasant spicy taste, which makes it popular for eating fresh.

• STAYMENS are large and have a rich red-colored skin. They are semi-firm and have a tart, spicy wine flavor. They are a relative of the winesap and store well.

• YORK (or imperial) apples are lopsided and have a red and green skin. Firm and tart, they are good cooked or baked.

• PIPPINS are good, tart cooking apples. They range in color from green to yellow.

• GRAVENSTEINS are the earliest ripening apple in most places on the West Coast. They turn from green to yellow to red as they ripen and are passable eating apples. Mainly used as a cooking apple.

• RHODE ISLAND GREEN is primarily a cooking and baking apple.

When buying apples, be aware of what you want. Eating apples should be fully ripe, but still crisp; cooking apples needn't be completely ripe, but will need more sweetener if they are green. Very unripe apples taste starchy, like a raw potato. They may also have a greenish tint just under the skin or throughout the flesh.

Supermarket apples are usually the fancier, more expensive grades which are free of blemishes and size irregularities. The wax which is used to coat the skin may be removed by peeling or extensive scrubbing in hot water. Some states have laws prohibiting the retail sale of very small or moderately blemished apples. These apples are usually sold for juice or allowed to rot, and can often be obtained very cheaply.

APRICOTS were called "the seed of the sun" by the ancient Persians. These small soft fruits are a beautiful golden orange when ripe and are a good source of vitamin A and iron (especially when dried). They have a nice flavor and texture, slightly tarter and drier than peaches. Good in fruit salads, smoothies, compotes, pies, preserved or juiced.

AVOCADOS are listed under "Succulent

Vegetables and Other Good Things" in the **VEGETABLES** section.

BANANAS are an excellent tonic for nervous depression when it is related to potassium deficiency: they provide a goodly amount of this essential mineral. Bananas which are imported into the U.S. are picked green and (for the most part) ripened in "gas chambers" with a poisonous gas similar to the gas they produce naturally when left to their own affairs. Ungassed bananas are available in some parts of the country, and they will ripen, given proper care. Changes in the color of the skin reflect the ripening process of bananas. As the fruit goes from green to yellow, starches are converted into sugars. When the tip and stem go from green to brown or black, and brown flecks appear on the yellow skin, the fruit is very near its peak, nutritionally and taste-wise. The fruit is easily bruised, and bruised areas will usually show as black areas on the skin. (However, not all black areas indicate bruises.) Bananas are extremely heat sensitive — a day in the sun or a warm space can progress a banana from unripe to overripe. Plastic or paper bags (which retain the natural gas) can hasten the ripening process. Overripe bananas acquire a strong smell and taste as they turn brown from the core out. The fruit is at its best when it is white or yellow white and uniformly soft. A hard center is a mark of under-ripeness. Bananas add a thick, rich texture to smoothies, and are a standard ingredient in fruit salads. See **Banana Cream Pie, Nanapea Chi** and **Zinnamaroon**.

BERRIES mold very quickly once they are ripe, so it's advisable to buy them very fresh, store them refrigerated, and use them right away. Ripe berries are usually soft and a uniform deep color. They may be served with milk, yogurt, or cream and a little honey; with granola and bananas; on top of pancakes, **Tortillas**, or **Chapatis**; as a topping for ice cream; or with other fruit in a salad.

CHERRIES are small round fruits which mature after the exquisitely beautiful blossoms have fallen from the tree. The sweet cherries are as delicious as any other fruit and are often eaten alone, for two reasons. First, they are difficult to pit, and therefore, time consuming to prepare for a salad; secondly, they have a great potential for psychological addiction. Unfortunately, they are also quite expensive in most places, which limits their use to special occasions. Bings, Tartarians, Black Lamberts, and other dark cherries will turn from bright red to a deep blackish purple as they ripen and get slightly soft at the peak of their development. Napoleons, Royal Annes, and other light varieties will get yellower or even shade to orange or red as they ripen. Softness is a clue to ripeness, but light varieties are generally not as sweet as the dark ones. Fresh cherries do not store well and should be eaten without delay when they become ripe. Sour cherries are used to make that all time favorite, cherry pie.

COCONUTS are rich nut-like things which can be cracked and eaten fresh or grated and dried. Avoid those with moldy spots or a weird smell. Before you buy a coconut, make sure it has milk inside: listen as you shake it. With a nail and a hammer, it is possible to make two holes and drain the milk. Then the hammer can be used to break the coconut into pieces, and a table knife can be used to remove the hull. See the **NUTS AND SEEDS** section for more details.

FIGS are one of the oldest foods of mankind. Whether fresh, canned, or dried they are tasty and nutritious. There are four major types of figs: Capri, Myrna, San Pedro, and Common. Capri figs are not grown for eating, but rather as homes for a certain kind of small wasp. These wasps develop in the Capri figs, which are picked and hung in baskets in Calimyrna and San Pedro trees. When the wasps leave the Capri figs, they enter the Calimyrnas or San Pedros and polinate them. They don't lay eggs and apparently don't harm the figs at all.

Calimyrna figs (the California Smyrna) are white or a beautiful yellow color and among the best and most sought after varieties for eating fresh or drying. They are large and have loads of crunchy seeds which impart a very nice, nutty flavor and texture to the fruit. San Pedro figs are a black fig, not very commonly grown in this country. Of the common figs, Black Mission most closely resembles the San Pedro, and it's superior taste and texture have made it far more popular. Black missions are smaller than Calimyrnas, but are quite good, either fresh or dried. Other common figs which are popular are the White Adriatic (used mainly for drying and in the baking industry); Kadotas, a white fig which is considered one of the best for canning; and the Brown Turkey, Celeste, Hunt and Magnolia varieties, which are grown in some regions of the Southern United States, primarily for canning and preserving.

Most of the commercial fig production in the United States is centered in California. When the figs are picked for eating fresh, they must be handled very carefully, and consequently, are expensive. Figs that are to be dried are allowed to completely ripen on the tree and go through a certain amount of dehydration. The ground underneath the trees is cultivated and rolled, and as the figs drop to the ground, they are harvested. After being more completely dried (in the sun or by a dehydrator), the figs are stored, usually in air tight compartments under fumigation. As orders are received, the fruit is mechanically washed in a hot water and steam bath which cleans, softens, and cooks them. They are then packed and shipped. Some organically grown figs are dried and shipped without being cooked. Because they have a lower moisture content, they keep better and are a better buy than the wet pack figs.

65

It's fairly simple to dry your own figs (and other fruits) if you have access to a large amount of fresh fruit. More information in the **CANNING AND PRESERVING** section.

Fresh figs are highly perishable. Ideally, they should be gently picked when completely ripe, and used almost immediately. Improper handling and prolonged storage will quite noticeably affect the palatability of this luscious fruit. Be aware that tightly packed figs often mold — check underneath the top layer when purchasing them in boxes at a marketplace. Some people dislike the taste of fresh fig skins.

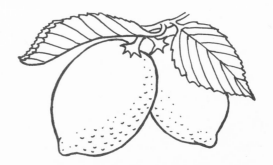

Dried figs are a super food. They are nutritious, store well, and can be enjoyed as a meal unto themselves or as part of other dishes. See: **Apple-Fig Goo, CANNING AND PRESERVING**, and the discussion of dried fruit in this section.

MANGOES are a rich, tangy tropical treat. They contain a reasonable amount of Vitamin C. The fruit is shaped like a flattened avocado and likewise has a large seed (which is firmly attached to the fruit). Mexican Mangoes are huge in comparison to the more commonly marketed Hawaiian varieties. The skin, which turns from yellow to red as the fruit softens and ripens, doesn't taste too good, but the insides are nice alone, in smoothies, or in salads.

NECTARINES have a smooth, shiny, plum-like skin which turns reddish gold as the fruit ripens. Inside is a delightful golden succulence which is reminiscent of its other parent, the peach. If one waits until the fruit gets slightly but uniformly soft, the tartness of the unripe fruit will be converted into a luscious sweetness which rivals the flavor of a good peach. When the fruit is ripe, the untasty skin may be easily removed with the teeth, fingers, or a table knife. If it doesn't come off in big pieces, the fruit is probably not ripe.

PAPAYAS are rather odd looking light bulb-shaped fruits with a thin, tough skin which is usually yellow mottled with green. As they get thoroughly ripe, the skin will get less green and more yellow (or even red, in the case of the large Mexican varieties), and they become slightly soft. After the myriad black seeds have been scooped out of the center of each half, the fruit may be eaten with a spoon, using the skin as a bowl. Papayas contain an enzyme called papain, which is said to be a digestive aid. In fact, it does break down protein molecules, but only under alkaline conditions. Papain is permanently de-activated by normal stomach acidity. Excellent in smoothies.

PEACHES are so exquisite it's hard to say anything suitable about them. Like other fruits, they aren't sweet unless they're ripe (and may not be even then, if they were heavily fertilized with nitrogen). Thanks to modern agri-technology, different varieties of peaches are available over a fairly long period during the summer and fall. The extremely early and late varieties usually aren't the best, but may well be worth eating. Peaches may be large or small, yellow or white inside, and have a free stone or a cling stone. The fuzzy skin can be easily removed in large pieces when the fruit is ripe. Messy to eat, but what a treat!

PEARS ripen off the tree, and should be picked carefully (they bruise easily) before they get yellow, and then (ideally) individually wrapped in tissue or newspaper. They get mealy when over-ripe. There are several varieties which are commonly grown.

• BARTLETT — large, excellent flavor and texture. Ripens early and is a good all purpose pear, except that it doesn't store well. Clear yellow with possibly a slight greenish cast when ripe.

• BOSC - Smaller and slightly later than the Bartlett. Yellow skin with a marked tendency to russet (turn rough and brown). Russeting is normal and does not adversely affect the quality of the fruit. Long tapering neck gives an appearance much different from other pears.

- COMICE — Some say it's the queen of the pears. Delicate flavor and melt-in-your-mouth texture. Bruises very easily and does not ship or store well. Usually available around Christmas, they are greenish-yellow when ripe.

- D'ANJOU — a midseason fruit which stores well. Creamy yellow when ripe, may russet.

- WINTER NELLIS — Small, often heavily russetted. Stores well, good flavor and texture.

PERSIMMONS are fantastically good, although perhaps too rich and sumptious for some. They will not pucker your mouth when they are ripe. Their reputation for puckering stems from people's impatience. As they are far too delicate to ship when ripe, one must wait, sometimes for weeks even, for store-bought fruit to get ripe. Wait until the skin gets translucent and the fruit is extremely soft with the common Hachiya variety, which has a pointed end. The smaller, flatter, tomato-like Fuyu loses its astringency before it gets super soft. Keeping the fruit in a closed container, especially with an apple, will speed the ripening process. Persimmons are good mashed with bananas, in fruit salads, or as an ingredient in frozen fruit ice creams.

PLUMS, like most fruits, occur in myriad varieties, and modern horticultural techniques are creating new types each year. Plums come with green, yellow, red, purple, or blue skins, and depending on the variety, are tangy or sweet and have edible or bitter skins. The pits are difficult to remove. European plums are thought to date back as much as 5,000 years. Two common European plums are the President, a dark purple late-ripener, and the Italian Prune plum. (Prunes are plums which

can be dried whole without fermenting.) The Italian prune is medium to large, tart, firm, dark purple, and good for eating fresh, drying, or canning. "Japanese" plums originated in China. Kelseys are large, good eating late-ripeners which are green inside and out. The popular Santa Rosa has a crimson to purple skin around its large, dark red and very tasty inside.

POMEGRANATES flourish in desert climates, but often do well in cooler places. The fruit is bumpily rounded and covered with a dark red skin which dries out and gets tough and leathery as the fruit ripens. Buy 'em when they shrivel up and get tough, and then they will be sweet. The jelly like stuff around the seeds is good, the pith is not. Cut the fruit in half, or try this super technique: thoroughly mash the inside with your thumbs without breaking the skin, then carefully cut a tiny hole with a sharp knife. The delicious juice can be sucked out without messing with the seeds or pith. Be careful, as the juice stains and will squirt out when you cut the hole.

DRIED FRUIT

Humans, like many other creatures, need to store away the abundance of spring and summer edibles for use in winter, when nature is not so bountiful. Long before supermarkets, home freezers, and canning jars manifested, people dried their food in the sun or near a fire. Dried fruit keeps very well if it is kept cool, dry, and away from animals. (Storage is discussed more completely in the **KITCHEN WAYS** section; the drying process itself, in **CANNING AND PRESERVING**.)

It is possible to reconstitute the fruit by soaking or cooking it in water or fruit juice — or one can eat it dry. It is perfect food for backpacking or taking alone in a sack lunch. As a candy substitute, dried fruit is great — but remember, just like candy, it sticks to the teeth and may encourage decay if allowed to "stick around" very long.

Most commercial dried fruit has been treated with sulfur and some form of chemical preservative or fumigants. Naturally dried fruit is often drier than the soft, chewy commercial product, which reduces the need for chemical preservatives. The lower moisture content makes the fruit tougher, but a light steaming will soften it right up. In the absence of sulfur, there is a tendency for the fruit to darken and discolor, but this doesn't affect the nutritional value or taste appeal. In fact, the natural dried fruit is probably a better bargain nutritionally, since it doesn't include as many chemical residues for the body to eliminate.

Naturally dried fruit may ferment in hot, moist, conditions — so try and obtain it from someplace where it is stored in a cool location. It's a good idea to wash the fruit, to remove dust, bug eggs and the like. Unfumigated dates and figs may be contaminated by worms or their droppings or eggs. Splitting them in half and checking for contamination before putting them in the mouth is highly recommended. With proper techniques (freezing or extended low temperature storage), unfumigated fruit

may be produced without significant contamination (otherwise, it wouldn't pass agricultural inspection.)

Spring and early summer is probably the worst time to purchase dried fruit, for two reasons. First of all, there's lots of fresh fruit to eat, and the body needs the water to help digest the sugars, especially when it's warm out. Secondly, spring is the time when the tail end of the dried fruit crop is available. The highest quality of any particular dried fruit will generally be available shortly after the end of the season of that particular fresh fruit. (Assuming free market economy conditions and the absence of stock-piling and other manipulation.)

Enough talk. Here are some recipes to help you use all these tree and vine ripened delicacies.

Banana Ice Cream

Freeze bananas in their skins until hard. Remove from the freezer and cut into 1 - 2 inch pieces. Slice the skin and peel it off (they may need to thaw a little). Or, peel before freezing and seal in a plastic bag. Put the pieces in small amounts into a blender and blend until smooth, or thaw a little and squish with a fork. Eat immediately or refreeze in a covered container. Top with **Carob Syrup**, fruit, nuts or whatever.

Nanapea Chi

5 ripe bananas, frozen
4 medium peaches

This is a fine treat for company or on a warm afternoon. It's easiest to make in a blender, but you can get by with a big fork or a wire whip and a strong arm (or an egg beater).

Let frozen bananas thaw slightly. Peel and chunk peaches, and puree. Then peel and slice the bananas, adding them to the peaches. Blend until mixture is a fairly uniform consistency, like ice cream. Eat as is or return to the freezer for a while to stiffen slightly. Yields approximately four cups.

Zinnamaroon

5 frozen bananas
1 pint box of bush or black berries
1/4 - 1/2 t cinnamon
1 - 2 nectarines (chopped)
handful of chopped, pitted dates

Peel and blend bananas. Fold in cleaned berries, cinnamon, dates and chopped nectarines. REALLY GOOD.

Variations: Use applesauce; other kinds of berries; thin with apple juice; add more dates or other dried fruit; add coconut.

Banana Popsicles

Cut chilled, firm, ripe, peeled bananas in half, crosswise. Insert popsicle stick. Freeze as they are or coat bananas with chilled or creamed honey. Roll in chopped cashews. Freeze unwrapped until solid, then store in freezer containers or plastic bags. Variation: dip in **Carob Sauce** after rolling in cashews (see **DESSERTS** for recipe).

Basic Fruit Parfait

Banana Ice Cream (**Zinnamaroon,**
  Nanapea Chi, or just plain frozen bananas
slightly crushed fruit (berries, peaches,
  papaya, persimmons, etc.)

Layer in glasses, creating stripes. Top with whipped cream or yogurt and a cherry. Grated lemon peel, cinnamon, or mace can be sprinkled at any level. Be aware of how the colors will look as you create — they can be very beautiful.

Banaple Parfait

For each serving:
  1 frozen banana
  1/2 C hot **Apple Sauce**
Optional ingredients:
  Carob Syrup
  chopped almonds
  chopped dates (soft)
  slices of fresh fruit

70

Peel the frozen bananas and mash into a smooth cream (you may need to let them thaw a bit). Swirl in individual serving dishes with the **Apple Sauce** (and **Carob Syrup** if used) and garnish with any of the optional ingredients, or layer the ingredients in parfait glasses (clear drinking glasses work fine). Serve immediately, as the contrast between the hot and cold ingredients is a delightful experience which is lost when the dessert is allowed to sit.

Raw Applesauce

apples
sweet cider
other fruit such as bananas, berries or
    pears (optional)
lemon juice (optional)

Wash, core, and chop apples, leaving skins on. Put in blender a few pieces at a time, adding enough sweet cider to make blending easy. Scrape sides of blender frequently and gradually add rest of chopped apples. Other fruits may be added as desired. A bit of lemon juice retards coloring and helps retain flavor. For best nutrition, color and flavor, raw applesauce should be prepared immediately before serving. It can also be added to cakes and breads, giving them a moist, rich texture.

Applesauce

apples
honey
cinnamon

Core and chop apples. Peel if skins are slightest bit bitter. Using the heaviest gauge pan you have (cast iron is best) put apples on lowest heat possible. Cover tightly. If only a light gauge pan is available, or quick cooking is desired, it may be best to add a small amount of water or apple juice. Simmer very slowly until water has come out of apples and they are beginning to soften. Add honey and cinnamon to taste. No amounts are given here because it depends on the size, kind and age of the apples. Cook until desired consistency; apples should be soft. If smooth applesauce is desired, beat with a wire whip or mash with a potato masher or blend in blender or put through a food mill. If apples are bland or old tasting or mealy, add a few drops of lemon juice to perk up the flavor. Serve warm or cold.

Variations: add raisins, sliced bananas, chopped dates.

Apple Fig Goo

4 C fresh figs
5 small apples, chunked
4 small pears, chunked
1/2 - 3/4 C dried apricots, chopped fine
1/2 C raisins
Optional seasoning:
    1/2 t powdered ginger
    1/4 t fresh ground cinnamon

Cut up the figs, discarding the stems. Simmer them, stirring occasionally, while you prepare the rest of the fruit. Add the apples, pears, apricots and raisins all at once, and stew over a medium heat, stirring frequently. When the apples are soft and the figs have cooked down into a sauce, add the seasonings, if you wish. (It is quite good without them, so taste first.)

Serve hot, alone, or with millet, hot or cold with yogurt, as a topping for ice cream or as a filling in bar cookies. It may be thickened by adding 2 T of arrowroot dissolved in a couple of tablespoons of water and bringing to a boil again for a pie filling. Yield: Approximately 5 cups. Serves 4 - 6 as a side dish or dessert.

Variations: Try adding 1/2 t dried lemon peel or the juice of half a lemon. Garnish with slices of uncooked bananas. You might want to substitute: berries for figs, peaches or plums for pears, prunes for dried apricots, dates for raisins, 1 - 2 t **Curry Powder** for other spices.

Winter Breakfast

12 C chunked cooking apples
1 C water
1 C shopped dates
1 C chopped, mixed dried fruit (raisins,
    prunes, figs, pears, etc.)
1/2 t cinnamon
4 medium bananas, sliced

Combine all above ingredients except bananas and cinnamon. Cook slowly in a covered kettle until apples are mushy. At this point add bananas and cinnamon. Cover, turn off heat, and let bananas steam until slightly soft.

Ginger Stewed Pears

1/2 C honey
juice and rind of 1 lemon and 1 orange
1/2 to 1 t ginger
4 pears, peeled and cored

Bring first three ingredients to boil. Add pears and simmer for five minutes, basting with the liquid mixture frequently. Serves 2 to 4. Good served with yogurt, cottage or cream cheese.

Honey Stewed Prunes

1 orange
20 large unpitted prunes
1/3 C honey
1 T arrowroot

Juice orange and cut peel into fine strips. In a saucepan combine prunes, 2 C water, orange peel and honey. Bring to a boil, cover and simmer 20 minutes until prunes are soft. Using a slotted spoon, remove prunes to a serving dish. Combine arrowroot and orange juice. Add to syrup in saucepan. Bring to a boil and cook, stirring until thick and smooth. Pour over prunes. May be served warm or cold. Good served with yogurt, cottage or cream cheese. Serves 4 to 6.

Peachy Fruit Soup

2 C water
1 C peeled peach slices
1 C plum slices
approximately 1/4 C honey (amount depends on sweetness of fruit)
2 T arrowroot
1 T lemon juice
1/2 t vanilla
3 C additional fruit: blueberries, peaches, plums, apples, bananas, etc.

Combine water with peach and plum slices in a saucepan. Bring to a boil and simmer 15 minutes. Mash fruit or puree in a blender. Add to peach and plum mixture. Add honey to taste. Mix arrowroot with a small amount of liquid and add it to the mixture. Bring to a boil, stirring to prevent lumping. Remove from heat, add lemon and vanilla and chill, covered. Just before serving, add additional fruit. Use 2 to 3 varieties for a pleasing color. Serves 4.

Baked Apples

Wash and core apples, leaving part of the core in the bottom of the apple to act as a plug. Fill the cavity with honey and sprinkle with cinnamon. Bake at 350° for 40 to 60 minutes (depending on the size of the apple), until apple is soft. If apples dry out, baste with apple juice.

Variations: stuff with raisins, dates, or other dried fruits or nuts. Use molasses or maple syrup instead of (or in combination with) honey.

Baked Banana Apples

2 medium bananas
1 T lemon juice
1/4 C honey
1/4 t ground nutmeg
6 medium baking apples

Wash and core apples and place in shallow baking dish. Peel and mash bananas and mix with lemon juice, honey and nutmeg. Fill apples with banana mixture. Bake at 375° for one hour or until tender. Serves 6.

Baked Bananas

2 medium bananas (about 6" to 7" long)
2 T lemon juice
2 T honey

Peel bananas and halve lengthwise. Combine lemon juice and honey and spread over bananas, coating them thoroughly. Bake at 400° for 10 minutes or until bananas are golden. Serves 2 to 4.

Variations: Use molasses instead of honey; to basting mixture, add a T or so oil or butter; add 1 t orange rind or 1/2 t ginger; or add 1/4 C coconut shreds.

Baked Curried Bananas

4 large bananas
1/4 C butter or oil
1 t **Curry Powder**
2 T honey

Cut bananas lengthwise, then in half crosswise. Melt butter or heat oil in shallow baking dish in preheated 350° oven. Stir in **Curry Powder** and honey. Dip banana pieces in mixture, turning to cover well. Bake about 15 minutes. Serves 4 (large servings).

Broiled Grapefruit

Wash and dry grapefruit and cut in half crosswise, allowing one half for each person. With a sharp knife, cut around the sections, separating the soft part of the fruit from the membranes. Spread the top with honey and dot with a bit of butter. Place under broiler until the honey begins to caramelize. Serve hot as a dessert or for breakfast.

Baked Peaches

1/3 C honey
1/4 C lemon juice
1 C water
6 to 8 medium peaches

Mix first three ingredients. Peel peaches, cut in half, and pit. Arrange them in a 2 quart casserole. Pour honey mixture over peaches. Cover and bake at 350° for 1/2 hour or until tender. Serve warm or cold. Serves 6.

Honey Baked Pears

4 large pears, halved and cored
juice of one lemon
1/4 to 1/2 C honey
1 t cinnamon
2 t oil

Mix last four ingredients and pour over pear halves in shallow, slightly oiled baking pan. Bake until soft at 350°. Serve hot. May be served with yogurt or cream.

Variations: use peaches instead of pears.

Curried Fruit

1 C pears, peeled and cut in half
1 C honey
1 C pineapple chunks
1 C peaches, peeled and quartered
2 to 3 t **Curry Powder**
butter or oil

Melt 1/4 to 1 C butter or oil with honey
and **Curry Powder**. Spread mixture on fruit
in a flat baking pan. Bake at 300° for an hour,
basting occasionally. Serve hot.

Variations: use bananas, apples, cashews,
or dates.

Fried Bananas

3 bananas
4 to 6 T flour
1/4 t mace
1 T milk, apple juice or water
1/4 C honey
1/4 t cinnamon
1/4 t lemon peel
oil

Add flour to honey until honey will hold no
more. Add seasonings. Add enough liquid (a
little bit at a time) to make a thick batter. Cut
peeled bananas lengthwise and then crosswise.
Coat in batter and saute in hot oil until batter
browns. Serves 4 to 6.

Variations: Substitute 1/4 to 1/2 t
turmeric for all the above spices.

ALSO REFER TO . . .

Fruit salad recipes in the **SALADS AND
SALAD DRESSINGS** section

Juice making instructions in the **JUICES**
section

Agar Jells in the **SALADS AND SALAD
DRESSINGS** section

Instructions for preserving fruit in the
CANNING AND PRESERVING section

Recipes for jams, jellies and pickled fruit
in the **CANNING AND PRESERVING**
section

Pie recipes in the **DESSERTS** section

Jyoti's Banana Bread, Almost

Apple Nut Muffins

Orange Honey Butter

Orange Jubilee

Date Milk

Krsna Drink

Banana Oatmeal Cookies

Aunt Anges' Applesauce Cake

VEGETABLES

VEGETABLE SECTION

NOTE: Vegetable salad recipes are in the salads and salad dressings section.

VEGETABLES

A vegetable is the edible root, stalk, leaf or flower of a plant. Corn (which is a grain) and the "fruits of the blossom" (such as tomatoes, beans, eggplants and squashes) are usually called vegetables, although technically they belong in other food classes. The word vegetable comes from a word which means "animating; hence, full of life" — an apt description of this group of foods.

Plants, as part of their life process, manufacture vitamins, proteins, and carbohydrates. They also draw up minerals from the earth. When we eat plant life, our bodies extract and use these nutrients, as well as benefiting from the cellulose or "bulk," a fibrous material which conditions the intestines and facilitates elimination. Cellulose must be broken down by juicing machines, chopping, shredding or cooking and thorough chewing in order to make available the nutrients which are locked up in the cells, as humans don't have any cellulose-digesting enzymes.

As important as these nutrients is another, subtler form of nourishment called prana, or life energy. Prana can be understood as an energy, similar to electricity but vibrating at much higher frequencies, which is present in all forms of life. It is said that prana is the animating force of the universe — the divine essence that nourishes us when we breathe and when we eat. Certain foods, fresh vegetables among them, are known to be good sources of the prana we need to insure our health and well being.

Produce that is organically grown and fresh from the garden is infinitely preferable to what is obtainable in the majority of stores, for, in most cases, flavor and nutrients (including prana) deteriorate during storage and transit and are adversely affected by the multitude of chemicals commonly used in commercial food production. Just as a freshly plucked leaf of lettuce is more "alive" than its limp, three-day-old counterpart, it is more capable of sustaining life. So, whenever possible, it is advantageous to invest some time and love in a garden, as there is a long term reward of health in addition to the immediate satisfaction of working with the elements and creative forces of nature.

When garden fresh vegetables are not available, the wise and careful shopper can obtain food of reasonable quality at a retail store. To help choose vegetables from the marketplace, we offer here a guide to the indicators of freshness and quality and hints on how and when to buy. First, some general comments:

• When shopping for vegetables, it is wise to check behind and beneath the stack. Often the freshest food is put there, in hope that people will buy the more accessible older food first. (Remember to carefully and lovingly restack the display, though, or you are liable to cause some bad feelings in the mind of your hard-working friend.) Compare what you find underneath and in back with the food in front, and buy what suits you best.

• Train your powers of observation. Learn to smell, touch, taste, look at and listen to the food: you can easily become a discriminating shopper. Generally, vegetables that are no longer crisp are less nutritious and flavorful than they were when fresh. Small vegetables are often better tasting than the huge chemically fertilized "eye grabbers". Good, normal coloring is important, though. (See descriptions of specific vegetables.) Beware of special "five for a dollar" type prices, as they are often the same or slightly lower than the regular price.

• Shop early in the morning, if you can, for the lights and relatively warmer temperatures of the display case hasten the loss of nutrients. Markets that do a lot of business generally have fresher food than smaller operations. Many rural communities have farm markets and roadside stands that buy directly from the growers and offer (at lower prices) food that is fresher and tastier than that in stores.

• When you arrive home after shopping, we suggest that you place your vegetables unwashed and untrimmed in tightly sealed plastic bags in the refrigerator. This practice helps retain nutrients as well as crispness. Many vegetables (especially cabbage and root vegetables) are still "alive" when you purchase them, and cold storage slows their metabolic processes and extends their lives, as well as maintaining their nutritional value. (Storage is more thoroughly discussed in the **KITCHEN WAYS** section.)

In the pages that follow, vegetables have been classified according to whether the most commonly eaten portion is a root, stalk, leaf, flower bud, or "fruit of the blossom," also called succulent vegetables. We have included serving suggestions and/or references to recipes whenever possible, as well as discussing what to look for when purchasing each vegetable. The recipes which follow the descriptions of the vegetables are grouped according to the cooking method they use. A discussion of each cooking method immediately precedes the recipes which utilize that particular method.

ROOT VEGETABLES

Fresh root vegetables are hard and firm: carrots, for example, will snap in half when bent sharply. Yellowed or limp leaves on root vegetables indicate that the food is getting old. Often, especially on beets, produce workers will cut off any yellowed greens — check near the root for places where the stalks have been cut. Usually, root vegetables sold in plastic bags with the greens completely trimmed away are very old and undesirable. (Carrots and parsnips are exceptions.)

Peeling root vegetables results in the loss of much of the vitamin content; scrubbing with a stiff brush under running water does an adequate job of cleaning and is also less time consuming. Note that root vegetables can accumulate many times the concentration of DDT (and other poisons) that is present in the surrounding soil, and that very little is known about the cumulative effect of these toxins on the human body. For this and other reasons, you may wish to obtain organically grown vegetables, or grow your own. On the whole, root vegetables tend to be somewhat starchy, and they may take longer to cook than other vegetables. Most roots can be added to soups and stews, and some, particularly potatoes and parsnips, will help to thicken the broth.

BEETS of all sizes, if they are firm and have crisp green tops, are a tasty addition to any meal. Grated raw, they are excellent in salads. Sliced or quartered and steamed, they can be served with a little lemon juice and salt, or butter, or glaceed with lemon juice, honey and orange or lemon rind.

CARROTS are one of the sweetest roots and can be used like beets, stir fried, or munched out of hand. Try them cooked with broccoli and zucchini, or new potatoes and peas. May be seasoned with mint, oregano, dill or thyme, or a hot sauce (simmer tomatoes with bell peppers, anaheims, or whatever kind of pepper you feel comfortable eating.)

Small tender carrots have a milder taste than the large, easy-to-cut-or-shred version. Carrots with splits or cracks may be bitter; rubbery ones are rather flat tasting. Soft, moldy places are very undesirable. Green areas at the top of the root are due to the presence of chlorophyll — an unusual type of "sunburn." Try grated carrots in salads, on sandwiches, or as a garnish.

CELERIAC is the root of a certain variety of the celery plant. It's good in **Borscht**, steamed, or baked like potatoes. Celeriacs from three to four inches in diameter are preferable to larger roots, which may be woody or hollow. Parboiling makes peeling much easier.

GARLIC is a very stimulating spice which is valued in illness for its cleansing properties. Not usually recommended for those who meditate. See ONIONS in this section and **FOOD AND CONSCIOUSNESS** for more information.

GIRASOLE is the root of a certain sun-flower plant native to Canada. It is also called the Jerusalem artichoke, due to historic mis-pronunciation of the Italian name. This tuber has a crisp, nutlike flavor when added to salads and is also good cooked. Choose as you would any other root; avoid soft spots and overall flabbiness. Clean well with a scrub brush — if necessary, break off the "knobs" to get at the dirt.

JICAMA is a root which is frequently used like potatoes in Mexico. Can be shredded and added to salads, or eaten raw like apple slices (peel and sprinkle with lemon juice.) Can be used like potatoes in almost anything. The roots are usually large, and may mold if not used up in a reasonable time. Trim the mold off, presto — the jicama is just like new (almost).

ONIONS are a stimulating food, similar to garlic (both contain "volatile oils," which impart the characteristic flavor). They create heat in the body, and many sages teach that onions, garlic, and similar foods have a nega-tive effect on the mind and recommend that they not be eaten by those on a spiritual path. For this reason, onions, garlic, chives, leeks, scallions and the like have been omitted from the recipes in this book. We have found that most dishes which traditionally call for one of these stimulating foods can be made even tastier without them. Onions and garlic, especially, tend to overwhelm the other seasonings. Bell peppers and spices are good substitutes for those who desire a mild "bite" in a particular dish. Sauteed celery resembles sauteed onion both in texture and appearance.

PARSNIPS look somewhat like old wrinkled carrots which have turned white. If they aren't too old, they are very sweet. They have a tough and sometimes bitter skin which can be rubbed off after they have been parboiled. Try them steamed and mashed, like potatoes, or in casseroles, or in steamed vegetable combinations. Parsnips can be sliced, dredged in flour, sprinkled with oil, and baked until tender. They make an excellent addition to soup stock. Can be used like kohlrabi, carrots or turnips. Look for firm roots, preferably less than one inch in diameter at the top.

POTATOES store best in a cool, dry, dark place. This fools them into thinking that they're still underground, and minimizes the chance of their getting soft and sprouting. They're still edible after they've sprouted, but they are better when they are still firm. Don't eat the sprouts, though — they are poisonous.

Like most vegetables, potatoes need not be peeled; a simple scrubbing will do. Potatoes may be baked at any temperature between 325° F. and 450° F., so they can easily be coordinated with other baked things. It is advisable to pierce the skin a few times before baking to prevent the tubers from exploding. The skins may be oiled prior to baking: it will make them softer. Potatoes are done when they are soft when squished (use a hot pad) or stuck with a fork. They'll cook faster with a large (16 penny), clean, ungalvanized nail stuck in the center. At 350°, allow about 1 hour for medium size potatoes to bake.

When steaming potatoes, allow lots of water, as they take a long time to cook, and really soak up water. Cooking times will vary; here are some estimates for steaming on the hottest flame or setting available:

For thin slices, 10 minutes
small cubes, 15 to 20 minutes
large cubes or quartered, 20 to 30 minutes
whole, the good Lord willing, they may
   eventually get done.
Serve as is, or mashed with the traditional milk, butter, and salt. (Some folks like salad dressing or sour cream on their potatoes.)

See **Alu Sabje**, and the potato recipes in this section.

RADISHES, like onions, garlic, and bell peppers, contain what are known as "volatile oils." They impart a slightly hot or tangy flavor, and are often used to jazz up a green salad. Good on the hors d'ouevres tray, too. The white radishes are much hotter than the average red ones. Some people feel radishes effect their meditation adversely and don't eat them.

RUTABAGAS belong to the turnip family. They have yellow insides, and although they have a much stronger flavor, they can be used in the same ways as turnips. Those three inches or less in diameter are best. Generally used in soups and stews. Try seasoning with caraway seed and nutmeg or basil.

SALSIFY is also known as the "vegetable oyster." It can be used as the base for a delicious vegetable burger. Simply grate it and mix with carrots or other vegetables, form into patties, and fry. May also be used like parsnips.

SWEET POTATOES are similar to yams, only somewhat lighter in color, and stringier. Some like them better than yams, some don't. More like a potato, not as sweet as yams.

TURNIPS that are small (1-1/2" maximum diameter) are preferred for a number of reasons. They are sweeter, more tender, and more easily digested than the large ones. Turnips can be steamed (and perhaps mashed, alone or mixed with potatoes), baked, or slivered, soaked and (with potatoes that have been prepared the same way) fried like hash browns.

To bake turnips as a casserole: steam twelve turnips for ten to twenty minutes. Place in an oiled baking dish and add 1/2 cup sour cream or yogurt and a teaspoon of basil. Bake at 350° for 20 to 30 minutes (until tender). Garnish with salt, paprika, and lemon juice.

Turnips can be stuffed with any of the following, after they have been steamed and hollowed out: the cooked insides mixed with potatoes or carrots, and perhaps a little sauteed bell pepper; any rice stuffing (see index); may be topped with grated cheese; or leftover steamed vegetables that have been pureed, topped with grated cheese or ground nuts.

YAMS may be baked or peeled, steamed and mashed, and served plain or with butter and/or honey or maple syrup. To candy yams, first scrub and steam them. Put into a sauce-pan and add oil, honey, a taste of citrus peel, and if you like, raisins and cinnamon or mace. Purple velvet yams are highly regarded. They can be identified by the purple "velvet" which shows through when the skin is scratched.

STALK VEGETABLES

ASPARAGUS is a member of the lily family.

81

The young tender shoots are quite a delicacy, either slivered (raw or cooked) into a salad or steamed and served with oil or butter. The entire stalk is very nearly as tasty as the tips; it just requires more cooking to reach the same state of tenderness. Asparagus that is limp has seen better days, and stalks that have a butt end larger than 3/4" in diameter are liable to be excessively fibrous. Choose stalks with tightly closed tips and smoothly rounded spears. It's said that a uniform green color is desirable, but never having tasted a uniformly green asparagus, we have no comment.

CELERY is a versatile plant, widely used as an appetizer (plain or stuffed with peanut butter, cheese, or any spread) and in salads, soups, stews and just about every other kind of dish that exists. The whole plant is edible, from the leaves (used in salads, soups or dried as an herb) to the root (see CELERIAC). The base of the stalk is just as good as the rest, although it is usually lighter colored. Crisp dark green heads that haven't been excessively trimmed are the best buy. It is somewhat difficult to grow at home. Does not shred well.

KOHLRABI is a member of the cabbage family that looks like a green turnip that decided to grow stems and leaves out of a number of places instead of just the top. Golf-ball to tennis-ball sized ones are generally more tender; the big ones get a very thick skin. Peel if oversized, steam (don't forget the greens) or dice and cook in a cream sauce. May be sliced and broiled for a potato chip type of thing.

RHUBARB: see **FRUITS**. (We put it in there because most folks use it as a fruit to make a sweet pie. Apologies to botany enthusiasts.)

LEAF VEGETABLES

All leafy vegetables can be used like lettuce in salads. Some — romaine, spinach, kale, endive and mustard greens, to name a few — can be stronger tasting or more bitter than others, and it may be advisable to use them in combination with the milder greens — red leaf, butter, and Australian lettuces, for example. It is widely believed that healthy green vegetables are a darker green than their supposedly less nutritious brothers and sisters. As far as we know, the validity of this theory has not yet won the approval of the scientific establishment, but organic gardeners report that nitrogen-deficient vegetables are identifiable by their lighter color. The amounts of other nutrients may also be associated with the coloring; streaks of red or brown in a leaf may indicate deficiencies of some kind in the soil. (Of course, they may also just be signs of decay that has set in after the vegetable was harvested.) Small amounts of "rusting" at the edge of the leaves is nothing to worry about, but it does indicate less than perfect quality.

Leafy vegetables last only a short time after they are harvested, shipped, displayed and sold. Careful handling is very important. Lettuce that is packed too tightly in crates will bruise and spoil. Greens need to be kept very cold to preserve their crispness and often they are sprayed with water during storage to prevent dehydration. (This may result in a loss of water-soluble vitamins.) Traditionally, discolored greens are trimmed before and during the period of their display at the market. It's fairly easy to judge the freshness of leafy vegetables by their crispness. Tired, wilted greens are not such a great buy at any price. The life force is leaving them rapidly, and taste and nutritional value are also deteriorating.

To preserve freshness, we strongly recommend storing lettuce and other greens in clean, airtight plastic bags in a cold refrigerator. Whether to wash them before storing or right before eating is a matter of personal choice: we wash our vegetables at the last minute, in order to preserve them as closely to their natural state as possible for the longest period of time. Other people prefer to wash the vegetables before storing them, on the theory that they keep better that way, or just to simplify and speed up preparing meals at a later time. In any event, wash them well, either under running water or by rinsing one leaf at a time in a bowl of water. Gritty salads are very unappetizing.

Wild greens, such as dandelion, sorrel, cress, and miner's lettuce, grow in almost every part of the world. Like other greens, they can be used in salads or steamed very briefly (two to five minutes). Wild greens tend to be slightly bitter. Most greens contain significant amounts of vitamin A and the B complex.

Greens shrink an incredible amount during cooking; be sure to buy enough. Beware of over cooking: greens take only a few minutes to cook, even at low heat.

BEET GREENS are often chopped and lightly steamed in their own juices (covered, at a low heat) or braised in a small amount of oil and water. May be curried slightly with mustard seeds (see **Curried Vegetables** for basic instructions). Beet greens, spinach, swiss chard, and some other vegetables contain significant amounts of oxalic acid. This substance is known to interfere with, and to a certain extent prevent, the assimilation of calcium and magnesium. Perhaps children who don't like spinach sense this intuitively. Certainly it is all right to eat foods with oxalic acid in them (carrots, oranges, celery and grapes also contain some oxalic acid), but it may be advisable to avoid habitually consuming large quantities of spinach, beet greens and chard. Cooking tends to reduce the amount of oxalic acid in a given quantity of food, probably due to dispersion of the acid into the cooking water.

CABBAGE stores fairly well, and often what is sold in markets has been sitting around in cold storage for many months. "New cabbage" which has been freshly picked is identifiable by its darker green color and dense, heavy heads. The "wrapper" leaves and the other dark outer leaves are the first to wilt, and usually they have been removed from old cabbage. When the heads have been trimmed a few times, only the lighter colored leaves will be left, and the stem will appear to be much larger than the stem of a fresh cabbage. Old cabbage which has small dark seeds in it is usually too bitter to eat.

In addition to the standard green smooth-leaved cabbage, crinkly savoy cabbage, long thin Chinese cabbage, and red cabbage are available in most parts of the country. Be on the lookout for worm damage in all varieties.

Cabbage stores as well as or better than any other vegetable. Good for snacking or shredded and served with **Russian Dressing**. May be added to salads, but will turn them bitter after a day or so. Cabbage is an expensive way to extend steamed or stir fried vegetables. Red cabbage adds a pleasing color accent to raw or cooked dishes. Cabbage leaves can be used for plates at large outdoor gatherings.

The Chinese cabbage that is sold in America is generally of two types. Bok choy or (pak choi) is a leafy vegetable with large celery-like stalks. The leaves are a darker green than the more familiar Chinese cabbage (often called Napa cabbage), which forms a firm head. All of the cabbage family contains appreciable amounts of sulfur, which manifests as a strong and unpleasant aroma and taste when the vegetables are overcooked. Steaming very briefly or simmering in milk or a cream sauce will cook the vegetable without causing the sulfur to become noticeable. Cabbage is excellent stir fried or sauteed with herbs.

See **Stuffed Cabbage**, **Cole Slaw**, and **Cabbage Pepper Stir Fry**.

SWISS CHARD is a variety of the common beet, sometimes called spinach beet. Surprisingly good as a salad green. The stems (which get rather large) can be used like asparagus, and the leaves may be cooked in the same ways as other greens. Has a tendency to get bitter when over mature. Smaller leaves are most tender, but many times quite large leaves can be used with excellent results. Be sure to nibble a corner of a leaf to test for bitterness before buying chard or taking the time to harvest it. Both green and red varieties are available. See BEET GREENS.

CHICORY is also known as witloof, witloof chicory, and French Endive. Chicory, endive, and escarole are all very closely related. Dark gray green leaves and beautiful violet-blue flowers characterize the wild chicory herb. Some varieties have an especially large root which can be washed, sliced 1/4" thick lengthwise and roasted until it is dark brown and brittle throughout (about four hours at 300° F) 300° F). The roasted roots may be ground and used like coffee.

The French (or Belgian) endive sold in stores has small whitish green torpedo-shaped heads. Its light color is the result of being grown in almost total darkness.

COLLARD is a variety of kale (or conceivably kale is a variety of collard, considering the amount of confusion in the literature in regard to such matters).

DANDELION GREENS add a snappy touch to spring salads. At other times of the year, they are best steamed for a few minutes. The root can be used like chicory for a coffee substitute. (See CHICORY.)

DOCK is a member of the buckwheat family (similar to sorrel) which grows in numerous places around the world. The narrow leafed varieties, such as yellow dock, are great in salads. The broad leaf varieties can be simmered several times (discarding the water each time) to reduce the oxalic acid content. (See BEET GREENS.)

ENDIVE — See CHICORY

ESCAROLE resembles leaf lettuce more than its curly cousin, endive. Technically it is an endive.

KALE (also called bore cole, cole and colewort) is probably the ancestor of domesticated cabbage. There are many varieties, colored green, blue, purple or even variegated red, green and yellow. It is commonly grown in the south and is a phenomenally good source of vitamin A, as are most strong flavored greens. Kale goes well in soups; it will help thicken them. Can also be used like other greens.

LETTUCE is the sweetest salad green. The many different types are usually divided into four classes.

• Crisp head resemble green cabbage. Iceberg is one of the commonest. Usually light green to white. This type of lettuce is popular because of its excellent storage characteristics and mild flavor. It also has less nutritious goodies than the more flavorful lettuces.

• Asparagus head types are rarely grown in this country. They are more of a stalk vegetable than a leafy green one.

• Loose leaf lettuce comes in many varieties: salad bowl; simpson; red leaf (or bronze); Australian; bib; Boston; and butter, to name a few. (Sometimes bib, Boston, and butter lettuce are considered a separate class.)

• Cos or romaine lettuce differs from the loose leaf varieties in that it forms a fairly tight head.

Each kind of lettuce has its own distinctive character. Romaine is crunchy, with a strong and sometimes bitter flavor; red leaf is sweeter and softer, as well as beautifully colored; butter lettuce is smooth and melts in the mouth (its darker green cousin Boston is very perishable); Australian and oak leave have interestingly shaped leaves, similar to endive and escarole but sweeter tasting; iceberg is great as "lettuce cups" to serve fruit or molded salads on.

Choose tender, lively-looking greens with good coloring. Yellow or rust colored leaves indicate either soil that was deficient in one or another nutrient, or else deterioration in a once healthy plant due to long or too warm storage.

MUSTARD GREENS, like most wild greens, are slightly pungent. They grow in many places. Some people feel they adversely affect their spiritual practices, and don't eat them.

PARSLEY is most often used as an herb, but its high vitamin content, and pleasant taste have made it popular as a salad green, too. Good in soups, steamed vegetables, sandwich spreads, and as a garnish.

SPINACH is available as lettuce in most places. We chop the stems off and compost them, and then wash the leaves very thoroughly. Otherwise, the spinach has a tendency to be sandy. Try chopped steamed spinach in **Vegetable Pakora** or in mashed potatoes.

TURNIP GREENS can be used like beet greens. Except for coloring they are very similar.

WATERCRESS grows wild (and is cultivated) on the sides of freshwater ponds and streams. Its small round leaves and little white flowers add eye appeal to salads, and its biting flavor appeals to many people.

GLOBE ARTICHOKES that are fresh and well developed have a fat stem and a flat or rounded (not conical) top. When they are fresh, the leaves are packed tightly together; as they get older, the leaves open up and the shape of the choke becomes more pointed. Soaking for a while (maybe an hour) in salt water will coax any worms out of the artichokes. Size usually doesn't have much to do with flavor, but it does affect the cooking time. May be steamed whole or in halves. (If no steaming rack is available, open up leaves and place stem up in 1/2 to 1'' boiling water, cover and steam until tender.)

Excellent served with **Lemon Herb Sauce**, salad dressings, **Margii Mayo**, or just lemon and butter. The soft lower part of the leaves may be scraped from the tougher part by running the leaves between the teeth. (Insert leaf, holding onto the tip with fingers. Close jaws, pull out leaf. Enjoy.) The leaves can be individually dipped in the sauce, or the 'choke can be cut in half (through the top and bottom, not between them) and the cavity filled with sauce. Once all the leaves are gone, remove the feathery part which is just above the heart, being careful not to waste any of the heart — it's the tastiest part. (This is very necessary. The feathery part tickles and sticks in the throat — aargh.) The stem is almost as good as the heart. Note: really small artichokes do not need to have the feathery part removed.

BROCCOLI is a green vegetable which is sometimes tinged with purple. Yellow or red broccoli looks pretty, but it's not as tasty or nourishing. The discoloration usually means the broccoli is old — either that it was left on the plant too long or that it has been stored too long or at too warm a temperature since being harvested. (Another sign of overly mature broccoli is flower buds that are no longer closely packed together.) Avoid limp or soggy broccoli. When the stalks are very tough, they can be sliced 1/8" thick (or quartered and sliced) and steamed along with the tops. (Add them a few minutes earlier, as they take a little longer to cook.) If the stalks are extremely tough, they can be peeled (the inner core will still be tender) or else saved for soup stock. Stalks with a rotted out core are good compost. Raw or cooked and cooled broccoli is fantastic in green salads. Steamed broccoli with lemon juice is also really good.

Try it with cheese or cream sauce or in combination with just about any other vegetable. Great for stir fry combinations or casseroles, too. One of the most nutritious vegetables.

BRUSSEL SPROUTS are buds which grow on a tall stem. They look and taste like little cabbages and are a member of the same family. Small, firm, dark green sprouts make the best eating. Soak in salt water to remove worms if you buy them organically grown [the ones that are poisoned (sprayed) hardly ever have worms]. Trim the stalk and steam lightly, perhaps sprinkling them with a tiny bit of tarragon. A very nice vegetable to serve by itself, with lemon and butter or **Lemon Herb Sauce**.

CAULIFLOWER is a delicacy. The flowerlets can be eaten raw, or steamed very briefly (till tender but still firm) and served with lemon juice. Select firm, tightly packed heads with a snow-white color. The heads get softer, separate, and turn a creamy color (sometimes spotted with brown) as they get old. The stalk is at least as good as the flowerlets; cook it

slightly longer. Like all of the cabbage family, it can be cooked in cream or cheese sauce, with delightful results. Great in steamed vegetable combinations, curried vegetables, and salads. See **Curried Brussel Sprouts** and **Cauliflower Casserole**.

SUCCULENT VEGETABLES AND OTHER GOOD THINGS

Succulent vegetables (often called fruits of the blossom) grow on vines, which bloom prior to fruiting. (Yes, they are classified by scientists as fruits.) Just for the sake of continuing the inconsistency, other non-vegetables (avocadoes, corn, and tomatoes) which are often treated like vegetables are included in this vegetables-that-aren't section.

If this all seems slightly confusing, please remember our dilemma: no matter how one tries, a round zucchini will never fit into a square hole. All systems of classification have little irrational idiosyncracies. Be happy. Love the vegetables (fruits?).

AVOCADOS are tender and sweet. The scrumptiously smooth-tasting avocado is truly a gift from Nature to humankind. This unusual pear-shaped fruit is an excellent source of fatty acids, both saturated and unsaturated. It can be mixed with or substituted for butter or salad oil in sandwiches, dressings, dips and some sauces.

Avocados ripen best when they are picked after they have matured but before they are ready to eat. Once the fruit has been picked, the ripening process is greatly affected by temperature. At certain stages, avocados may be held in cold storage and prevented from ripening, but when they are close to being ripe, refrigeration only slows the process down. For best eating quality, it is probably wise to avoid refrigerating nearly-ripe avocados.

It is possible to gently grasp an avocado at each end, and see if it "bends" slightly, to determine if it is ripe. Be gentle — pinches cause bruises. Avocados have a thick skin which gets rough and very black when they are ripe. Choose those with the stem still attached. When buying unripe Hass, look for yellow dots on the green background: they indicate that the fruit was allowed to mature before being picked. Sun or wind burned Hass may have shiny discolored areas on the skin, but this usually doesn't affect the insides.

Overall softness is the best way to judge the ideal state of ripeness. Usually, the sides are the last place to get soft, and eventually the whole fruit will become squishy and soft, except for the skin, which often gets hard and brittle. The degree of ripeness each person likes best can only be determined by experimentation. Hass are the favorite commercial variety, at least partly because of their relatively long period of "eatability." They can be held at moderate temperature for a few days or be refrigerated for about a week when plenty ripe enough to eat, with very little loss of quality.

Fuerte is the other commonly produced commercial variety. It has a smooth green skin which is thinner than that of the Hass, and the fruit is much easier to bruise. The skin of Fuertes may turn black or partly black when ripe, but often doesn't. Again,

softness is the best clue to ripeness. Be wary of letting Fuertes get too ripe, as they don't last well at all once they're ready to eat. Avocados that are watery and stringy have probably been frozen on the plant. This seems to be more of a problem with Fuertes than with other varieties.

Mac Arthurs look somewhat like Fuertes. They are a lighter green, have a lumpy stem, and a taste slightly different from the Fuerte. They are ripe when they get soft, lose their shine, and show yellow spots on the skin. (The skin may also get mottled with black.)

Rincons are also similar to the Fuertes variety. They have a higher oil content and a longer neck, the latter making them look like green light bulbs.

Avocados are a welcome addition to just about any salad. Because their oil content is sufficient to slow down digestion, some people choose not to eat them with other fruits, but they do add a luxurious touch to salads made with peaches or persimmons. For a green salad, they can be sliced, diced, or made into **Avocado Dressing**. When the fruit is ripe, it can easily be peeled by cutting just through the peel and then removing the strips of skin. Not quite ripe fruit will be difficult to peel in this manner. To prepare avocados that are going to be mashed or eaten "in the shell": cut in half (through the stem and blossom end, not across them), remove the pit, and scrape the goodies out with a spoon.

See the **SANDWICHES AND SPREADS** section for more ways to use avocados.

BEANS can be divided into two groups: those with edible pods are usually eaten fresh, while beans with inedible pods are most often shelled and dried.

Edible pod or snap beans are also known as string beans. However, thanks to modern technology, beans are now available with no strings attached. Snap beans are also called green beans, except when they are purple or yellow. Whichever color you buy, get fresh ones that are still crisp and healthily colored. If they don't "snap" when you break them, they're not very fresh — try growing your own. Reddish brown flecks, shrivelling, and limpness are signs of age. The string may be removed from string beans by breaking or cutting a chunk from the stem end and pulling, sort of like unzipping a coat.

Rinse beans briefly by handfuls (if they are organically home grown) or scrub each one meticulously (if they've been sprayed or you're really enthusiastic about cleanliness). Steaming the beans whole preserves the most nutrients, but they can be cut up and cooked with other vegetables. The classic gourmet touch is to cook sliced or slivered almonds with cut up beans.

Inedible pod beans may also be eaten fresh. Limas and fava (or broad) beans are especially good in casseroles, mixed vegetable dishes, or just by themselves. Choose fresh looking medium to large sized pods that clearly have good sized beans in them. (The ones that look empty really are.) Shell right before using. See **Muth**.

Fresh CORN is very perishable. Homegrown corn that's eaten right after it's picked is sweet and rich, succulent and juicy: something to be enjoyed while sitting in the sunshine on a beautiful day. Within a few hours after being picked, however, much of the sugar in the corn has turned to starch, and cooking is necessary to sweeten up the flavor. Butter helps to recreate the original taste of the fresh raw corn, but it's not quite enough. Corn can be briefly steamed or baked, in or out of the husk. To bake husked corn, wrap tightly in aluminum foil (after brushing with oil or butter) and bake for approximately 20 minutes at 350°. Don't overcook this wonderful vegetable, or it will taste like cardboard.

When shopping for corn, look for the fresher ears, which should have a good healthy green husk with a lightly colored tassel. Pale husks and/or dark, shrivelled tassels are signs of old age. Most people like to peel the tasseled end down slightly to check for worms. At the same time, the kernels can be checked to see if:

• they come all the way to the end of the ear

• are small and tender (not puckered)

• are a medium yellow (in most varieties grown commercially, white kernels indicate immaturity, and sun yellow indicates over maturity).

If the corn is to be baked in the husk, it won't dry out as much if the husk is left undisturbed. When scraping corn off of the cob, go deep enough to get the corn germ, which is stuck way down in the bottom of each little socket.

Corn combines well with almost all other vegetables, and its bright yellow color and sweet flavor add a nice touch to almost any dish. See **Saffron Spread**, and **Broccoli Corn Salad**.

CUCUMBERS are nice to munch raw (Maybe with a little salt) or cut up in a salad. The only time we ever cooked one, we wished we hadn't. It wasn't good at all.

Select firm very dark cucumbers without soft spots. If the skin is bitter, it can be peeled. Lemon cucumbers look like knobby yellow golf balls, and taste sweet and somewhat lemony.

EGGPLANTS are an exotic relative of the potato. Native to India, they have been cultivated for over 4000 years and are an important crop in China, India, and Japan. Eggplant is a staple food in the Mediterranean and Balkan countries, and many recipes for this vegetable originate in these regions.

There are many varieties of eggplant besides the large (purple) American kind. Two of the most common are the small white Japanese (which is shaped like the American ones) and the long, thin "aubergines" of France (which are also called Japanese eggplant in some grocery stores). Choose lightweight eggplants which have a good, dark color and are free from serious skin defects. Unripe eggplants (yes, they are berries, masquerading as

vegetables) are heavy for their size and may have a bitter taste, which can be eliminated by peeling, overcooking, or laying slices on a few paper towels to let the bitter juices leak out. See **Eggplant Parmesan**, **Vegetable Pakora**, and **Lemon Rice**.

OKRA are greenish colored pods, popular in Creole-style cooking. The smaller ones (1-1/2" - 2" long) are most tender. Properly cooked, they are really great.

PEAS, like beans, come either with or without an edible pod. The edible pod varieties (called sugar or snow peas) are picked before the peas get very large.

Avoid limp or shrivelled up peas, and be careful not to overcook them, if you cook them at all. Fresh raw peas are really good in salads. See **Curried Peas and Cauliflower**.

PEPPERS all turn red when they get ripe. ANAHEIM PEPPERS are long, skinny, and dark green in color. Although they resemble the more common bell pepper, they are hot and are traditionally used for Chili Rellenos. BELL PEPPERS are mildly spicy and can be used to replace onion in most recipes. The green bell pepper is an unripe version of the sweeter red bell. The wax with which both kinds are often treated during commercial processing can be removed by peeling (somewhat laborious) or by industrious scrubbing under hot running water. The top can be cut out with a paring knife to facilitate chopping. May have some limited use in sauces for those people who really like to get zapped. Bells are very high in vitamin C. See **Stuffed Peppers**. ITALIAN LONG GREEN PEPPERS look and taste like a cross between an Anaheim and a bell pepper. JALAPENO

PEPPERS are generally only an inch or two long, and are even hotter than Anaheims.

SQUASHES of all kinds are extremely easy to grow and are an excellent choice for those who like to garden but haven't very much time to spend on soil preparation, weeding, etc.

Summer squash have a soft skin, do not contain much starch, and are about 95% water. When small and tender, they are quite good raw, as a snack or in salads. They can be steamed or sauteed. Oversized summer squash are good candidates for stuffing. All varieties of summer squash can be used interchangeably. The most common varieties are:

Zucchini (or cocozelle or Italian marrow) is the most popular variety of summer squash. Select those with a good dark green (maybe even almost black) color which are firm. Any that are larger than about six inches long are suspect; they may not have as much flavor as they once did. Can be grated into salads, breaded and sauteed, or used to give body to soups and stews. See **Zucchini Vegetable**, **Stuffed Zucchini**.

Scallop Squash (also called patty pan or green bush squash) has a nice shape and lends itself well to breading (try corn meal) or dipping in a batter and sauteing.

Yellow (Straight or Crookneck) squash has a bumpy skin and adds a nice color to whatever it is used in. Tastes a little sweeter than the other summer squashes.

WINTER SQUASHES have a hard rind and a high carbohydrate content. They store incredibly well without refrigeration if they are kept cool and dry. When they're ripe,

they're very sweet. Generally, those that are of average size, shape and color are the best buys, as they are less likely to be pithy or bland. The rind should be hard, not just firm. Softening of the rind often indicates internal decay. When buying cut pieces of squash at a supermarket, beware of blemishes on the skin, a shrivelled inside, or mold on either the inside or the skin.

The different varieties can be substituted for each other in almost any recipe; i.e., pumpkin pie can be made with any winter squash. Winter squash are most often cooked in one of the following ways.

• After cutting into pieces, bake in a covered casserole,

• cut and steam in a covered casserole on a rack,

• cut and bake uncovered (makes for very dry squash),

• Bake whole, if you can't cut them. Done when a fork slips through to the center.

Cut pieces may be basted with honey, maple syrup, butter, orange juice, or whatever seems appropriate. Acorn squash halves may be filled with goodies — nuts, dried fruits, etc. Alternately, the squash can be pureed (after steaming or baking) and mixed with a sweetener or oil and salt.

There are many popular varieties of winter squash. ACORN, so called because of its shape, has a dark green rind. It is usually slit in half (parallel to the ridges) and baked. Each half serves one or two people. BANANA squash have a pale beige to orange colored rind and are usually so huge that they are sold in cut up portions. BUTTERNUT has a butterscotch or caramel colored rind and has a taste similar to its name. GOLDEN NUGGET squashes look like miniature pumpkins and have an excellent flavor. HUBBARD has a dark green skin and is often sold in pieces wrapped in plastic.

TOMATOES are really an acid fruit but are usually treated as a vegetable. They can be very good eaten as a fruit, especially the yellow-orange, low-acid varieties such as Golden Jubilee. Vine ripened tomatoes are best, but those that are picked mature but unripe will ripen to a reasonable state if stored out of direct sunlight at room temperature. Avoid tomatoes with bruised or soft spots. However, overall softness is an indication of just-so ripeness. This versatile food is at home in vegetable salads, cooked vegetable dishes of all kinds, casseroles, served alone, raw or broiled. One of the easiest ways to create a sauce is to add tomatoes to whatever you're cooking. See **Spaghetti Sauce**, **Zucchini Vegetable**, and **Stuffed Vegetables**.

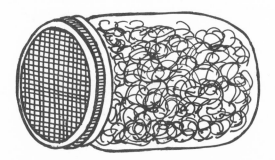

Bean sprouts are a dietary staple in some Far Eastern countries, and they are becoming increasingly popular in the Western world — for some very good reasons. Sprouted seeds, grains, and beans are alive, and contain valuable enzymes, as well as being an excellent source of prana (energy). Many sprouts (especially alfalfa) have a high mineral content and almost all are rich in vitamins. Sprouts often contain more nutrients than the parent seed, compared on a moisture-free weight basis. They can easily be grown at home in a matter of days, and are inexpensive, easy to digest and — surprise! — taste good, too. Many nutrients present in the unsprouted seed are present in two or three times the original quantity in the sprouts.

A FEW CAUTIONS: For best results, it is important to use good quality seeds and beans when growing sprouts at home. Preferably, use the current year's crop for sprouting, to insure the maximum yield and minimum spoilage — those that don't unfold, may mold. Most important of all, though, is that the seed be unhulled (except for sunflower seeds) otherwise, the chances of germination are very low.

We have experimented with various methods of sprouting and have found that there is one way which is (for us, at least) significantly more reliable and somewhat less trouble than the others. Other methods which follow the same general principles will probably work though. The materials needed are easy to obtain — a wide-mouth quart Mason jar with a ring, and a piece of plastic screening (or old nylon stocking or cheesecloth) which is somewhat larger than the jar opening. If you can't get a Mason jar, any wide-mouth jar will do — a rubber band will serve to hold the screen in place.

The procedure is simple. Place the appropriate amount of washed seed, grain, or sorted beans (see below for amounts) in the jar with a good amount of cool to lukewarm water — roughly three times the volume of the seed. (Distilled water is best, but not a necessity.) Place the screening or cheesecloth over the jar opening, and secure it with the ring or a rubber band. Let the seeds soak (overnight unless otherwise noted below), and then pour off the soaking water (save it for soup stock, cooking water, etc.). Rinse the sprouts by adding more than enough water to cover, gently agitating the jar, and pouring off the water. Repeat until the water is clear. (This helps prevent mold.) Keep them damp, rinsing from one to three times a day, depending on the weather and the type of sprout. Keep them in a well-ventilated place out of the direct sun until they reach the desired length. (This will take from one to seven days, depending on the circumstances.) Ideally, the jar should be tilted enough to let excess water run out.

If you like, expose the sprouts to filtered sun for a few hours at the end of their growing period. This will radically increase the prana and chlorophyll content. The sprouts are now ready to eat, or they may be stored for a few days in an airtight container in the refrigerator. Most sprouts are excellent raw in salads. Some sprouts are easier to digest after they have been lightly steamed. All sprouts are excellent cooked with whole grains, added to bread dough, or incorporated into loaves and casseroles. We have included suggestions for

using the different kinds of sprouts in the following pages. Sprouts can be substituted for many vegetables in the recipes in different sections. Be creative — the best dishes are often improvisations on a recipe.

ALFALFA sprouts can be made with a minimum of effort. They are far and away the most popular type of sprout. Start with two to three tablespoons of seed per quart jar, and soak them overnight in a small amount of water — one-half to three-quarters of an inch in the bottom of the jar is fine. In the morning, pour off the soaking water (freeze it and save for soup stock). Rinse the sprouts often enough to keep them moist — once a day is enough, unless you live in hot, dry country. Be sure to drain the sprouts, and keep them in a cool, well-ventilated place away from sunlight. Let them get about an inch and a half long — this usually takes three to six days. Alfalfa sprouts are good in or on almost anything. Try them raw in salads, sandwiches (especially toasted cheese or avocado), and juice combinations, or as a garnish for steamed vegetables, soups, and casseroles. There is a fantastic recipe for **Alfalfa Dressing** in the **SALADS AND SALAD DRESSINGS** section.

RED CLOVER is very similar to alfalfa, and is sprouted in the same way. Although the taste and texture of the two differ slightly (red clover has a "bite"), they can be used interchangeably.

CRESS, ENDIVE, RADISH, MUSTARD, FENNEL, and FENUGREEK are also sprouted like alfalfa, but the sprouts of all these seeds are somewhat bitter or pungent. They may be added in small quantities to salads, mixed with other sprouts, or used to flavor curries.

UNHULLED SESAME SEEDS may be sproutable, but we haven't had much luck with them.

HULLED SUNFLOWER SEEDS which are not broken may be coaxed into life, and they are a nice addition to salads or baked goods such as cookies and breads. Unhulled sunflowers like to be soaked for about twenty-four hours in warm (not hot) water. Then, proceed as for alfalfa. Really sweet and very nutritious.

WHEAT can be soaked for three to five hours and then sprouted in another twenty-four hours. If the sprouts are allowed to get longer than three-eighths of an inch, they start losing flavor (and, presumably, nutritive value). After two days or so, the main sprout will begin to be covered with fine auxiliary roots, which tickle on the way down one's throat. (In cold weather, these changes take longer.)

For a quart of sprouts, wash and remove the chaff from about three-quarters to one cup of wheat berries. (Hard red wheat has more protein and may sprout more easily twice during the growing period. Can be mixed half and half with alfalfa sprouts and topped with **Russian Dressing** for a quick salad. Wheat sprouts are excellent in breads (see recipe for **Sprouted Wheat Bread**).

RYE gets the same treatment as wheat, except that it can be grown slightly longer.

CORN: proceed as for rye, only soak longer — overnight will do.

OATS, RICE, BARLEY, MILLET, and BULGUR bought at a foodstore will not sprout. Except for bulgur (which has been steamed), they have all lost an outer hull during processing. Maybe if you harvested your own, you could sprout them — let us know if it works.

BEANS take longer to sprout than other seeds, and they tend to mold if they aren't babied along. It is important to carefully sort out all hulls, funny-looking or broken beans and rocks before attempting to sprout any kind of bean. Thoroughly wash (about 1/2 cup per quart jar), soak overnight in a jar full of water. Then rinse until the water is clear. Thereafter, rinse 3 - 4 times daily until the water is clear, being very careful not to break off any of the delicate sprouts. Remove any broken or moldy beans as soon as you notice them. With a lot of love, an equal amount of luck, and moderate weather, they'll be ready to eat in three to five days. It's a good idea to wash the sprout jar thoroughly with soap and hot water in between batches of beans. This helps reduce mold problems.

LENTILS are easier to sprout than most other beans. They are great when lightly steamed and added to a salad, or steamed in combination with other vegetables, such as carrots, cauliflower, and squash.

SOY AND MUNG beans are very similar. Both are difficult to sprout, but well worth the effort. (The long sprouts in the Chinese section of the produce display at the super-market are mung sprouts. So far, we haven't ever gotten any that long.) We usually cook them for a while, either by steaming or sauteing them, but lots of folks eat them raw.

Most raw beans contain "inhibitors" which block the action of some digestive enzyme that is needed to break the bean down. Cooking de-activates these inhibiters. Sprouting may or may not de-activate the inhibiters — any bio-chemists out there have a definitive answer on this question?

WHOLE PEAS AND CHICK PEAS (GARBANZO BEANS) will sprout, but we've found LIMAS, KIDNEYS, PINTOS, GREAT WHITE NORTHERNS, and BLACK BEANS fairly difficult to sprout. Don't let our difficulties keep you from experimenting though — love and perseverance are irresistably strong.

Sprouted beans can be substituted for unsprouted beans in most recipes (they'll need less cooking), and they can add a nutritious gourmet touch to your favorite main dishes. (See also **Muth.**)

MISCELLANEOUS NOTES: We have successfully sprouted combinations of seeds, combinations of grains, and combinations of beans, but have not gotten very good results when we combined the different groups. Some folks do get good results sprouting combinations of seeds and beans, though.

If your sprouts don't sprout, make sure that:

• They are getting enough water

• The seed is fresh, untreated, and unhulled

• The temperature is moderate

• They are out of direct sun

• They are properly soaked and rinsed at the appropriate intervals

• Are you loving them enough?

	Amt. of seed for 1 qt. jar	Type of seed	No. of days	Best length (in inches)
QUICK REFERENCE	3 T	Alfalfa	3 - 4	1 - 2
CHART	1 C	Garbanzo beans	3	1
FOR SPROUTING	3/4 C	Lentils	3	1/2 - 1
	1/2 C	Mung beans	2 - 3	2 - 3
	1 C	Soybeans	3	1/2 - 3/4
	1 C	Wheat	2	1/4 - 1/2

STEAMING VEGETABLES

Steamed vegetables are more nutritious, look nicer, and taste better than boiled vegetables. There are basically two reasons for this. First of all, steaming involves much less water than boiling, and the water has less opportunity to dissolve nutrients and flavor than it does in boiling. Secondly, it is easier to control the amount of cooking the vegetables undergo when they are being steamed. Since the vegetables are less likely to get overdone, they are more likely to taste good and look nice. Vitamins which are unstable to heat and/or soluble to water are less likely to be lost in steaming than in boiling.

There are three basic methods of steaming vegetables:

• In a steamer basket or on a rack over hot water, in a pan with a tight fitting lid.

• In "waterless cookware," which has a vapor seal lid. Use a little bit of water, and medium heat. Watch carefully.

• In a pressure cooker. Be extremely precise about cooking times if you want to avoid overdone vegies.

NOTE: Whenever one is cooking several vegetables together, it is a good idea to add them to the pot at different times, based on

the amount of cooking time needed. First add those which need the most cooking, and last, those which need the least cooking. It is also possible to adjust the size of the pieces, so that all the vegetables will take the same amount of time.

Steamed Vegetables:
Suggested Combinations

Number one. For each serving: 1 carrot, 1 small beet, 1 small to medium stalk of broccoli, cauliflower (about the same amount as broccoli, a large handful or so). Scrub the carrots and beet with vegie brush, wash other vegetables. Slice carrots and beet thin, cut broccoli, and cut cauliflower into small hunks. Place in a steamer rack, carrots and beet on the bottom. Steam until done.

Number two. Use string beans on the bottom, corn in the middle, and add zucchini when beans are almost done.

Number three. Use new potatoes, peas and carrots. Scrub but don't peel potatoes; slice or cube and place first in steamer rack. Put scrubbed carrots, sliced 1/8" thick, next. Add peas on top. Steam.

Number four. 1 bunch steamed broccoli (about 1-1/2 lb.) topped with one recipe of cheese sauce will serve 4 to 6 people.

. . . and so on, ad infinitum. Generally, we try to combine a root vegetable, a stalk or leaf vegetable, and a flowerbud vegetable or "fruit of the blossom." This tends to give a balance of nutrients.

Suggestions for Leftover Steamed Vegies

Leftover vegetables can be:

- Pureed and used in soups

- Used whole with noodles in soup

- Added cold to salads

- Pureed for sandwich filling or baby food (maybe mixed with avocado)

- Mixed with cooked grain, top with shredded cheese and baked until hot

- Put between two **Chapatis** or one folded chapati and fried

- Pureed and added to bread, protein loaves, or stew

Summer Spectacular Steamers

For each serving:
1 ear of corn, kernels cut off
1 medium to large stalk broccoli
1/2 C whole cherry tomatoes

Peel stalk of broccoli if tough and cut into thin slices. Put in steamer rack first. When almost tender, add broccoli flowerlets, then corn kernels. At the last minute, add cherry tomatoes and steam 1 to 2 minutes longer.

Browned Almond Cauliflower

1/3 C slivered almonds (preferably blanched)
1/3 C butter
1 medium head cauliflower, steamed

Melt butter and add almonds. Cook until butter is lightly browned and almonds are crisp (check crispness of almonds by eating one: undone ones will be tough). Pour almond butter over hot cauliflower and serve. Serves 4 - 6.

Honeyed Turnips

6 small turnips, steamed whole
1 T honey
1 T oil
1/4 t each nutmeg and/or cinnamon

Steam turnips whole. Mix honey and oil in pan. Sprinkle with nutmeg and cinnamon and turn the turnips into the glaze until well coated.

Honey Orange Parsnips

1 pound parsnips (small ones are best)
salt
2 T butter or oil
1 T honey
1 t grated orange rind
2 T orange juice

Peel parsnips and cut in 1/4 inch diagonal slices. Steam until tender. Place in saucepan, add remaining ingredients and simmer a few minutes. Serves 4.

Sweet 'n Sour Beets

A bunch of beets (enough for the people
   you are serving)
1 T arrowroot
1/2 - 1/2 C lemon juice
a few whole cloves
3/4 C honey
1 T butter

Scrub, slice and steam beets. Mix all ingredients except butter until arrowroot is dissolved. Bring to a boil and boil for five minutes. Add butter. Stir until melted. Pour over beets and let stand 20 minutes. Serve hot. Yield: Makes a little over a cup of sauce, so can cover enough beets for about 5 people. More than that? Double the sauce recipe.

Gingered Carrots

6 medium carrots
1/2 t honey
1 pinch of ginger
2 T lemon juice
2 t dried parsley
2 T butter

Scrub carrots and cut into thin slices diagonally. Steam until just barely tender. Mix other ingredients and toss with steamed carrots. Serves 4.

Minted Carrots

2 pounds carrots
1/4 C butter or oil
salt
1/4 C honey
1 t lemon juice
1 T fresh mint leaves, minced

Scrub and slice carrots. Steam until just tender. Melt butter and add remaining ingredients. Add carrots and heat, turning frequently, until lightly glazed. Serves 4.

Caraway Beets and Peas

2 pounds fresh beets
salt
1 to 1-1/2 cups hulled peas (fresh are best
   but frozen are okay)
2 T butter
1/2 t caraway seed
1 T lemon juice
1/2 C cultured sour cream or thick yogurt

Cut off beet tops above crown; don't remove roots. Scrub thoroughly and steam whole 30 to 40 minutes until tender. Rub off skins; cut off tops and roots and slice beets. Heat butter and add peas. Steam on low heat until barely tender. Add all other ingredients except sour cream. Heat thoroughly. Serve topped with sour cream. Yields 4 servings.

Lemon Chilled Broccoli

2 t lemon juice
2 T olive oil
1/8 t salt
1 t minced parsley
1 t chopped green pepper
2 C steamed and chilled broccoli

Combine all ingredients except broccoli.
Pour mixture over broccoli.

STIR FRYING

Stir frying is done in an uncovered pan without water. A wok is best because the stirred vegetables will not get stuck in the corners of the pan. Heat the wok. Put cooking oil in a squeeze bottle and make a small ring of oil around the upper edges of the pan so it can drip down to the center, coating the sides as it goes down. Add vegetables and stir until hot but still crisp. If desired, 1 T water may be added to starchy vegetables; or sliced tomatoes can be placed on top of the other vegetables and the whole thing can be covered and cooked until done. (See BRAISING, this section.)

The main idea of stir frying is to stir the vegetables continuously to avoid overcooking them. To do this the vegetables need to be cut the same size. Longer cooking vegetables need to be put in first and shorter cooking ones later. Sesame oil is the best oil and peanut oil next. These oils have a high breaking point so they don't burn or smoke as readily at the high temperature needed for stir-frying.

An easy sauce can be made by putting cut ginger in first, cooking the vegetables, and then adding about a tablespoon of arrowroot to a cup of water and pouring in at the end of cooking. Stir in until clear and bubbling, salt to taste.

Celery Bell Pepper Stir Fry

2 C celery, sliced 1/4'' thick on the diagonal
1 C bell pepper, cut in long slivers
1 T oil

Heat oil in wok or heavy cast iron pan until sizzling hot. Toss in celery and saute on high heat, stirring quickly, for one minute. Add bell peppers and continue cooking, stirring constantly over high heat, for 2 - 3 more minutes.

Stir Fried Cabbage

4 C shredded cabbage
1-1/2 T oil
1/2 t salt

Heat oil in a wok or cast iron pan until very hot but not smoking. Stir in cabbage. Add salt and stir constantly for 5 minutes. Turn down heat. Cover briefly until cabbage is just soft. Do not overcook.

Variation: STIR FRIED CABBAGE SOUP may be made by adding water at the end of stir-frying, bringing to a boil and adding more salt to taste. Very simple, light and good.

Cabbage Pepper Stir Fry

3 C shredded cabbage
1 green pepper, thinly sliced
1 T oil
lemon juice
salt

Heat oil until very hot. Add vegetables and stir quickly over high heat for 3 - 5 minutes, or until crisp-tender. Add lemon juice and salt to taste just before serving. Serves two generously.

Stir Fried Sprouts

2 T oil
1/2 C minced green pepper
1/2 C minced celery (optional)
2 C sprouts
1 t thyme or basil

Heat oil in pan and stir in green pepper and celery. Cook for one minute. Add sprouts, stirring often for another minute. Add herbs and continue cooking until done. Cover and steam if a very soft sprout is desired.

Red and Green Stir Fry

1 C tomatoes (cut into sections)
1 C slivered green bell peppers
1/4 C minced parsley
1 T oil

Heat oil in a wok or cast iron pan until sizzling. Toss in bell peppers and fry on high heat for 2 minutes. Add tomatoes and parsley. Toss well and continue to cook 1 more minute.

Creole Stir Fry

2 C whole tiny okra (about 1/2 pound)
2 C sliced zucchini (3 - 6 inch zuchs)
2 C corn kernels
2 T oil

Heat oil to sizzling in a wok or cast iron pan. Toss in okra and stir fry for a minute or so. Add zucchini and corn and continue stir frying 3 to 4 more minutes until vegies are crispy tender. Yield: 2 - 3 servings.

Variations: Stir-fry some **Tofu** and then add the rest of the vegetables as per directions.

Sweet 'n Sour Vegies

Sauce: (make first)
2 - 4 pureed tomatoes (about 1 C)
1 - 2 T pineapple juice
1 T honey
1 t salt
1 T arrowroot (mix with 1 - 2 T water to make a thick paste)

Mix above ingredients and simmer for five minutes.

1 - 2 C celery, sliced on the diagonal
1 green pepper, chopped in 1/2 inch pieces
1/2 - 1 C snow peas (edible pod)
a few water chestnuts, sliced (or roasted and sliced chestnuts)

2 - 3 stalks of bok choy, chopped
1/2 C bean sprouts
2 - 3 T oil

Heat oil in a cast iron pan or a wok until sizzling hot. Add vegies and keep turning them constantly for 2 - 3 minutes. Pour sauce over vegetables and cover and simmer until vegetables are just tender.

SAUTEING

Sauteing is similar to stir-frying but takes less attention because it is done at a lower temperature. The oil seals in the juices, holds the flavors and helps develop a crust on the vegetables. Heat 2 - 4 T of oil and/or butter in a large frying pan. When hot, but not smoking, add the vegetables and stir. Reduce the heat to medium or low and continue cooking, stirring occasionally. Cover if desired. When done as you like, remove from pan or turn off heat. The vegetable will be crispy tender and will have a lot of fresh flavor.

If you are using several kinds of vegetables, adjustments need to be made. The vegetables can be cut in different sized pieces according to their cooking time (with hard vegetables like carrots cut thin and quick cooking vegetables like cabbage cut larger) and all cooked at once; the vegetables can be added one type at a time, in order of the length required for cooking (say carrots, then broccoli, broccoli, then celery, then cabbage) leaving some time between each addition; or different vegetables can be cooked completely separately and put in a warm place while the others are cooking.

Different fats give different flavors: olive oil gives a rich flavor, safflower, soy, and corn have a light flavor. Butter gives nice flavor but burns easily when not mixed with oil.

Crunchy Cooked Salad

sliced carrots
chopped green pepper
lentil sprouts
small chunks of broccoli
cubed summer squash
salt to taste
thyme
parsley
oregano
marjoram
summer savory
lemon juice

Saute vegetables together, adding the salt and pinches of each of the herbs (amount will vary depending on amount of vegetables used). Add a generous squeeze or two of lemon juice and remove the vegetables from the heat while they are still slightly crunchy. Cool and serve at room temperature or chilled, or serve hot with a grain.

Carrot-Cabbage Saute

3 T butter or oil
1 small head cabbage (about 1-1/4 lb.),
  finely shredded
3 large carrots, scrubbed and coarsely grated
  (about 3 C)
1/2 t dill weed
1/2 t tarragon
2 t lemon juice
salt to taste (about 1/2 t)

Melt butter or heat oil on high heat in wok or cast iron skillet. When hot (but not burning or smoking) add cabbage and carrots, stir and lower heat to medium. Saute, stirring frequently until halfway tender (about 4 minutes). Add dill, tarragon, and salt, tossing to mix. Continue sauteing until crispy tender — about 4 more minutes. Toss with lemon and serve.

Country Fried Winter Squash

1-1/2 pound winter squash (a medium sized
  butternut, hubbard, banana or pumpkin)
  peeled and sliced 1/4'' thick
1 stalk celery, minced
1 medium bell pepper, minced
2 T **Butter Oil Spread** or butter
salt to taste

Heat butter in a heavy skillet. Add squash, bell peppers and celery. Sprinkle with salt. Turn to coat with butter. Cover and cook over medium heat turning 2 to 3 times until lightly browned and tender (about 15 minutes). Serves 3 as a side dish.

Zucchini Parmesan

1/4 C oil
8 - 9 medium zucchini, thinly sliced
1 green pepper, minced
1/2 C celery, minced
2 T chopped parsley
1/2 - 1 t salt
1/4 t oregano
1/4 t rosemary
4 C tomatoes, finely chopped
1/2 C grated parmesan cheese

Heat oil in large heavy skillet. Add all ingredients except tomatoes and cheese. Saute over medium heat, stirring frequently, until vegetables are tender (about 20 minutes). Toss in tomatoes and continue to saute until tomatoes are thoroughly heated (about 5 minutes); pour into a serving dish and sprinkle with parmesan cheese. Serves 8 to 10.

BRAISING

Braising involves the use of oil, as a sealer for the juices of the vegetables, and water, to slowly steam them the rest of the way done. Heat oil in a heavy pan or wok. Add chopped vegetables and quickly stir them around in the oil (use about 2 t oil per packed cup of vegetables). When they are well coated, cook a little more. Add a few tablespoons water (the amount will vary, depending on pan surface and time left steaming) and cover. Continue cooking at a low heat until done. Watch that the water doesn't all dry up. If you figured things right, the water will all be gone at just the time when the vegetables are ready to serve. Better to err on the side of too much water than too little.

Spicy Braised Vegetables

2 C cauliflower, chopped (1 small head)
1 C choped cabbage
1 C chopped bell pepper (1 large pepper)
1 C carrots (sliced nituke style)
1/2 C lentil sprouts
2 T oil
1/2 t salt
1 t turmeric
1 t ground coriander
3 - 4 whole cloves (approximately 1/4 t ground)
1/2 t ground cinnamon
1/2 t black mustard seed
1/2 t cumin seed
1 t fenugreek (optional)

Prepare and measure the vegetables, as noted above. Heat the oil and spices in a saucepan (at least 2 quart size, with a tight-fitting lid). When the mustard seeds begin to pop, reduce heat and add the vegetables, all at once, stirring rapidly as you pour them in. Saute briefly, then add two T water, cover and let the vegetables steam until they are tender. This dish may be garnished with nuts or raisins and served with **Chapatis** or a cooked grain.

Golden Squash

2 pounds winter squash, peeled and diced
  (about 4 C)
1/4 C oil
1/2 t black mustard seed
1/2 t whole cumin seed
1/2 t ginger
1 t paprika
1/2 t turmeric
1 t salt
2 T honey
juice of 1 lemon
1 minced green pepper (optional)

Heat oil in a heavy pan (cast iron is good) with a lid. Add seeds. When mustard seeds dance add all the other ingredients except honey and lemon juice. Cover pot, lower heat and simmer squash until very tender (about 15 minutes). Uncover, add honey and lemon juice, and serve. Makes 4 cups, about 4 servings.

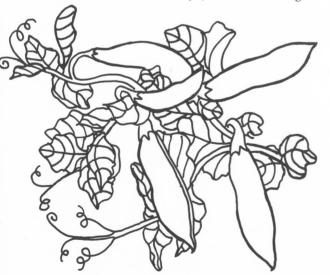

Green Beans Oriental Style

1 pound green beans (choose thin pods with
  undeveloped beans)
1/3 C water
1/4 t shredded ginger root
1 pound green beans (choose thin pods with
  undeveloped beans)
1 T oil

Combine water and ginger. Wash beans, remove tips and string. Cut in half lengthwise. Heat oil in a wok or cast iron pan and add beans. Cook 3 - 4 minutes stirring constantly. Pour ginger water over beans. Cover and cook 15 minutes.

Cabbage Amandine

1/4 C butter
1/3 C slivered, blanched almonds
4 C shredded or finely sliced cabbage
1 - 2 T lemon juice
salt to taste

Heat butter in large heavy skillet until lightly browned. Add almonds and saute, stirring until golden. Remove with slotted spoon and set aside. Add cabbage, cover and braise until cabbage is crispy tender (about 5 minutes). Add lemon juice and salt to taste. Fold in almonds and serve. Serves four as a side dish.

Summer Vegies

1-1/2 C summer squash (3/4 inch cubes)
1/2 C shelled peas
1 C cherry tomatoes or large tomatoes cut
    into 1 inch cubes
1 C mung sprouts
1 - 2 T oil

Heat oil until sizzling in a wok or cast iron
pan. Saute squash, stirring constantly, for
one minute. Add peas, tomatoes and sprouts.
Toss well, cover and turn down heat. Allow
to steam until peas are just tender, but still
crisp. Don't overcook or tomatoes will
be mushy.

Green Winter Vegetables

2 C broccoli, cut into flowerlets and thinly
    sliced stems
1 C chinese cabbage, shredded
1 C celery, cut in 1/4" slices on the diagonal
1 T oil
3 - 4 T vegetable water

Heat oil in a wok or cast iron pan. Toss in
broccoli and stir well. Saute for 1 minute.
Add celery, toss well and saute for 1 more
minute. Add cabbage and vegetable water.
Cover and steam 3 to 5 minutes over a medium
heat. Be careful not to burn the vegies.

Zucchini Vegetable

12 zucchini (not more than 6" long; about
    50" total length)
3 T oil
2 t turmeric
1 t salt
2 large or 4 small potatoes, scrubbed and cubed
1 red bell pepper (green is OK), chopped
4 tomatoes, cubed

Heat oil in a heavy pan. Add turmeric and
salt. When oil is sizzling add cubed potatoes.
Coat well in oil. Turn heat down, cover and
simmer 4 to 5 minutes. Add bell pepper and
zucchini. Mix in thoroughly, cover and simmer
until vegetables are just tender. Add tomatoes.
Stir in well. Steam for another minute or two.
Serves 4 as a side dish.

Alu Sabje

4 medium potatoes, scrubbed and peeled
2 bell peppers, chopped
1/4 to 1/2 C oil
1 t fennel seeds
1/2 t whole cumin seeds
1 t black mustard seeds
2 t turmeric
1 t salt
a bit of water

Heat the oil in a heavy pan. Add seeds. When mustard seeds dance, add all other ingredients except water. Toss potatoes well to coat with hot oil. Add a few drops of water, cover and turn down heat. Simmer checking and stirring frequently until potatoes are done. Serves 4 to 6.

Curried Vegies

6 C chopped vegies
1/4 C oil
1 t black mustard seeds
1/2 t whole cumin seeds
2 t turmeric
1 t salt

Heat the oil in a heavy pan. Add seeds. When mustard seeds dance, add other ingredients, stirring quickly to avoid burning. Turn heat down, cover and simmer until vegetables are tender. (If you are using some vegetables with a high water content, such as zucchini or tomatoes, no water will be needed, but if vegetables are all dry, such as cauliflower, add a little water before covering so that vegies will not stick and burn.) Excellent served as a main dish with **Chapatis** or **Puris**. Serves 2 - 3 as a main dish.

Curried Peas and Cauliflower

2 C fresh hulled green peas
3 C cut up cauliflower
6 T oil
2 t whole cumin seed
1 t black mustard seed
2 t salt

Heat oil in a heavy pan and add seeds. When mustard seeds dance, add vegies and salt. Stir thoroughly, cover and turn heat way down. Simmer, stirring occasionally, until vegies are tender, (about 15 minutes). Serves 4 as a main dish, 6 as a side dish.

DEEP FRYING

Tempura

1 C whole wheat flour
1 t arrowroot
1/2 - 1 t salt
1-1/4 C water

OR

1 C whole wheat pastry flour
1 t arrowroot
1/2 - 1 t salt
1 C water

Combine one of the above sets of ingredients and mix well. Chop into slightly larger than bite-size pieces some of the following:

broccoli
cauliflower
squash
zucchini
fresh green beans
carrots
celery
eggplant
green pepper
or any other vegetable that will keep
   its sturdiness

Preheat at least two inches of cooking oil (peanut, sesame or the like) in a deep pan such as a wok or a dutch oven. When the oil sizzles when a drop of batter is added, that will be the right temperature to keep it all during the cooking process.

Stir some of the vegetables into the batter until covered with it. Drop piece by piece into the oil. Don't fill the pan so full that they stick together. Fry on one side until golden brown (this may take anywhere between 3 - 8 minutes) and then turn over and fry until the other side is golden brown. Remove and set on an absorbent material (paper towel, paper bag, or whatever) to drain. Eat while still warm. Can be kept warm in the oven, but they will lose some of their crispness.

Vegetables Pakora

Pakora Batter:

1 C garbanzo (chick pea) flour
1 t salt
1 t turmeric
3/4 to 1 C water

Mix ingredients, using 3/4 C water. Should be consistency of batter. More water can be added if it seems necessary.

Possible vegetables or fruits:

eggplant (1/4 inch slices)
carrots (long thin pieces)
broccoli flowerettes
potatoes (slice very thin)
cauliflower flowerettes
quartered bananas
thinly sliced apples

Use any or all of the vegetables shown. Dip in pakora batter and fry in deep fat at about 350° until slightly brown. Drain on paper towels. Eat hot. To tell if the fat is the right temperature: it should brown a one inch cube of bread in 20 to 30 seconds. May also be heated in a well seasoned cast iron skillet with a small amount of oil.

BAKED VEGETABLE DISHES

Winter Squash Supreme
(a holiday special)

2 medium acorn squash (butternut, golden
  nugget or any smallish winter squash will do)
2 t butter, melted
1/2 C heavy cream
1/2 C maple syrup or honey

Cut squashes in half lengthwise. Remove seeds and put halves cut side up in oiled baking dish so they won't tip over. Brush inside of each half with butter. Mix cream and syrup and fill each squash cavity about half full. Bake uncovered at 350° until tender (approximately one hour). Serves 4.

Almond Squash

2 medium sized butternut squash (about 2-1/2
  pounds of any winter squash will do)
5 - 6 T butter or oil
3/4 - 1 C pure maple syrup or honey
1/2 C toasted, slivered almonds

Peel and seed squash. Cut in large chunks and steam until tender, or bake whole at 350° for one hour and then peel and seed. Add butter and mash squash until very smooth. Stir in maple syrup or honey, and pour into oiled 1 - 1/2 quart casserole. Sprinkle with almonds. Bake at 350° for 20 minutes until well heated. Serves 8.

Stuffed Baked Potatoes

3 large baking potatoes (3 - 5 inches long)
1/3 C hot milk
3 T oil
1/2 t salt
3 T sharp cheddar cheese, grated
paprika

Thoroughly scrub potatoes and bake at 400° until soft (about 1 hour). Slit potatoes lengthwise and carefully scoop out pulp. Add milk, oil and salt. Whip until fluffy. Stuff potato shells with mixture and sprinkle with cheese and paprika. Return to oven (350°) and heat through until tops are toasty. Serves 3.

Herbed Potato Boats

4 large baking potatoes
1/2 C cultured sour cream or thick yogurt
salt to taste
1/2 t marjoram
pinch of thyme
paprika

Scrub potatoes thoroughly and bake at 400° for about 1 hour until tender. Cut in half and spoon out pulp, leaving shells intact. Mix potato pulp with sour cream, salt, marjoram and thyme, until smooth. Spoon mixture into potato shells and sprinkle with paprika. Serve immediately or reheat in 350° oven. Makes 8 halves.

Dilled Mashed Potatoes

4 C riced or mashed hot potatoes
1 C yogurt
2 t parsley flakes
2 t lemon juice
2 t dill seed
salt to taste
butter

Mix all ingredients except butter. Put in shallow 1 quart oiled baking dish and dot with butter. Bake at 350° for 20 minutes. Serves 4.

Irish Potatoes

4 medium sized potatoes
salt
thyme
parsley
1 - 2 T oil
1-1/2 C milk (non-fat reconstituted fine)

Thoroughly scrub potatoes and cut into 1/8 - 1/4 inch slices. Place 1 layer in an oiled baking dish. Sprinkle very lightly with salt, thyme and parsley. Repeat process with each layer. Sprinkle with oil and add milk until it barely comes to the top layer (approximately 1 - 1/2 C). Bake one hour and 15 minutes at 350°. Serves 4 as a side dish.

Nutty Candied Yams

6 large yams
1 C honey
1/2 C water
1/2 t salt
2 T oil
pinch of cinnamon
1/2 C shelled nuts

Bake yams in jackets until almost tender (350 - 400° for about 1 hour). Cool slightly, peel and cut into thick slices.

Boil all other ingredients together for 5 minutes. Pour syrup over potato slices in a shallow pan and bake uncovered at 375° for 30 minutes, occasionally basting slices with sauce in pan.

Orange Yam Casserole

6 baked, peeled and sliced yams
1/4 C butter or oil
2 small oranges, sliced finely, but not peeled
1/2 C honey
1/2 C orange juice
1/4 C bread crumbs
oil

Place one layer of yam slices in an oiled casserole. Dot with butter and top with a layer of orange slices. Repeat layers of yams and orange slices until all are in the pot. Mix honey with orange juice and pour over all. Cover with slightly oiled bread crumbs. Cover and bake 20 minutes at 375°. Then uncover and cook an additional 10 minutes.

Baked Eggplant Slices

2 medium eggplants (washed, but unpeeled)
6 T oil (preferably olive)
2 T lemon juice
1/2 t oregano
1/2 t salt
2 C grated parmesan or romano cheese
    (1/2 to 3/4 pound)

Cut eggplants crosswise into 3/8 inch slices. Place slices one layer deep in a shallow baking pan. Combine oil, lemon juice, oregano and salt, thoroughly. Spoon 1/2 of mixture over eggplant (about 1/2 t per slice). Let stand 15 - 30 minutes. Turn slices over and spoon on remaining dressing. Let stand another 15 - 30 minutes and then sprinkle generously with cheese. Bake at 400°, 15 - 25 minutes (depending on thickness of slices) until eggplant is soft. Serves 4 - 6.

Scalloped Tomatoes
(a way to dress up those home-canned tomatoes for company fare)

2 C cooked tomatoes
1/2 t salt
1/2 t thyme
2 t honey
2 T butter
1 C fine bread crumbs

Cover bottom of oiled casserole with a layer of tomatoes. Sprinkle with salt and thyme, drizzle with honey, and dot with butter. Cover with a layer of bread crumbs. Repeat layering. Bake 20 minutes at 375°.

Curried Brussel Sprouts and Cauliflower Casserole

1-1/2 C steamed cauliflower
1-1/2 C steamed brussel sprouts
1 C vegie water (water used for steaming)
2 T oil
2 T **Curry Powder**
2 T whole wheat pastry flour
1 C thick **Yogurt**
salt
1/4 C slivered almonds

Blend oil, **Curry Powder** and flour. Simmer while stirring for a few minutes. Gradually add vegetable water, stirring until smooth and thickened. Fold in **Yogurt** and heat slowly (too fast will cause curdling). Season to taste

with salt. Place vegies in oiled 1-1/2 quart casserole. Pour sauce on top and sprinkle with almonds. Bake at 400° for 15 minutes until well-heated with golden brown nuts. Serves 6.

Rainbow Cabbage
(good all-vegie main dish)

2 small or 1 large cabbage
5 medium summer squash, diced
2 medium turnips, grated
3 medium carrots, grated
1 yam (or potato), grated
1 green pepper, chopped
1 C fresh parsley
2 tomatoes, chopped
1 t thyme
salt

Steam cabbage whole until just barely tender. (This will take from 30 to 60 minutes.) Steam all other vegies except parsley and tomatoes. When cabbage is done, cool a bit until "handleable"; cut out core and carefully pull out cabbage leaves from inside, leaving 1/2 - 1 inch thick walls. Chop about 1/4 of the inside cabbage leaves and combine with parsley, tomatoes, other stamed vegies, and thyme. Season to taste with salt. Stuff cabbage, coat with oil, and reheat in a 350° oven 10 to 40 minutes (depends on how hot stuffing was). Remaining inside leaves can be eaten cold with salad dressing or reheated and served with another meal. Serves 6 - 8 generously.

Broccoli Au Gratin
(made from broccoli stems!)

1 bunch broccoli stems (with solid, not
    hollow insides)
salt (optional)
1-1/2 C thick **Cheese Sauce** (made with
    cheddar cheese; see **SAUCES**)
2 T finely crushed dry bread crumbs

Peel stems if they need it and cut crosswise into thin slices (about three cups).
Steam until just tender. Put in baking dish.
Cover with cheese sauce and sprinkle with
bread crumbs. Bake at 450° for 10 to 15
minutes or until top is well browned and
casserole is heated through. Serves 4.

ALSO REFER TO . . .

Instructions for juice making in the **JUICES
    AND BEVERAGES** section

Vegetable salads in the **SALADS AND SALAD
    DRESSINGS** section

See the **MAIN DISHES** section for heavier
    recipes and soups using vegetables and
    legumes.

INFORMATION ON BEANS and COOKED
    BEANS (basic recipe) in the **MAIN
    DISHES** section.

Saffron Spread

Soyspread

Eggplant Spread

Humus Tahini

Vegetable Broth

Easy Tomato Sauce

Spaghetti Sauce

Vegetable Herbs

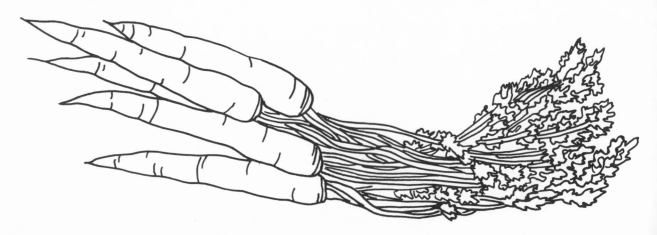

JUICES
and
BEVERAGES

JUICES

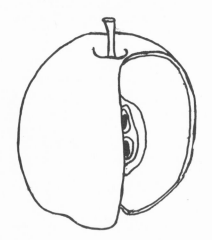

Fresh raw fruit and vegetable juices are wonderful sources of physical nourishment. They are extremely easy to digest and assimilate and contain most (if not all) of the available nutrients in the food from which they are taken.

Fresh raw juices are reputed to be good cleansers and purifiers. Pasteurized juices have similar effects, but to a lesser degree. Bottled juice will keep for a long time unopened, but once opened, it should be refrigerated to help prevent fermentation. Bottled juice which is not stored under refrigeration at the store is very likely pasteurized. Some raw juices are packaged in containers and shipped cold to different places. (A bloated plastic container is indicative of fermented juice).

Citrus juice can conveniently be made with a plastic or glass hand juicer. Some fruits (berries, grapes, peaches, etc.) can be liquified in a blender. Other fruits and vegetables respond best to juicing in a machine. We know of four major types of juicing machines:

• hand cranked juicers: slow, ecologically sound. We've never used one, but some people really seem to like them.

• centrifugal: grates food and separates liquid by "spin-drying" the pulp. Must be cleaned frequently.

• Pulp-ejector: shoots pulp out one direction and juice in another. More convenient than centrifugal types,but may be less efficient.

• triterator (grinder) and hydraulic press; very expensive, does a fantastic job of getting the juice out.

FRESH JUICE PREPARATION

Here are some general things we have learned about the preparation of fresh juices:

• Prior to juicing, all fruits and all vegetables should be cleaned (except citrus), bad spots removed and skins, if bitter, removed.

• Fresh produce has more flavor and is more nutritious than wilted produce.

• The yield of juice from a particular fruit or vegetable varies according to the freshness of the produce: dehydration takes place continuously after harvest.

• Fresh raw juices are best when drunk immediately. Unless a press-style juicer is used, the juice will deteriorate fairly rapidly after 24 hours.

• A grinder and press-style juicer extracts the most juice and nutrients from the produce. Centrifugal and pul-ejector style juicers are cheaper than presses, but don't produce as much juice, and the juice doesn't stay fresh as long, probably because more anti-oxidents get left in the pulp.

Some hints for juicing of specific fruits and vegetables:

• ALFALFA SPROUTS can be juiced with vegetables.

• APPLES with bad tasting skins should be peeled. It's advisable to core apples before juicing them because the seeds contain a fair amount of arsenic. Delicious apples are least desirable for juice.

• CARROTS with bad tasting skins should be peeled if the skin is browned at all or bitter. Dilution with celery or other juice cuts the "sticky sweetness."

• CHERRIES need to be pitted; this is easiest with a mechanical cherry pitter.

• GRAPES which are really ripe make juice which is almost too sweet. Mixing with apple juice or using slightly underripe grapes will help solve this problem. Grape seeds add a bitter flavor to the juice. Allowing the sediment to settle and then decanting the juice will improve the flavor. Or, try using seedless grapes (like Thompson Seedless). Wine grapes, which are usually not sold in markets, can often be obtained very cheaply from growers. They usually make excellent juice.

• LEAFY GREENS which are juiced in combination with other vegetables should be fed into the machine first, so that the bulkier vegetables can help push the greens through.

• RADISH juice doesn't keep very well.

• SPINACH and other greens should be washed very, very thoroughly before they are used.

• WHEAT GRASS juice is made by sprouting wheat, growing the grass 6 - 8 inches tall, "mowing," and juicing the grass.

Here are some basic juice combinations which we have enjoyed. Other possibilities are limited only by your imagination.

• BASIC VEGETABLE JUICE: 3 - 5 stalks celery and 1/2 bunch parsley to one quart carrot juice

• CHLOROPHYLL JUICE: add 1 bunch spinach or a handful of alfalfa leaves to the ingredients of BASIC VEGETABLE JUICE.

• CARROT BEET JUICE: 3 - 4 parts carrot juice to one part beet juice.

• CARROT, BEET AND CELERY: 1 part beet, 1 part celery, and 3 parts carrot.

• CARROT APPLE: One to one.

• GRAPE APPLE: one grape to two apple.

• CARROT ALFALFA: one to one (if you can handle it).

• PINEAPPLE APPLE: one part pineapple to 1 - 2 parts apple.

• CANTALOUPE WATERMELON: two to one.

• MELON MIXTURE: 1 part each of three different melons (honeydew, cantaloupe, watermelon, etc.)

Smoothies are fruit drinks made by blending fruit and fruit juices into a thick, rich, milk-shakey-type thing. Just about any combination of flavors and consistencies is possible. We have included recipes for a **Sweet Fruit Smoothie** and a **Citrus Cooler** to spark your imagination.

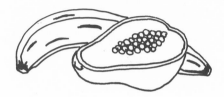

Basic Sweet Fruit Smoothie

1 banana
1 large, sweet fruit (apple, persimmon, papaya, etc. Two fruits if small), or 3/4 C berries or cherries.
3/4 - 1 C apple or other fruit juice (the amount depends on the juiciness of the fruit or berries)
2 - 3 pitted soft dates (optional)

Blend. Drink right away or store in an airless container in the refrigerator.

Citrus Cooler

1 quart citrus juice (any kind)
1 pint box strawberries, washed and stemmed
1 banana (optional)

Blend together and enjoy.

Hot Cider

Use this amount of seasoning for up to 1
quart of apple cider or juice:

1 2-inch long stick of cinnamon
1 whole nutmeg
3 - 4 whole cloves
3 - 4 whole allspice
Optional: 1/2 t ground orange or lemon peel
   or small slice of fresh peel or 1 t to 1 T
   fresh lemon juice.

Boil the juice or cider with the spices for a
minute and then simmer for five to fifteen
minutes, depending on the amount of juice
used and your experience of the taste.

Variations: Use cherry cider or grape juice.

Hot Lemon Water

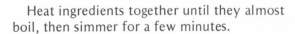

2 lemons, peeled and chopped
2 T honey
1/8 t cinnamon
2 - 3 whole cloves
5 C water

Heat ingredients together until they almost
boil, then simmer for a few minutes.

NOTE: Lemon water to be taken during a
fast (to relieve nauseous feeling) is made from
lemon juice, water, and salt only.

ALSO REFER TO . . .

Herb Teas under **HERBS AND SPICES**

Tomato Juice in the **CANNING AND AND PRESERVING** section

Orange Jubilee

Spirited Spiffy Carob

Carob Milk

Date Milk

Ginger Buttermilk

Krsna Drink

Spiced Nut Milk

Golden Milk

Date Milk Shake

Vegetable Broth

salads
and
salad
dressings

SALADS AND SALAD DRESSINGS

Remember the colorful jello salads filled with delicious fruit that used to be so appetizing before you became a vegetarian? Well, thanks to the bountiful ocean, even the strictest vegetarians can enjoy jelled salads. The secret is agar-agar, a clear seaweed product which serves the same function as the gelatin in jello. We have included several sample recipes to illustrate the principles described in the BASIC DIRECTIONS FOR AGAR JELL.

It is our hope that everyone who uses this book can learn enough about the basic processes of food preparation (such as making agar jells) to feel comfortable experimenting with variations on the recipes. Really, especially with salads, improvisation is the key to interesting and appetizing meals. To provide a base for further exploration, we have included a reasonable number of recipes for fruit and vegetable salads which we felt were unusually good. Please, please feel free to substitute ingredients if you're tired of our idea of what tastes good, are missing an ingredient that is called for, or have tried the recipe before and have an idea for changing it. Salads which are made from the ingredients at hand often have a magical feeling, a sort of attunement to the unique flow of the particular time and place of their birth.

Even if you're not feeling like experimenting, each of the salads can be varied substantially by serving it with different dressings. The fruit salad dressings follow the FRUIT SALADS. The vegetable salad dressings follow the VEGETABLE SALADS.

Because they are made primarily from raw foods, salads should ideally be preapred immediately prior to serving. Once the fruits or vegetables have been cut up and exposed to the air, the oxidation of valuable vitamins and the loss of prana (life-force) begins to occur. If a salad must be made ahead of time, the deterioration of flavor and nutrients can be minimized by pouring a small quantity of lemon (or other freshly squeezed citrus) juice over the salad and storing it in a covered container in the refrigerator.

If the salad is to be stored before it is eaten, or if leftovers are anticipated, wilting can be minimized by not mixing the dressing in with the salad. When a salad is prepared from raw and cooked vegetables, it is advisable to mix each serving individually and store the leftovers in separate containers. Otherwise the cooked vegetables will cause the raw vegetables to deteriorate faster.

BASIC DIRECTIONS FOR AGAR JELLS

Agar is a sea weed that can be used as a thickener to replace gelatin (which is an animal product). Agar commonly comes in three forms: granulated, flakes and kantan sea vegetable bars. Granulated is the least expensive form. Here are the equivalents:

• 1 T granulated agar = 2 T powdered gelatin

• 1 T granulated agar = 2 T agar flakes; each will jell 3-1/2 - 4 C liquid

• 1 bar of kantan (about 1/4 oz.) will jell 1-1/3 C liquid

119

To prepare an agar jell, have the fruit cut before starting (about 2 C fruit per 4 C liquid) as the jell sets very rapidly. Stir the agar into half or all the liquid and let sit for 1 - 2 minutes. Then bring to a boil for two minutes, stirring constantly. Cool, and then add fruit juices you do not want to cook, and stir in fruit. Refrigerate until set, which takes only an hour or so.

Agar jells stay solid at room temperature. They are best eaten fresh for there tends to be some separation overnight. The fruit will spoil if not refrigerated, but the jell can be taken on trips or the like when plain. Substitution of one kind of fruit or juice for another (with similar properties) gives any number of variations to the recipes which follow.

Fruit Jell

1-1/2 C water or fruit juice (use the water
   drained from canned fruit if possible)
4 - 6 T honey (less if juice is very sweet)
1/4 C lemon juice
1-1/2 C drained fruit
1/2 T granulated agar

Follow BASIC DIRECTIONS.

Mint Jell

Pour 1 C boiling water over 1/4 C crushed mint leaves and allow to steep 5 - 10 minutes. Strain and use with papaya, peaches or bananas.

Orange Agar Jell

3-1/4 C orange or grapefruit juice
2 T honey
1 T granulated agar
2 oranges, peeled and chunked

Combine juice, honey and agar. Let sit two minutes. Bring to boil and boil two minutes, stirring frequently. Cool. When cool, stir in oranges.

Cherry Orange Jell

2 T agar flakes
1-1/2 C cold water
1-3/4 C orange juice
2 C pitted fresh, raw, sweet cherries

Mix agar and water. Let set 1 minute. Bring to a boil and boil 2 minutes, stirring. Cool. When cool, stir in orange juice and cherries. Sets very rapidly. Refrigerate. 1 - 2 T honey may be added to orange juice for a sweeter dish. Makes four servings.

Lemon Plum Jell

2 C cut and skinned plums and liquid
3 C water
5 T lemon juice
3 T honey
1 T granulated agar
2 frozen bananas, smashed

Combine water and agar. Let sit 2 minutes. Bring to a boil for two minutes, stirring frequently. Cool. When cool stir in plums and juice, lemon juice, honey, and frozen bananas.

Grape Pineapple Jell

1-1/2 C grape concentrate
1/4 C honey
3 C chopped fresh pineapple
4 C cold water
1-1/2 T granulated agar.

Follow BASIC DIRECTIONS.

FRUIT SALADS

Ambrosia

1 C pineapple chunks
1 C fresh grapes, cut up
1 C grated coconut
1/2 C honey
2 T agar flakes
1 C cold water
1 C oranges, chunked
1 C thick yogurt
1/2 C finely chopped nuts or
    sunflower seeds
1 t grated lemon or orange rind
1 C hot water

Mix agar with cold water. Let sit for 1 minute. Add to hot water and boil for two minutes. Let cool slightly and add other ingredients. Pour into mold and refrigerate for 12 hours or so before serving. Serves 8 as a dessert.

Downright Delicious

6 T agar flakes
5 C water
3 C orange juice
1 C lemon juice
1 C honey
1 large cantaloupe, scooped into balls or cut
    into bite-sized pieces
1 pint basket of strawberries, washed and
    halved
(or replace cantaloupe and strawberries with
    4 C of chopped fruit of other kinds)

Mix agar flakes and water in a pan. Bring to a boil and boil 2 minutes. Cool to room temperature. Add orange and lemon juice, honey and fruit. For a stronger orange tasting dish, use 1 6-ounce can undiluted orange juice concentrate plus 2 T water to replace 1 C of the orange juice.

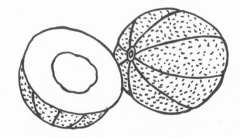

Waldorf Salad

2 red apples, cored and chunked (not peeled)
1 large stalk celery, chopped fine
1 T honey
1 t lemon juice
1/2 C chopped pecans or walnuts
2 T eggless mayonnaise or yogurt (omit
    lemon juice if using yogurt)

Blend mayonnaise, honey and lemon juice. Add to celery and chopped apple. Mix well and top with nuts.

Guacamole

1-1/2 C mashed avocado (about 3 medium)
1 medium to large tomato, chopped, or
    2 T lemon juice, or both (makes it tangy)
1 large bell pepper, finely minced
1/2 t ground coriander
1/2 t ground cumin
1/2 t oregano
1/2 t salt.

Combine thoroughly. Makes four generous portions as a salad or may be used as a dip.

Variations: May be extended in the salad direction by the addition of other chopped vegetables. Parsley, celery, sweet red peppers, and sprouts are especially good.

Spring Sweet Fruit Salad

8 medium apples, chunked
4 - 6 bananas, peeled and sliced
3/4 C raisins or currants
3/4 C chopped dates
3/4 C chopped prunes
1 shredded fresh coconut
4 baskets of strawberries, sliced

Combine above ingredients and serve with the following (or any other) dressing: 1/4 C honey, 1/2 C apple juice. (Makes more than enough for this salad.)

Variations: Add figs to the salad as it is or substitute for some of the dried fruit. Add an avocado or two for a very substantial meal. Add or substitute other sweet fruits in season: pears, other berries, peaches.

Tropical Delight

1/2 pineapple, peeled and chunked
1 grapefruit, peeled and chunked
2 oranges, peeled and chunked
1/2 to 3/4 C dates, pitted and chopped
1 avocado, chunked
1 large spoonful of honey

Combine ingredients and mush around to mix juices. The avocado and citrus juices make a creamy dressing. Serves 4.

Fourth of July Salad

7 plums (skinned and chunked or squished over bowl)
3 peaches (peeled and chunked)
7 apricots (chunked)
2 nectarines (sliced or chunked)
2 bananas (sliced)
3 medium apples (chunked)

Wash fruit. Just before serving prepare fruit as directed and mix in a bowl.

Applelessalad

3 bananas (sliced)
6 plums (peeled and squished)
7 apricots (sliced)
4 peaches (peeled and chunked) or substitute some nectarines
1 box strawberries (remove stems and slice)

Wash fruit. Just before serving prepare as directed and mix in a bowl.

Winter Fruit Salad

3 sliced bananas
6 small to medium chunked apples
1/2 C cashews or other nuts (optional)
1/2 to 3/4 C chopped dates or other dried fruit (raisins, figs, prunes, etc.)

Mix ingredients and top with **Banana Honey Dressing**, another fruit dressing or just a T or so of honey. If apples are old or slightly over-ripe, a squeeze of lemon juice perks up the flavor and helps keep them from discoloring.

123

Banana Orange Salad

1 large orange
1 T honey
1 large banana, sliced

Peel and chunk the orange. Mash a few chunks to draw out the juices. Mix well with honey and add sliced banana. Serves 2.

Cantaloupe Surprise

1 well ripened fresh cantaloupe
2 C diced fresh pineapple
1/2 C honey
lemon juice to taste
2 bananas, sliced
1 t vanilla

Cut a hole in the cantaloupe at the stem end. Empty out the seeds with a small spoon. Take out the fruit with a spoon, leaving some behind. Mix cantaloupe with other ingredients and spoon back into the cantaloupe shell. Put in plug and seal with butter. Refrigerate for a while, allowing flavors to blend. Then let sit out until almost room temperature, and serve fruit on slices of cantaloupe shell. Serves 4 to 6.

Indian Fruit Salad

2 large pears, chopped
1 C fresh grapes, sliced
1 chopped apple
1 sliced banana
1/3 C cream
1/2 t vanilla
seeds of 2 cardamom pods or 1/4 to 1/2 t
    ground cardamom
1 pinch saffron (or 1-2 t
    American saffron)
1/2 C cashew pieces
2 T honey

Mix ingredients. Serves 6.

FRUIT SALAD DRESSINGS

Banana Honey Dressing

2 large bananas
1/4 C cashews
2 T honey
2 t lemon

Large quantity:
10 bananas
1/2 C honey
1 to 2 C cashews
1/2 lemon, juiced

Mix in blender until smooth.

Spicy Fruit Salad Dressing

1 C honey
1-1/2 t salt
3 T lemon juice
2 C oil
2 T mustard powder
2-1/2 T poppy seed
1/2 C lemon juice

Shake up very well or blend in blender. For a sweeter dressing add 1/4 C more honey. Yield: 3 C or slightly more.

Fruity Fruit Salad Dressing

Here is one of the simplest ways to make fruit salad dressing (if one has a blender). Take whatever type of fruit is particularly abundant at the moment and blend well in a blender with enough bananas, dried fruit, or honey to create a sweet syrup. The addition of berries or other brightly colored fruit can contribute to eye appeal. Peaches, bananas, and berries is a real nice combination.

Avocado-Yogurt Dressing

1 avocado
1/4 C dried coconut
1/2 C yogurt
2 T honey

Blend until smooth. Makes enough for a large salad for 6 - 8 people.

VEGETABLE SALADS

Raw vegetables are usually served in the form of a salad, but they are also good appetizers. Broccoli, cauliflower and zucchini, just to name a few, are quite comfortable beside the traditional carrots and celery. Served with one or more of the spreads from the **SANDWICHES AND SPREADS** section, raw vegetables can be the highlight of a meal.

If you aren't used to the flavor of a new vegetable, you might find it easier to eat it chopped fine in a salad at first.

Basic Vegetable Salad

1 head red leaf lettuce, cut or torn into
   bite size pieces
2 large carrots, grated
2 beets, grated
1 C alfalfa sprouts
4 stalks celery, chopped
2 medium zucchini, thinly sliced
   (quarter them first if you like)

Combine ingredients and toss. Eat plain or with any of the dressings included in this section. Serves 6.

Variations: These depend on what is available. Any kind of lettuce will do. Jerusalem artichokes may be substituted for either the carrots or the beets. Cucumbers or any summer squash may replace the zucchini, and any kind of sprouts may be added to or substituted for the alfalfa sprouts. Avocados, tomatoes, peppers, fresh raw sweet corn and any number of other goodies can be added when they are available. However, the basic salad keeps well under refrigeration, and many of the suggested variations don't. Sesame seed meal, sunflower seeds, or other nuts can be added as garnish to make a more substantial salad.

Solid Salad

1 large carrot, grated
1/2 pound green beans, cooked and chopped
1 C cooked soy sprouts
a handful of alfalfa sprouts
1 stalk celery (optional)

Toss together with some olive oil, a squeeze of lemon juice, a good sprinkle of **Salad Herbs** and perhaps some salt. Nuts, seeds, and other goodies can be added if desired. Can be made with other vegetables: try peas, asparagus or corn, fresh or canned. Serves two.

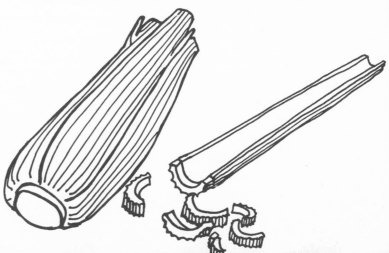

Buffet Salad

This salad is great for guests or an informal family meal. On a serving table put the following:

1) **Basic Vegetable Salad**
2) Bowls of chilled, cooked vegies (broccoli, cauliflower, corn, lentil sprouts, etc.)
3) Bowls of sesame meal, sunflower seeds, artichoke hearts, cashews, pitted olives, etc.
4) Chunked or grated cheese
5) Sliced tomatoes
6) Containers of a couple different dressings (Guacamole, Humous, etc.)

Can be served with bread or dessert or as a meal unto itself.

Super Salad

1-1/2 C lentil sprouts
1 large carrot, quartered and sliced
2 medium stalks of broccoli
1/2 head (medium) red leaf or butter lettuce
optional: steamed peas, tomatoes, romano cheese, sunflower seeds

Lightly steam the broccoli, carrots and sprouts. Cool; chop the broccoli. Chop or tear the lettuce into bite size pieces, and put a layer on a good sized plate (three plates, or six when part of a meal). Mound the cooked vegetables on top of the lettuce and toss each plateful once lightly. If you like, add a sprinkling of grated romano cheese, steamed peas, sunflower seeds, or chopped tomatoes. Very good with **Alfalfa Dressing** or **Avocado Dressing**. Serves three as a main dish or six as part of a small meal.

Italian Salad

1 large bunch broccoli, steamed and cut into bite-sized pieces
1 large bunch cauliflower, steamed and cut into bite-sized pieces
3 medium large carrots, sliced thin
3 stalks celery, chopped
1/2 C sunflower seeds
1 C black olives, halved and pitted
2 C artichoke hearts, chopped (optional)
1-1/2 T lemon juice
1/2 T crushed fennel
1/2 C chopped parsley
1/4 t salt
1 T oregano

Directions: Combine ingredients and toss. Serves 4 without artichoke hearts, six with them.

Sadhu Salad

8 good sized swiss chard leaves
4 small tender zucchini
a few handfuls of green beans (1 to 2 cups cooked and chopped up)
3 medium carrots
1 or 2 small stalks broccoli
Russian Dressing

Steam the green beans and the broccoli. When they are cool, cut them up. Slice the zucchini very thin, in 1/4 or 1/2 inch circles, shred the carrots, and chop or tear the chard. Toss all the vegetables with about 3/4 C Russian Dressing. Serves 6.

Carrot Slaw

Mix well:
2 C shredded carrots
1 C minced celery
2/3 C mashed avocado

Divide into four portions and serve mounded on lettuce leaves. Can be used as a sandwich spread, or, for an excellent raw main dish, try adding sunflower seeds and chopped almonds.

Coleslaw

2 C grated red cabbage
1 grated carrot
1 stalk celery, finely minced
2 - 4 T **Margii Mayo**, commercial eggless mayonnaise, or sour cream and herbs
juice of 1 lemon (optional)
1 t or less of honey (optional)

Combine ingredients well.

Potato Salad

4 medium-size potatoes, cooked with skins on and cubed when done
1 stalk celery, minced
1 grated carrot
dill weed, basil, thyme
salt
Margii Mayo, commercial eggless mayonnaise or sour cream

Combine vegetables together. Sprinkle on some herbs and salt. Add enough dressing to make it moist, but don't overdo it.

Broccoli Corn Salad

1 good sized stalk of broccoli
3 large ears of corn
3 small carrots
4 leaves of chard
4 leaves of romaine lettuce
8 leaves red-leaf lettuce
1 C alfalfa sprouts

Wash the broccoli and steam the flower buds and some of the stalk (diced). As soon as the broccoli is started, husk the corn and slice off the kernels. Add the corn on top of the cooking broccoli. Wash the greens and tear or chop them. Wash and grate the carrots and toss them with the greens and sprouts. When the broccoli and corn are done, put them in another bowl to cool. Serve the cooked and raw vegetables in separate bowls to avoid wilting the greens. Good undressed. Serves 4 - 6.

VEGETABLE SALAD DRESSINGS

Avocado Dressing

1 medium size ripe avocado
approximately 1/2 C oil
1 T lemon juice
1/2 t salt or to taste
2 t oregano
1/2 t sage
1/2 t savory
1/2 t dill weed
1/4 t coriander
1/4 t thyme

   Peel and mash the avocado in a measuring cup. Add enough oil (approximately 1/2 C) to make a total of 1 C oil and avocado. Mix well with the lemon juice, salt, and herbs. Restir just before serving over salad. Yield is a function of desire.

Basic Vegetable Salad Dressing

1 part lemon juice or vinegar
2 - 3 parts oil
Salad Herbs or any combination you like
salt to taste

   Combine ingredients in a wide mouth jar or other container. Add herbs to taste. You can probably add more than you think since salad dressing goes a long way. The flavors will come out more as they sit. The herbs will then harmonize and be absorbed by the oil and lemon juice. Shake well immediately before use.

Lemon Honey Dressing

1/2 C lemon juice
1/2 C honey
1/2 t salt

   Mix all ingredients together. Yield: 1 C. Good with a mixed vegetable salad.

Alfalfa Sprout Dressing

1 C alfalfa sprouts
1/2 C oil or mashed avocado
1/2 lemon (juice and pulp) or more to taste
1/2 t vegetable salt or 1/4 t salt
1/2 t savory
1 t oregano
1 t basil
1 t thyme

Blend together. Yields 3/4 - 1 C.

Kate's Green Dressing
(for sprout salads)

3-1/2 C greens (spinach, chard, beet greens, etc.)
1/4 C parsley
1/2 C lemon juice
2 C water or vegetable juice
1 t salt or more, to taste
2 avocados
thyme
dill

Blend together in blender. Makes: a lot, restaurant proportions.

Tapasvini's Squeeze Bottle Salad Dressing

1/2 C lemon juice or 1/3 C vinegar
1-1/2 t salt
7 T honey
8 ounces **Tofu**
4 T sesame seeds
4 T water (approximately)

Combine all ingredients in blender and blend until sesame seeds are ground. Tastes great on cooked vegetables or fresh salads. Keeps for a couple of days in the refrigerator. It is thick and smooth so comes out of a squeeze bottle great (kids will love this).

Variations: Substitute yogurt for sesame seeds and water or use sunflower seeds or other nuts instead of sesame seeds.

Russian Dressing
(tomato)

1/2 C oil
2 T lemon juice
1/2 C tomatoes, thick tomato juice or puree
2 t salt
1/8 to 1/4 t **Salad Herbs**
1/4 to 1/2 t paprika

Blend well. Yields about 1 C.

Margii Mayo

1/2 C evaporated milk or cashew milk (we
    don't usually recommend canned food,
    but evaporated milk is one of the
    better ones)
1/4 t salt
1/4 t celery seed
1/2 t paprika
pinch of turmeric
1 t honey
2/3 C oil, approximately
2 T lemon juice

    Blend milk, seasonings, and honey together.
Gradually and very slowly add oil as the
mixture is blending in the blender, until
mixture becomes thick. Stir in the lemon
juice last.

ALSO REFER TO . . .

Tofu Mayonnaise

Salad Herbs

SPROUTS

Notes on individual fruits and vegetables under
    their respective sections

nuts and
seeds

NUTS AND SEEDS

Many strict vegetarians expect nuts and seeds to provide all or most of the protein in their diet. In order to help people decide whether this is a wise course of action or not, we have compiled a handy, dandy chart. The chart shows the percentage of the food which is protein; the extent to which the protein is utilizable, which is referred to as the NPU (Net Protein Utilization) value; and the prduct of these two numbers, which gives us the number of grams of complete protein per 100 gram portion. In other words, the values in the third column are almost directly comparable to grams of egg protein, the standard to which other proteins are compared. (See the NOURISHMENT section for further details). Remember that 100 grams is equal to approximately 3-1/2 ounces (28 grams per ounce. One-half cup of cottage cheese weighs slightly more than 100 grams.) Values for cottage cheese and tofu are included to provide a basis for comparison.

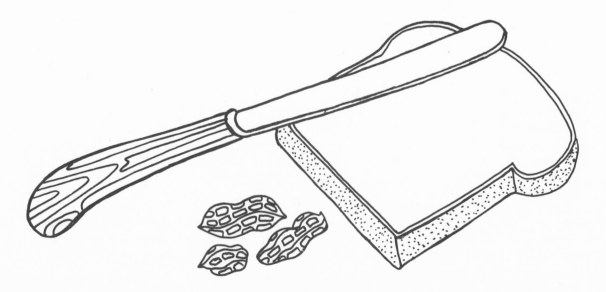

COMPARISON OF PROTEIN VALUES

	Grams of Protein Per 100 grams edible portion (% Protein)	Approximate Percent of protein which is completely utilizable (NPU)	Grams of complete protein per 100 gram portion (% Protein X NPU)
Almonds	19.0	30%	5.7
Black Walnuts	20.5	50%	10.3
Brazils	14.3	50%	7.2
Cashews	17.2	60%	10.2
English Walnuts	15.2	36%	5.5
Peanuts	26.0	36%	8.4
Sunflower Seeds	24.0	60%	14.4
Tofu (soybean curd)	8.0	60%	4.8
Cottage Cheese	17.0	75%	12.8

(Note: Data is from USDA Handbook No. 8, **Composition of Foods**; USDA Home Economics Research Report No. 4, "Amino Acid Content of Foods"; and **Diet for a Small Planet**, by Francis Moore Lappe.)

We can see from the chart that to get 30 grams of high quality protein from a single food, one would need to eat about 10 ounces of cashews or black walnuts, about 7 ounces of sunflower seeds or about 9 ounces of cottage cheese.

The rest of this section is a mini-encyclopedia of seeds and nuts. Ways for preparing individual nuts are included under the heading of each nut. A recipe for **Nut Milk** is included in this section. Others are listed at the end of this section.

ALMONDS are part of the rose family, which includes the peach, plum, and cherry. The part of the almond fruit which corresponds with the flesh of the peach is compressed, dry and velvety. It splits open to show the stone, which is light-weight, beige, and fairly smooth. Inside this is the edible kernel.

Nutritionally, almonds are one of the best nuts. They are a good source of thiamin (B_1), niacin, iron, phosphorus, potassium and protein. They have more riboflavin and calcium than other nuts.

The kernel can be blanched by soaking in boiling water for two minutes and then rubbing off the skin. Almond milk can be made from the blanched almond. (See recipe at end of this section.)

BRAZIL NUTS (betholletia) come from a globular fruit, 2 - 4 inches in diameter, that contains 8 - 24 seeds arranged like sections of an orange. The individual seed has a three-sided, dark brown shell. The kernel is long, cream-colored inside, and has a brown outer protective skin. Brazils are imported from South America, where they grow (especially in Brazil) along the Amazon and Orinoco Rivers.

Brazil nuts are well supplied with unsaturated fatty acids, but low in carbohydrates. They contain enough extra tryptophan and methionine (essential amino acids) to make them a valuable complement for bean protein.

CASHEWS are the seeds of the cashew apple, a brilliant red or yellow swollen receptacle to which the kidney-shaped nut is attached. The cashew nut is surrounded by two shells. The inner one contains an acrid oil that is removed by heating before the nuts are taken from the shell. Cashews are imported from India and Africa and are only sold in their shelled state.

Cashews are higher in carbohydrates and lower in fats than other nuts. They can be eaten raw, roasted, or oiled and salted. Cashew oil is a delicate table oil. Cashews contain surplus tryptophan, which makes them a good complement for milk protein. They are easy to digest and have more of an alkaline residue than other nuts (see **NOURISHMENT** section).

CHESTNUTS have a thinner shell than most nuts. They are starchy instead of oily, and lower in protein, fat and calories than other nuts. They are grown in the United States and also imported from Southern Europe. They are usually available only in the winter.

Chestnuts can be roasted in their shell. First, slash through the shell on the flat side of the nut. Then place the nuts, cut sides up, on a baking sheet. Roast at 400° until tender (about 20 minutes). Insert a fork through the cut to test for tenderness. They can also be boiled.

To remove skins, blanch for two minutes in boiling water, drain, and peel with a paring knife. Or remove skins after roasting.

Chestnuts are perishable at room temperature, but will keep several months in the refrigerator in loosely covered containers or ventillated plastic bags. Shelled, blanched chestnuts can be frozen for longer storage. Pack in tightly closed containers and freeze at 0° or lower. Can be used in cooking without thawing.

COCONUT (Cocos nucifera) is a large nut with a smooth outer husk which is slightly ridged and flat at one end. The inner shell is oval and fibrous with small "eyes" that can be punctured to obtain the liquid inside. When the nut is picked green the meat is very soft and the water clear and delicately flavored. When it is picked ripe, the meat is harder and the milk cloudy and sweet. Coconuts are imported from the West Indies, Central America, and the Philippines. They grow on palm trees.

Coconuts are lower in protein than other nuts. They are higher in calories and saturated oils

To shell a ripe coconut, puncture the "eyes" with a large nail and a hammer. Drain off the liquid through the holes and drink it or use it in cooking. The nut can either be cracked open immediately or propped in a pan and put in a 350° oven for 12 to 15 minutes to loosen the meat from the sides. Scoop out the meat and peel off the outer skin with a vegetable peeler. Grate the coconut at room temperature or warmer.

Fresh coconuts in the shell retain good quality up to a month in the refrigerator. Fresh coconut meat and coconut milk can be kept up to a week in the refrigerator if covered.

To toast coconut, spread grated coconut on a baking sheet and place in 350° oven for about 10 minutes. Stir frequently. To reconstitute dried coconut, cover with milk and refrigerate for 6 hours. Drain before use.

To make coconut milk, combine the grated meat of a ripe nut with its natural milk. Place in 325° oven and let heat thoroughly. Remove and cool, strain and put solids in cheese cloth to squeeze out all the remaining liquid. The coconut cream will rise to the top and form a hard cake within 24 hours (be sure to refrigerate). This is higher in coconut butter than the rest of the milk. Coconut oil and coconut butter are manufactured from the oils of the coconut meat.

FILBERTS (hazelnuts, cobnuts) are a hard nut, medium brown, small and smooth. Filberts are larger than hazelnuts and are grown in Washington, Oregon and imported from Spain, Italy and Turkey. Hazelnuts grow wild around the U.S. but are usually too small to eat. They are one of the most flavor-ful nuts, sweet and buttery, and are a good source of minerals.

135

The skin of the filbert can be removed by roasting for 10-15 minutes at 300°, stirring occasionally. Cool slightly and slip skins off. Filberts with skins may be toasted for 10 - 12 minutes at 400°.

GINKGO NUTS, (bok gwar), are used in Chinese cookery and are imported from the Orient. Their shell is hard. The kernel is encased in a pinkish skin that must be blanched to be removed. They can be purchased in the United States in Chinese markets. To blanch, cover with boiling water and let stand for five minutes. Drain, dry and rub off skins. Ginkgo nuts can be used in soups, casseroles and vegetable dishes.

HICKORY NUTS - see PECANS

MACADAMIA NUTS are grown mostly in Hawaii, though they are native to Australia. The ripe fruits grow in clusters, like grapes, with a thick green husk containing a hard dark-brown shell. The kernel is almost white. It is usually prepared with coconut oil and salted. They contain a high percentage of fat and are a good source of calcium, phosphorus, and iron.

PEANUTS (goobers, goober peas, ground-nuts) are an annual pod-bearing plant of the legume family, so they are actually beans rather than nuts. After blooming, the tips of the plant hang down to the ground, and the peanuts grow underneath the soil. There are three main types: the Virginia Peanut is long and slender, the Runner is small and stubby, and the Spanish peanut is round. Peanuts are lower in iron than other nuts and seeds (they have 1/5 as much iron as the same weight of sesame seeds).

Peanuts can be purchased in the shell, raw or roasted; shelled, raw, roasted, or oiled and salted; in the form of peanut butter, peanut flour (popular in Europe), or peanut oil. Their flavor is heavy, so they can dominate the flavor of a dish or baked good, unless they are used very sparingly. Peanuts combined with whole wheat (in equal quantities, by weight) contain all the essential amino-acids in a fairly good balance.

To remove skins, blanch in boiling water for 3 minutes. To roast, spread in shallow pan and place in 350° oven for 15 - 20 minutes, stirring occasionally.

Peanut Butter

Peanut butter can be made in a blender using 1-1/2 to 3 T of vegetable oil and 1/2 t salt for each cup of unsalted peanuts. Put in the first cup of nuts and turn the blender on high speed. Add up to one cup more nuts and the oil after the first cup has become chopped. Blend until of the correct consistency (smooth or crunchy).

PECANS are a large species of the hickory nut. They are oblong and cylindrical in shape with a light, easily breakable shell. Inside are thin partitions enclosing a red-brown seed.

Pecans are high in unsaturated fats and are easily digested when thoroughly chewed. They contain quite a few enzymes and calories but not many carbohydrates.

PINE NUTS (piñon, pinyon) are oily brown seeds, 1/2 - 2/3 inches long. In some ancient cultures, they were used more frequently and in greater amounts than any other nut.

PISTACHIOS are members of the cashew family. They are the yellow-green seeds of a small, reddish, dry and wrinkled fruit. They are grown in Texas, Mexico, Florida, the West Indies and the Mediterranean area.

They are higher in potassium and iron than most nuts. They are high in protein and contain little indigestible cellulose.

PUMPKIN and SQUASH SEEDS come in various sizes depending on the variety of squash. Most purchased seeds are larger than Jack O'Lantern seeds and easier to remove from the shell. They can be eaten raw (though they need to be dried first) or can be roasted. They are high in protein and iron.

SESAME SEEDS originated in Africa. They were one of the first seeds grown for oil by human beings. There are many varieties with a range of 45 - 63% edible oil and 16 - 32% protein. Sesame oil is noted for its naturally "long shelf life."

The meal or oil cake remaining after oil extraction is rich in protein, calcium, phosphorus and niacin. It is used chiefly as cattle feed. Unhulled sesame seeds generally cannot be digested whole, so they should be slightly ground before eating.

SUNFLOWER SEEDS are one part of a very useful plant. The leaves can be used for fodder, the flowers yield yellow dye, and the seeds can be used for oil and food for both humans and animals. Sunflower oil is considered about equal to almond and olive oil as a table oil. The seeds are grown mostly in the U.S.S.R., England, other parts of Europe, and in India. About the most nutritious of all seeds, they contain more protein, phosphorus, iron, sodium, potassium, thiamin, and riboflaven than most nuts.

Sunflower seeds are difficult to chew properly, and it may be advisable to sprout or grind them into butter if you're eating a lot of them.

WALNUTS came from ancient Persia and were brought to the U.S. by Spanish missionaries around 1700 A.D. They have a hard, woodlike outer shell covered in the growing stages by a green hull. The two-part kernel of the nut is sweet and oily. It is covered by a thin brown protective covering called a pellicle. When the outer shell is removed in most factories a pellicle substitute which is tasteless and colorless is applied to check rancidity. It is claimed to be harmless and acts as an anti-oxident. Walnuts contain about 15% protein and 15.6% carbohydrate. Black walnuts are hard to find. English walnuts are easier to shell than black.

A fresh walnut kernel snaps when broken. Rubbery or grey ones may be rancid. The nuts are harvested from September to November, after which they are sold shelled, chopped or in the shell. They can be made into a mash for poultry feed or into walnut oil.

Walnuts can be frozen, but once they have been thawed, they should not be refrozen. To toast, drop the kernels into rapidly boiling water and boil for three minutes. Drain well. Spread kernels evenly in a shallow pan and bake at 350° (stirring often) for 12 - 15 minutes or until golden brown.

Nut Milks

1 quart water or milk
1 T honey
1 C nuts (cashews, blanched almonds, or other nuts)

Combine in blender and liquify until smooth. It may be strained but we don't recommend it.

ALSO REFER TO . . .

Almond Yogurt Coffee Cake
Almond Squash
Cabbage Amandine
Sesame Grain Pancakes
French Toast
Sesame Seed Sauce
Chestnut Stuffing
Nut and Lentil Loaf
Spiced Nut Milk
Whole Wheat Gravy
Sunseed Sauce
Buttered Almond Sauce
Nut Bars
Peanut Butter Fudge
Honey Spice Nuts
Gomasio (sesame salt)
Granola
Ethereal Cereal
SPROUTING
Muth

   Under the individual nut and seed listings,
see:

Blanching ALMONDS
Roasting CHESTNUTS
Grating COCONUT
Making COCONUT MILK
Skinning FILBERTS
Blanching GINKGO NUTS
Making PEANUT butter
Toasting WALNUTS

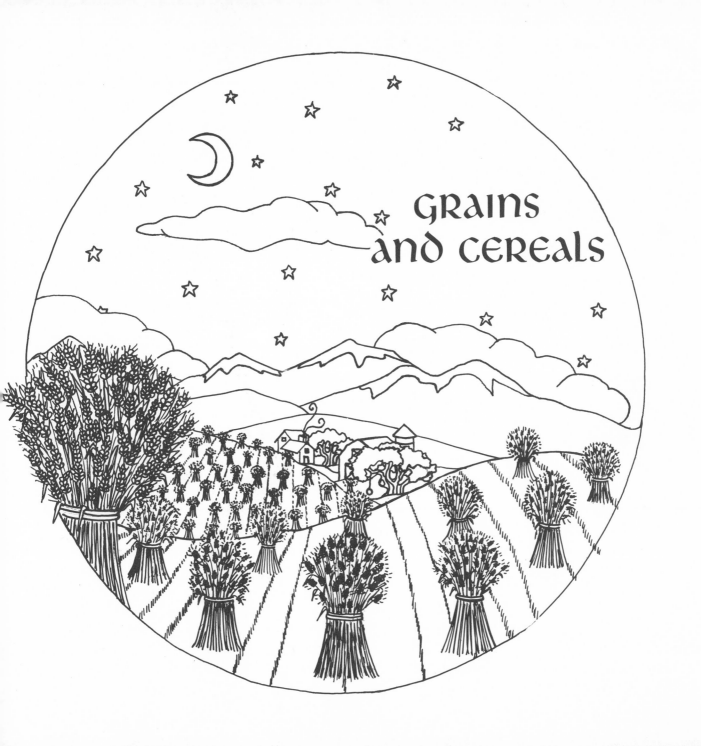

GRAINS
AND CEREALS

The following are brief descriptions of grains and grain products to help you in identifying, selecting and using these foods.

BARLEY is an extremely hardy grain. It is perhaps the oldest cultivated grain. Cooked whole, it is used in soups and stews. It is used as a flour by people allergic to wheat. It gives a sweet, moist, cake-like texture to breads, cakes and cookies. Barley grits can be quickly cooked for cereals and the like.

BRAN is the outer coating of the wheat kernel (see diagram, this section). It is a good source of vitamins and minerals, but may also contain a lot of pesticide residues. It is a good source of fiber to balance out low-bulk diets. It is less irritating to the intestines when it is soaked well or cooked before use.

BUCKWHEAT groats are three-cornered seeds. They are extremely hardy and blight-free and therefore are not generally sprayed with insecticides. They can be used as a stuffing, a breakfast cereal or a rice substitute.

BULGUR is cracked whole wheat that has been steamed. It can be soaked for 30 minutes or so and used in salads or cooked into a cereal similar to rice.

CORN is used both as a vegetable and as a cereal grain. Cornmeal is coarser than corn flour and various grinds of each are available. The color of the flour varies according to the type of corn used. Flaked corn requires only a short amount of cooking before it can be eaten.

COTTONSEED FLOUR contains quite a bit of protein, but since cotton is not classified as a food, it is sprayed with enormous amounts of pesticides. The flour can be substituted for about 1/4 of the flour of any recipe.

CRACKED WHEAT is similar to bulgur, but it has not been cooked. It needs to be cooked before it is used.

GLUTEN FLOUR is wheat flour with the starch removed. It is used most in making breads. The gluten forms a very cohesive elastic mass which traps the bubbles produced by the yeast. This results in a lighter bread. A high protein patty can be made by mixing gluten flour or wholewheat flour into a stiff dough with water. Soak and knead in cold running water to remove the starch. When no more cloudy starch runs off with the water, you have pure gluten. This will take much longer with the whole wheat flour than it does with the gluten flour. The remaining ball of dough can be sliced, and steamed or parboiled; then sauteed or ground and shaped into patties or loaves.

GRAHAM flour is a type of whole wheat flour similar to pastry flour, but with more bran in it. When a recipe calls for graham flour, pastry flour can be substituted if graham flour is unavailable.

GRITS are very coarsely ground grains that can be cooked into a cereal or used in cooking.

GROATS. See WHOLE GROATS.

MEALS are generally ground coarser than flours, but we have not discovered any definite standards specifying the point at which the two terms overlap.

MILLET is a tiny, pearl shaped grain (usually yellow or white) that grows easily in a variety of soils. This ancient grain is very nutritious and can be cooked as a whole grain or ground coarsely (in a blender or grain mill) and substituted for 1/10th of the whole wheat in a recipe. Millet is very

sweet and therefore popular as a breakfast grain. Pearl millet contains a reasonable amount of good quality protein.

Oat groats can be cooked whole for cereal, though it takes a long time. They can be sprouted and are available flaked or rolled (see FLAKED OR ROLLED, this section).

RICE is available in various forms. Brown rice is husked but not polished. Sweet rice is a glutenous rice used for oriental dessert dishes. Converted rice is similar to refined rice in texture and taste but retains many of the original vitamins because it has been parboiled.

RICE POLISH is the inner layer of bran that has been removed during the refining of white rice. It is high in thiamin, B vitamins and minerals and has been used as a cure for Beri-beri. Use it like wheatgerm.

ROLLED and FLAKED cereals have been steamed and put through rollers. Quick cooking rolled grains are chopped before this process.

RYE is generally grown in areas where wheat cannot survive. Often it is combined with wheat flour for bread.

SEMOLINA is a pale yellow meal made from the middlings of hard wheat. Couscous is similar but slightly coarser.

STONE-GRINDING of flour takes place at slower speeds than steel-grinding. Stone-ground flour is more nutritious than steel-ground flour because the heat involved in steel-grinding destroys heat-sensitive vitamins.

TRITICALE is a cross between rye and wheat which is very high in protein. It has just recently become widely available. Its flour can be substituted for part of the wheat flour in most recipes for a more nutritious food.

WHEAT is the most commonly used grain in America. There are many varieties. Harder types have more protein (gluten) and so make better breads. Softer types are used to make pastry flour, which is less glutinous. The wheat "berry" or groat can be soaked and used in breads. The berries can be cooked like rice and served warm with vegetables or the like. They can be sprouted and used in salads, cooking and breads.

WHEAT GERM is the embryo of the grain. It is removed from white flour during processing. Wheat germ should be refrigerated in airtight containers to prevent oxidation and resultant rancidity. If it is not vacuum packed and very fresh, it may already be rancid by the time you buy it.

WHOLE GROATS (grains) contain all the nutrients found in the grain, since nothing but the husk has been removed. Groats keep better than chopped or ground grains because the oil and other nutrients are protected from oxidation. See the diagram in this chapter of the parts of a whole grain.

BASIC COOKING METHODS

FOR GRAINS

FIRST: Wash the grain thoroughly by rinsing in a colander or stirring in a bowl and pouring off the water. Repeat until water is clear. For the first three methods, use a heavy saucepan with a tight fitting lid. NOTE: Before cooking grain by any of the first three methods, it is possible to toast it in a cast iron frying pan, or saute it in just a little bit of oil, and possibly some spices. This lends a distinctive flavor to the grain, which some people consider well worth the extra trouble. Also, herbs and spices may be added to the cooking water. The amount of water used will determine how moist the grain is when it's done. If you are cooking vegetables with the grain, add a little more water than you normally use. Grains are done when they are soft all the way through, and no longer taste like raw starch. (Usually, they will "puff" also). If grains are sprouted before cooking, they will get done much faster than usual.

METHOD 1: Put water, grain and salt into a pan and bring to a boil. Stir once, cover, and turn heat down as far as possible. Simmer without uncovering and without stirring until the water has been absorbed and the grain is tender (see chart for approximate amount of time). The reason for not stirring is that as the grain expands, it forms a network of steam tunnels. If these are disturbed, the grain will cook unevenly, with the bottom soggy or burned and the top not done.

METHOD 2: Bring salted water to a boil. Add washed grain so slowly that the water never stops boiling. Stir once, lower heat, cover, and simmer until done. Grains cooked this way will end up fluffier and less sticky than grain cooked by method 1.

METHOD 3: (The fast way) Use the maximum amount of water specified in the chart on page 150. Put water, grain, and salt (if desired) in pan and bring to boil. Cover and hold at a boil for 5-10 minutes. (it will probably be necessary to reduce the heat somewhat to keep the pan from boiling over.) Reduce to medium heat and continue cooking until about one half the allotted time has passed. Check grain to see if it's done. If not, recover and watch very carefully. This method occasionally results in burned grain. That's the price of being in a hurry.

METHOD 4: (Thermos method). Soak 1 C grain (whole or cut) for 5 - 6 hours. Then add additional water until you have 3 C grain and water mixture. Bring it to a boil and add 1 t salt. Pour into pre-heated thermos. (Let hot water sit in it, then dump out water just before filling thermos.) Cap and lay thermos on its side. In 8 - 10 hours, the grain will be done. This is a good way to serve a hot breakfast while camping. If it is cold out, wrap the thermos or use it as a footwarmer.

METHOD 5: (Pressure cooking.) Combine the grain, minimum amount of water shown on chart, and salt in the pressure cooker. Bring to full pressure, turn down to simmer and cook for time specified in last column of chart. Remove from heat and let pressure go down. Grain should be done when opened.

BREAKFAST CEREALS

Cereals can be prepared from a combination of grains with similar cooking times. Soy grits can be cooked with cereals to increase their protein value. Cereals can be soaked overnight to cut down on the cooking time in the morning. Wheat germ can be added just before serving. Raisins, dried fruit, or nuts can be cooked into the cereal - add near the end of the cooking time. Spices can be added for flavoring. Salt, particularly **Gomasio** (sesame salt) can be added as a flavoring instead of sweetening. Leftover grains and cereals can be fried (see **Fried Cornmeal Mush**). Other things to add are: coconut, honey, maple syrup, date sugar, milk, banana, apples and other fruit.

Rice Cream Cereal

To make powder:

Wash brown rice and dry roast in a heavy, well-seasoned skillet until it is golden-colored and begins to pop. Grind in an electric blender at high speed or grind by hand in a grain mill.

1 C rice cream powder
4 - 4-1/2 C boiling water
1/4 - 1/2 t salt

Dry roast powder in a heavy skillet over a medium flame until it gives off a nut-like fragrance. Bring pan to sink and cool by setting in another pan of cool water. Add boiling water and salt. Mix thoroughly to remove lumps and return pan to heat. Cover and cook over a low heat for 35 - 45 minutes. Stir occasionally to prevent burning. Mix thoroughly before serving.

Variations: use other whole grains.

Cornmeal Mush

1 C cornmeal
4 C cold water
1 t salt

Mix 1 C cornmeal with 1 C water and make a smooth paste. Boil the other 3 C water and add salt. Gradually add the paste while stirring. Simmer approximately 10 - 30 minutes until the water is absorbed, stirring frequently to avoid lumping.

Variation: Add 1 C raisins.

Fried Cornmeal Mush

Put left-over cornmeal in a loaf pan and refrigerate. When solid, turn out of pan, slice and fry on lightly-oiled, well-seasoned griddle until brown. Serve with syrup.

Variations: Substitute leftover oatmeal, rice cream or other cereal for the cornmeal.

Toasted Wheat Germ

Method 1: Put wheat germ in a loaf pan and place in the oven at 300° for 10 to 20 minutes. Stirring will allow a more even toasting. Watch carefully.

Method 2: Place wheat germ in a well-seasoned frying pan over medium heat. Stir until toasted.

For sweet wheat germ: mix in 1/2 C honey, warm, to 4 C wheat germ before toasting in oven, or after toasting in a frying pan.

Homemade Familia

1 C quick oatmeal
1 C rolled wheat
1 C toasted wheat germ
1/2 C millet meal (optional)
2/3 C almonds, sliced thin
1/2 C raisins
2/3 C date sugar
3/4 C ground dried apples

Mix above ingredients and store in a tightly closed container. Add milk about five minutes before serving. For camping, add 1 C instant milk to the above mixture and then add water when serving.

Muesli

1 T cream
honey to taste
juice of 1/2 lemon
1 T oats
1 large apple
1 T grated nuts

Mix cream, honey, and lemon juice with oats. Grate apple into mixture. Sprinkle nuts over top.

Granola

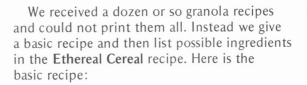

We received a dozen or so granola recipes and could not print them all. Instead we give a basic recipe and then list possible ingredients in the **Ethereal Cereal** recipe. Here is the basic recipe:

3 T oil (or more)
1/2 C honey
3 - 4 C rolled oats
1/4 t salt
1/2 vanilla (optional)
1/2 t cinnamon (optional)

Combine wet ingredients in one container, dry ingredients in another. Combine the two mixtures. Roast in a shallow pan at 250° for 25 - 30 minutes in the oven, or in an electric frypan for one hour. After roasting add dried fruit or nuts.

For crunchy granola, use 1 C unsweetened coconut and 1 C sesame seeds in place of 1 - 2 C oats.

Ethereal Cereal

If you like to experiment or have your own favorite ingredients for granola, you will find this recipe more to your liking. Look back to the **Granola** recipe for directions and to remind yourself of the basic balance required.

Use 4 - 6 C dry ingredients for each 1 C wet ingredients, and (optional) 1 C fruit. Take your choice of the ingredients below, but include the basic ingredients of the **Granola** recipe.

DRY INGREDIENTS: rolled oats, rolled wheat, rolled rye, wheat germ, bran, assorted flours, meals, grits, sesame seeds, pumpkin seeds, sunflower seeds, chia seeds, flaxseed, chopped or sliced nuts, shredded coconut, powdered milk, date sugar, salt.

WET INGREDIENTS: melted butter, oil, molasses, honey, warm water, vanilla, coconut milk.

Fruit: shredded apples, fresh shredded coconut, raisins, chopped dates, apricots, or other dried fruit.

Tomato Wheat

1 C whole wheat berries
3 C tomato juice
1/4 t cumin seed
1 chopped green pepper
pinch of oregano.

Wash wheat berries and add to boiling tomato juice. Cover, reduce heat, and simmer for 3 - 4 hours. Then add other ingredients and continue simmering until green peppers are tender.

Burt's Buckwheat
(Kasha)

1 bell pepper (minced)
2 T oil
1 C buckwheat groats
1 chopped tomato (optional)
1 t salt
2-1/2 - 3 C water

Heat oil in a heavy pan. Add buckwheat groats and minced bell pepper. Stir for a minute over high heat. Add salt, water and tomato. Cover and simmer until done (about 20 minutes). Yield: about 2 C.

Kate's Fried Rice

2 C brown rice
1 t salt
2 T oil
1/2 C minced green pepper
1/2 C minced celery
1 t thyme or basil

Fry rice in oil until it turns slightly brown and smells roasted. Add 4 C water, cover and steam 20 minutes. Add other ingredients and steam another 15 - 20 minutes. Serves 6.

Rice Pilaf

1/4 C butter
1-1/2 C brown rice
1/2 C uncooked whole wheat **Noodles**
   or vermicelli
3 C boiling water or vegetable stock
1/2 C chopped celery
1 C chopped vegetables
salt to taste
1/2 C **Yogurt**
parsley (to garnish)

Melt butter in medium sized saucepan. Add rice and toast over medium heat for 10 minutes, until rice is lightly browned. Add **Noodles**, boiling stock, vegetables and salt to taste. Bake in a covered casserole for 30 minutes at 350°. Then fold in **Yogurt**, garnish with parsley, and bake another 10 minutes or until tender. Serves 4 - 6.

Yogi Rice
(sweet)

2-1/2 - 3 C water
1 C brown rice
handful of raisins
bit of fresh ginger
1 cinnamon stick
5 whole cloves
3 pods cardamom
honey

Put all but the honey together and cook by grain cooking METHOD ONE. Remove whole spices which will have come to the top Add a spoonful of honey to taste and stir.

Variation: **Curried Yogi Rice** — Cook as above adding 1 chopped apple. Add 1 sliced banana, curry powder, turmeric and butter to taste (with the honey) at the end.

Lemon Rice

1 t salt
1 t black mustard seed
2 t turmeric
1/4 C butter or Ghee
1/2 C red or green bell pepper
1 C peeled, diced eggplant
handful of shelled green peas
3 C cooked brown rice (about 1 C raw)
juice of one lemon

Add salt, mustard seed, turmeric to butter; heat and stir until mustard seeds dance. Add vegetables and cook until almost tender. Add rice. Stir until all is heated; then add lemon juice and serve. Serves 4 - 6. An excellent, colorful company dish.

Chinch Bhat
(Rice and Yogurt)

Oil
1/2 t mustard seeds
1/2 t fennel seeds
1/2 t cumin
Yogurt
1 t turmeric
salt to taste
1/4 - 1/2 t cayenne
2 to 3 C cooked rice (2/3 - 1 C raw)

Put 1/2 inch oil in bottom of 10-inch frying pan and add mustard seeds; when they dance, add spices, then cooked rice. When heated through, add a large serving spoonful of **Yogurt**.

Herbed Rice

1-1/2 - 2 C water (more water for softer rice)
1 C brown rice
1 t salt
1/2 t rosemary
1/2 t marjoram
1/2 t thyme
1 T butter

Bring water to a boil. Add rice very slowly. Stir in other ingredients. Cover and turn down heat as far as possible. Cook for approximately 40 minutes until all water has been absorbed.

Noodles

3 C whole wheat flour
2/3 - 1 C cold water
1 t salt

Mix ingredients well. Add additional water if necessary to make a workable dough. Knead dough 10-15 minutes. Roll out very thin on a well floured board. Cut into strips (wide for lasagne, thin for noodles . . .) let dry out completely and store until needed. Cook in boiling water until just tender.

Variations:

1) Noodles may be cooked immediately after making. Will not take as long to cook.

2) 1 C of whole wheat flour can be replaced with another kind of flour such as buckwheat or rye.

Poppy Seed Noodles

8 ounces noodles
1 T butter
2 T poppy seeds

Cook noodles in boiling water until done. Drain. Return to pan. Add butter and poppy seeds tossing lightly to mix.

Variation: Substitute 2 T slightly ground sesame seeds.

Crisp Fried Noodles

(a great way to use left over noodles)

4 t butter or oil
8 ounces noodles, cooked

Melt butter in heavy skillet over low heat. Cook noodles on one side without stirring until browned. Using a dinner plate, invert noodles so that the browned side is on top. Slip noodles back into pan, cooking another 5 minutes or until bottom is browned. Serves 4.

ALSO REFER TO . . .

CRACKERS AND BREADS section
DESSERTS section
Food of Intuition
Stuffed Cabbage
Macaroni and Cheese
Spaghetti
Lasagne
Whole Wheat Gravy
Tempura

GRAIN NUTRITION COMPARISON

GRAIN	VOLUME IN CUPS	WEIGHT (in grams)	CALORIES	PROTEIN (In grams)	CHO (grams)	CALCIUM (mg)	IRON (mg)	VITAMIN A (I.U.)	THIAMIN (mg)	RIBOFLAVIN (mg)	NIACIN (mg)	FAT (grams total lipid)
All-purpose flour	1	110	400	12	1	84	18	3.2	0	.4	.2	3.2
Barley	1	203	710	17	17	2	160	32.0	0	.25	.17	6.3
Bran flakes	1	25	117	3	t	32	25	2.0	0	.1	.1	3.4
Corn meal, yellow	1	118	360	9	4	74	6	1.8	500	.4	.1	2.0
Farina (enriched and cooked)	1	238	100	3	3	t	21	10.0	0	.11	.07	1.0
Oats, rolled	1	236	150	5	3	26	21	1.7	0	.2	t	.4
Rice, brown	1	208	748	15	3	154	78	4.0	0	.6	.1	9.2
Rice, converted	1	187	677	14	t	142	53	1.6	0	.3	t	7.6
Rice, white, enriched	1	191	692	14	t	150	46	1.6	0	t	t	1.6
Rice polish	1	100	264	12	12	46	70	16.0	0	1.8	.2	14.0
Soy flour, (full fat)	1	110	460	39	22	33	218	8.8	121	.9	.3	2.3
Wheat germ	1	68	245	17	17	7	34	57.0	0	1.4	.5	3.1
Whole wheat flour	1	120	390	13	2	79	49	3.9	0	.6	.2	5.1

Abbreviations: CHO = carbohydrates; t = trace amount; mg = milligrams; I.U. = International units

QUICK REFERENCE GUIDE FOR COOKING GRAINS

1 Cup Grain	Water (Cups)*	Cooking time** (in minutes)	Pressure Cooker*** (in minutes)
Barley, hulled	2 - 2-1/2	30 - 60	30 - 40
Brown rice	1-1/2 - 2	40 - 60	30 - 40
Buckwheat groats	2 - 2-1/2	20 - 40	Not recommended
Bulgur	1-1/2 - 2	15 - 20	Not recommended
Corn meal	4 C	20 - 30	Not recommended
Cracked grains	1-1/2 - 2	15 - 20	Not recommended
Millet	2 - 3	20 - 30	25
Oats, rolled	2	5-15	Not recommended
Oats, whole	1-1/2 - 2	40 - 60	30 - 40
Rye, whole	2 - 2-1/2	60 - 90	45
Triticale	2 - 2-1/2	60 - 90	45
Wheat, berries	2 - 2-1/2	60 - 90	45
Wheat, cracked	1-1/2 - 2	15 - 20	Not recommended

* Amount of water varies according to method used for cooking.
** Amount of time required varies according to method used.
*** Certain grains, due to their size and consistency, tend to plug the safety valves of pressure cookers, which may cause them to explode. For this reason, we recommend that these grains NOT be pressure cooked. Be sure to read the manufacturer's instructions carefully before using a pressure cooker.

BREADS
and
CRACKERS

152

BREAD INGREDIENTS

Hearty, nutritious bread is an important part of a vegetarian diet. To make a good bread, it helps to know a little about the ingredients that will be used. Wheat flour is usually the basis for breads. There are two types of wheat: soft wheat and hard wheat. Flour made from soft wheat is silky when rubbed between the fingers; hard-wheat flour feels slightly gritty. Soft wheat flour is called pastry flour and is not the best choice for yeast bread because there is not as much gluten as in hard wheat flour (see below). Whole wheat flour contains the germ or live part of the wheatberry and the bran or outer coating. Unbleached white flour has had the bran and the wheat germ removed, and does not contain as many nutrients as whole wheat flour. Bleached enriched flour has also had the germ and bran removed, along with the vitamins, minerals, and essential fatty acids contained in the germ and bran. (See diagram in GRAINS AND CEREALS.) Bleached enriched white flour had some of the natural vitamins replaced by synthetic ones.

From the dictionary: "Gluten is a tenacious elastic substance, especially of wheat flour, that gives cohesiveness to dough." It is developed during the kneading and forms a stringy mass that holds in the bubbles (of carbon dioxide) that result from the growing yeast or other leavening agent. There is a higher gluten content in wheat than in any other grain, and this is why wheat breads are usually lighter than breads made with other grains. When you are using grains with a low gluten content, you may wish to add gluten flour to help make the bread lighter and hold together better. This substance is available from El Molino Mills. It is made as follows: a stiff dough is made of hard wheat flour and it is immersed in water. Then the starch is kneaded out, and the gluten is dried and ground into flour.

Rye flour is next to wheat in gluten content. All other grains have very little gluten, but each adds its distinctive touch to bread. Soy flour adds protein. Breads containing it brown faster and remain fresh longer. Rye flour is silky and helps work in other granular grains such as corn meal, rolled oats. Pure rye flour tends to make a sticky dough. Corn flour adds sweetness and a more crumbly texture. Millet flour makes bread more crunchy as well as sweeter. Rolled oats make bread stay moist longer. They add to the texture and make the bread slightly chewy and sweeter. Barley flour added to breads makes them more cakelike. For non-yeasted breads, cakes and pastries, barley flour is an excellent substitute for wheat flour. Use an equal amount to replace wheat flour. The finished product will be very slightly heavier than if it were made from wheat, and more cake-like than bread-like. The flavor is not much different from that of wheat. Buckwheat (not related to wheat) makes breads very heavy: it is best used in small amounts. It adds a good flavor and an interesting texture. Bran is best soaked an hour or so before it is added to the bread. (It adds flavor, texture, and bulk).

You may also want to add whole or cracked grains to your bread. These must be soaked or better yet, cooked before adding. Whole grains can also be sprouted and added (whole or ground) to the bread dough.

To enrich bread nutritionally: for each cup

of flour add 1 T soy flour, 1 T powdered milk, and 1 T wheat germ.

Flours from large commercial firms are ground quickly by heavy steel rollers which generate a lot of heat. This tends to "burn" off the heat sensitive vitamins and the oil in the grain. Stone ground flours fare better in this respect, but also often contain minute particles of stone, which wear down teeth. Freshly ground flour tastes better and is more nutritious than stale flour. There are small hand grain grinders available for twenty dollars and up. Your local natural foods store should carry them. (You can't grind enough at a time in your blender). The coup de grace is to hook up an old bicycle frame so that you can power the grinder with your legs, which don't get tired as fast as your arms do at this task.

There are two types of yeast which are used in making bread: cake yeast, and dry powdered yeast. (Sourdough starter is different and is discussed later. Nutritional yeast, torumel, and brewer's yeast will not cause bread to rise). The cake yeast must be fresh. If the cake is slightly brown, smells yeasty, and crumbles easily, it is probably still fresh. Dry yeast purchased in bulk form is the most economical. Many natural food stores carry it in bulk, and El Molino sells 1/2 pound and 1 pound packages. Keep unused portion in an airtight can or jar, preferably refrigerated. 1 T dry yeast equals one cube cake yeast or one small package dry yeast.

Yeast produces carbon dioxide as a by-product of its growth. The CO_2 causes the bread to rise. The yeast feeds on the sweetener in the bread (the small amount of sugar present in grain is not enough). Its activity is practically controlled by the salt in the bread: if not enough salt is used, the bread will rise too quickly and run out of its pan (maybe), producing large-holed, coarsely-textured bread; if too much salt is used, the bread will not rise enough, and it will be heavy. An over-refined product like white sugar will feed your yeast, but contribute many calories and not nutrients. We recommend a natural sweetener such as honey, sorghum, blackstrap molasses, maple syrup, barley malt, or date sugar. These add nice flavors and minerals. The thicker ones, such as honey, also help keep the bread moist. Remember to cut down liquid 1/4 C when substituting a cup of honey for a cup of sugar.

Fat is added to the bread (3/4 to 1 T per cup of flour) to give a richer flavor. Again, we recommend natural products such as unrefined, cold-pressed oil. Butter isn't too good for your body, but does add a lot of flavor.

The last necessary ingredient is liquid. A little water (at least 1/4 C) must be used to activate the yeast. The rest of the liquid can be water, milk, fruit juice, vegetable juice, or whatever you can think of. Breads made with milk are more nutritious (powdered milk can be used) and have a velvety texture. Raw milk should be scalded to kill off any undesirable types of wild yeast that might sour the bread. (Scalding means heating just below the boiling point — the milk steams and tiny bubbles rise at the edges of the pan). Try substituting coconut or nut milk for the animal milk. Breads made with all water as the liquid have a thicker, crisper crust and resemble French bread in texture. Within reason, the less liquid used, the better the texture of the bread will be. More liquid is required when using whole grain flours (whole wheat, rice flour), as the bran of the grain absorbs more liquid than the rest of the grain. Also, the amount of water that the flour can absorb (and the amount of flour the water can absorb) depends on the temperature, humidity, and amount of gluten present in the flour.

1 T lecithin per 4 C flour can be added to the bread as a preservative and nutrient. You can also add chopped or ground nuts, sunflower seeds, sesame seeds, grated apple, raisin, currants, dates, shredded coconut, chia seeds, and other goodies to any basic recipe.

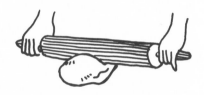

Wheat Rice Crackers

2 C cooked rice (approx. 2/3 C raw)
3-1/2 T oil
1 C whole wheat flour
1 T water
1 t salt

Crumble cooked rice until grains are separated. Mix thoroughly with other ingredients. Knead well (by handfuls is easiest) until mixture sticks together. Roll out about 1/8 inch thick (about the thickness of a cooked millet grain). Cut into circles or squares and put on a greased cookie sheet and bake at 300° until golden brown. Makes about 3 dozen 2 inch round crackers.

The thinner they are rolled, the crisper they will be. Holes can be pricked in the center to improve crispness.

Rolling is easiest between two pieces of wax paper or a plastic bag that has been sliced open, forming two sheets. The dough can also be rolled out on the greased cookie sheet and cut into squares.

Cheese Cracker

1/2 C butter
2 C grated cheddar cheese
1 C whole wheat flour (or 1/2 C whole wheat flour and 1/2 C rye flour)
1 t salt
1 t dill (optional)

Mix and divide into two balls. Work into two long rolls 1 inch in diameter. Wrap in waxed paper and chill in freezer for 30 minutes. Slice wafer thin. Put on buttered baking sheet. Bake 10 minutes at 350°.

Sweet Millet Crackers

3-1/2 T oil
2 C cooked millet
1 C flour
1/4 C honey

Crumble cooked millet until grains are separated. Mix thoroughly with other ingredients. Knead well (by handfuls is easiest) until mixture sticks together. Roll out about 1/8 inch thick (about the thickness of a cooked millet grain). Put on greased cookie sheet and bake at 300° until golden brown. Makes about 3 dozen 2 inch round crackers.

Graham Crackers

2 C graham flour
1-1/2 C whole wheat flour
1/2 t salt
1/2 t cinnamon (optional)
1/2 C oil
1/2 C milk
1/4 C molasses
1/4 C honey

Combine flours, salt and cinnamon. Work in oil. Mix together milk, molasses and honey. Add to dry ingredients and mix well. Knead on lightly floured board and roll out. Cut into squares, place on a cookie sheet and prick with a fork. Bake in 300° oven for about 25 minutes, until golden brown.

OTHER UNLEAVENED BREADS

Tortillas

3/4 C cornmeal or flour
3/4 C whole wheat flour
1/4 - 1/2 t salt
1/2 - 3/4 C water

Mix together corn meal, flour and salt in a bowl. Dribble in water, mixing with fingers until it can be formed into a ball. Knead a minute or two, then set aside for 10-20 minutes. Just before frying, roll out into circles about six inches in diameter. If the edges tend to split, roll out extra large balls of dough and cut around a bowl or small plate to make the tortillas circular. Keep all the discarded edges to roll into the last tortilla. Makes about 6.

Fry in oil (either just a little or deep fry in 1/2 - 1 inch oil). If you don't mind stiff tortillas (they break when bent) you can dry roast them in an iron skillet.

Serve with **Refried Beans**. Using the tortillas to scoop up beans or roll the beans up in the shells. These can be eaten as is or topped with grated cheese and baked at 350° for 20 - 30 minutes.

Tortilla Chips: uncooked circles may be cut into sixths, spread in an even layer on oven racks or cookie sheets and heated until crisp. Salt if desired. Can be served with **Guacamole**. They can also be deep fried for chips.

Chapatis

This bread is an Indian staple. It takes time but is worth it.

1 C whole wheat flour
1/4 t sea salt
1 or 2 T water
ghee

Combine flour and salt with enough water to make an elastic dough. Knead roughly. Then break off a plum-size piece and roll out as thin as you can. Cook as follows: Coat the griddle or frying pan with oil; fry about 20 seconds on the first side, flip and press with a spatula for 20 seconds; flip, brush with ghee, fry for 3 seconds, flip, brush with ghee, fry for 3 seconds, continue flipping and brushing till it is done as you like. Continue in the same style with the rest of the dough.

Variation: when rolled out very thin, brush with ghee and fold in half; brush new surface and fold in half again; you now have a triangular shape; roll into a circle and fry as before. Chapatis can be used as plates for large gatherings.

Puris
(Indian deep-fried bread)

1 C whole wheat flour
1/4 t salt
1/4 C water

Mix flour and salt in bowl. Gradually drip in water, mixing with your hand until you form a ball. Knead until smooth, about the consistency of an earlobe (really). Cover and let sit for approximately 30 minutes. Divide into 5 balls.

Put about 1-1/3 inches of oil (safflower or sesame) in a skillet (preferably cast-iron) and begin heating it.

Roll a ball between your palms until smooth. Flatten a little into a rounded patty, coat each side sparingly with flour and place on a board. Gently roll from the center out into a circle, turning over frequently. Stop rolling when it is slightly less than 1/8 of an inch thick. If you are making them ahead of time, oil lightly and do not stack more than three high.

When oil is very hot (but not smoking), slip puri into oil from side, so it doesn't splatter on your hand. You can use a spatula to hold it under the oil and encourage the bubbles to expand. Small bubbles should start and then spread so that the puri is one big puff. About this time it should just be turning golden brown: carefully turn it over (so you don't splatter), and fry the other side. When bubbles stop in the oil around the edges of the puri, this is a good indication that it is time to turn it over or take it out. Set on paper towels to cool and drain.

Don't be discouraged if you can't get them to puff the first time you try. Try varying the way you roll them, the temperature of the oil, or the mixing and kneading of the dough.

Serve with **Curried Vegetables**, **Lemon Rice**, **Indian Gravy**, **Peas and Cauliflower** or any Indian recipe, soups or stews. Indians use puris to scoop up food.

Carrot Molasses Muffins

1 packed, finely grated raw carrot (1 large
   carrot) or 1/2 C cooked mashed carrots
1 C chopped nuts
1-1/2 C pastry flour
1/2 t cinnamon
1 C chopped dates
1/2 C soy flour
1/2 C molasses
2 T oil
1/4 C water

Combine dry ingredients stirring well to separate carrots and dried fruit. Mix wet ingredients and add to dry ingredients. Mix well. Fill muffin tins almost full. Bake 40 - 45 minutes at 350°. Makes 1 dozen muffins.

Remembrance Holy Bread

4 C whole wheat flour
salt to taste
3 C hot water
approximately 3 C other ingredients
   (see instructions)

Add flour to water to make a thick batter. Beat vigorously for about 20 minutes (while sitting happily in the sunshine) until batter becomes somewhat elastic. Add soya flour, brown rice flour, rolled oats, corn flour, corn meal, wheat germ, rice polishings, raisins, honey, chia seeds, etc. Add salt to taste. Let stand about ten minutes. Knead and turn into oiled pans. Turn oven to 300° and put bread into cold oven. Bake about 1-1/2 hours or longer. Experiment with different flours, substitute milk or vegetable water or fruit juices for the water. Add grated apples or carrots.

Iowa Heavy Bread

5 C whole wheat flour
1 C soy flour
1 C corn meal
1 C wheat germ
1 T salt
6 T oil
handful of sesame seeds
4 C water
Gomasio

Mix flours, corn meal, wheat germ, and salt in a large bowl; mix in the oil, sesame seeds, and water. Pour into oiled bread pans. Sprinkle **Gomasio** on top. Bake at 350° to 400° for 1-1/2 to 2-1/2 hours.

Sprouted Wheat Bread

1 C wheatberries
a bit of flour

Soak wheatberries and sprout (for more detailed instruction see SPROUTS). When 1/4 inch long, grind with the fine blade of a food mill. Sprinkle a board lightly with flour and knead wheatberries until they stick together. Form a small, very flat loaf. Let rise several hours. Bake at 250° for 2-1/2 hours. The bread will be crusty on the outside and soft and chewy on the inside. The results will vary depending on the weather, age and absorption of moisture in the sprouts, and the ideation of the cook. Can be baked in the sun if it's very hot outside.

QUICK BREADS

Biscuits

2 C flour
1 t soda
1/2 t salt
1/4 C powdered milk
1/4 C butter
2/3 C water

Preheat the oven to 400°. Mix the dry ingredients together. (If you don't have powdered milk, leave it out and use milk instead of water.) Melt the butter and pour it on top. Using a strong fork, mix it in thoroughly (until the whole mixture has a texture like cornmeal). Add the water and stir. The dough should be just wet enough to hold together but not be sticky. Put some flour on your hands and on the counter, and use a rolling pin or a glass to roll the dough out about 1/2 inch thick. Then cut out your biscuits by pressing the top of a glass through the dough (touching it to the flour in between to prevent sticking). Put biscuits on an oiled cookie sheet and bake at 400° until done.

Easy Frozen Biscuits

Cut rolled biscuit dough with small empty juice cans. Fit the rounds of dough back into the washed and dried can and seal the ends with foil and freezer tape or the like. Freeze. To use, remove from can by pushing from one end. Bake immediately.

Cornbread or Corn Muffins

2 C whole wheat flour
2 C cornmeal
1/4 C oil
1 T honey
1/2 t salt
dates, nuts (optional)
1 t baking soda
milk to thin batter (about 1 C)

Mix everything together (make sure the baking soda gets mixed up). Use enough milk to make the batter about the texture of peanut butter. Makes a dozen big muffins. Bake at 350° for 20 - 30 minutes. If you don't have a muffin pan, make cornbread in a square pan.

Honey Muffins

2 C whole wheat flour
1 t salt
3 t baking powder
1 C milk
4 T honey
1/4 C oil

Sift together dry ingredients. Mix together wet ingredients and add the dry, stirring only enough to moisten. Bake at 400° for 25 - 30 minutes or until delicately browned.

Variations:

BLUEBERRY MUFFINS - add 1/2 C fresh blueberries to sifted dry ingredients.

FRUIT MUFFINS - add 3/4 C chopped citron to batter. Brush muffins lightly with honey before baking.

HONEY-FILLED MUFFINS - put a drop of crystalized honey in the center of the batter of each muffin.

PEANUT BUTTER MUFFINS - blend 1/4 C peanut butter with the honey and add to the milk mixture.

SOYBEAN MUFFINS - replace 1/2 C flour with 1/2 C soybean flour.

ORANGE MUFFINS - Replace the milk with orange juice and add 1 t orange rind.

Apple Nut Muffins

1-1/4 C packed grated raw apple (1 large apple)
1 C chopped nuts
1-1/2 C pastry flour
1/2 t cinnamon
1 C raisins, chopped figs or dates
1/2 C soy flour
1/2 C molasses
2 T oil
1/4 C water or apple juice

Combine dry ingredients. Add fruit, stirring well to separate (and coat with flour) dried fruit and apples. Mix wet ingredients and add. Mix well. Fill muffin tins almost full. Bake 40 - 45 minutes at 350°. Makes 1 dozen muffins

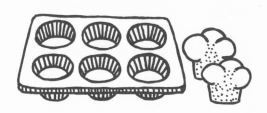

Fig Rye Muffins

2-1/2 C rye flour
1 t salt
1 t soda
1 C ground figs
1/4 C molasses
2 T oil
1 C water

Mix dry ingredients thoroughly. Add figs and stir enough to coat the fruit with flour. Add wet ingredients. Stir until dry ingredients are moistened. Spoon into oiled muffin pans. Smooth dough down. Top may be oiled slightly. Bake 30 minutes at 350°. Remove immediately from pan and cool on a rack. Makes 12 muffins.

Variations: substitute other dried fruit for figs (such as prunes); substitute milk or fruit juice for water; substitute whole wheat flour or other for rye; add 1 t cinnamon or allspice or lemon peel.

Bran Raisin Muffins

1-1/2 C bran
1-1/2 C milk
1/2 C molasses
2 C flour (whole wheat pastry)
1 t soda
1/4 C oil
1 C raisins

Soak bran in milk for 10 minutes. Add oil and molasses. Combine flour and soda and add. Mix in raisins.

Variations: for cleansing muffins add 3 T flax seed chopped in blender with oil. Substitute prunes for raisins.

Fritters

1 C whole wheat flour
1/2 t salt
1/2 t baking soda
1/2 t spice or herb if desired (like cinnamon for apple fritters)
2 t honey
6 T yogurt or soured milk (amount could vary according to consistency of yogurt)
deep frying oil

Combine dry ingredients in bowl and mix well. Add wet ingredients and beat well. This should form a thick batter. Add grated or finely chopped fruit or vegetables and stir until well coated. Drop by tablespoonfuls into one or more inches of hot oil. Test the heat of the oil by dropping a bit of batter in and seeing if it floats to the top and sizzles quickly. If it is too hot, the oil will begin to smoke, and the fritters will brown too fast and be raw on the inside. Cook until medium to dark brown. Test one and make sure they are getting done inside. Remove from oil with a slotted spoon so that oil drains off, and drain on a paper towel or bag.

Jyoti's Banana Bread, Almost

3 large or 4 small bananas
1/2 C melted butter or oil or
   Butter-oil Spread
1/2 C honey
1 t vanilla
1/2 C date sugar (1/2 C honey can
   be substituted)
1 t salt
1 t soda
1 t mace (optional)
1-3/4 C pastry flour
1 C chopped nuts (optional)

Puree the bananas through a food mill, in a blender, or mash well. Add the other ingredients in order listed, mixing thoroughly after each addition. Bake at 350° in a greased pan. A large loaf pan takes 45 - 60 minutes (45 for moist, 60 minutes for dry and crusty) and small ones, 35 - 40 minutes. Makes one large or two small loaves.

Easy Pumpkin Bread

Follow Jyoti's Banana Bread Recipe and substitute 1 - 1-1/4 C pureed cooked pumpkin or winter squash (less if watery) for bananas.

Boston Brown Bread

2 C corn meal
3 C sour milk
1/4 pound butter
1 t salt
2 C graham flour
1 C molasses
2 t soda
1 C raisins (optional)

Combine above ingredients. Put in coffee cans with covers. Set on rack (with water underneath) in large kettle. Cover. Steam for three hours.

YEAST BREADS

BASIC YEAST BREAD PROCEDURES

Mix the ingredients (which should be room temperature). Add the yeast to some lukewarm water (to test the temperature of the water, drop some on the back of your wrist; if you can't feel the temperature or if it feels just like warm, it is the right temperature.) Add the sweetener to this water, and let it sit for ten or fifteen minutes while you get everything else ready. (This gives the yeast a chance to get growing.) Add the salt and the liquid that you are using, and then add as much flour as you can mix in. Add nuts, etc., (see BREAD INGREDIENTS) with the flour.

Now you are ready to KNEAD THE BREAD. Your working surface should be at the height at which your hands rest comfortably. If you are using a board on top of another surface, a wet towel will keep it from slipping. Spread some flour out on a clean smooth surface. (A cutting board is not good because the bread dough will work into the cuts and perhaps mold.) Dump the bread dough out on the flour, push it down, fold over and push it down again. Repeat. This is kneading. Add more flour to the kneading surface occasionally to replace the flour picked up by the dough. Do not add flour to the top of the bread (it will get folded in and make a pocket of dry flour). Also, the bread will tell you when it has had enough flour added because it will stop picking it up from the table. If you add flour to the top, you may add more than the bread dough needs. The purpose of kneading is to develop the gluten in the flour. Breads with little or no wheat flour in them require longer kneading. Kneading is done when the dough is smooth, satiny, and not sticky. It should be the consistency of an earlobe or a plump baby's bottom: warm, rounded, soft yet springy. Touch lightly with your index finger — the mark should not disappear. Usually ten minutes of kneading is enough. Overkneading will cause the bread to be poorly textured.

LET IT RISE. Oil the kneaded bread and place in a clean large bowl (large enough so when dough doubles, it won't go over the top). Cover with a paper or cloth towel, or plastic wrap. Leave the dough in a warm place, free of drafts, to rise (on top of a pilot light is good). Depending on the bread and the weather, it will take from 25 minutes to several hours for the bread to rise. If you do not have a warm nook for the bread, put a bowl in your sink and fill the sink with warm water. Place the dough in the bowl, adding hot water as the water in the sink cools. Be careful not to get the bread wet. The bread should be evenly heated while rising (especially while in the pans). If bread rises unevenly, it will crumble when sliced. Protect it from too much heat in the summer. The bread is ready to shape into loaves when you can insert two fingers half an inch into the dough and have the indentations remain. If dough has risen too long, it will be very sticky, and more flour will have to be added before the dough is manageable, resulting in a dry loaf of bread. If it is not convenient for you to shape the bread when it is ready, punch it down (which lets the gas out so the yeast doesn't suffocate), cover as before and let rise again. Remember that each time the bread rises, it does so in a shorter period of time. To shape loaves: pull off a piece of dough that half fills the bread pan. Larger bread pans take 2-1/2 pounds of bread; medium ones take 1-1/4 pounds; a 2-pound coffee can holds 2-1/2 pounds bread dough. There are several methods to shape the loaf. The bread dough may be stretched out and two edges folded under. Then you may put it in the pan, or first roll the folded bread up the long way and then put it in the pan. Or, without folding, round the dough in your hands, tuck any rough edges under, and put it in the pan. The important thing to remember is to put all rough edges and seams on the bottom, and oil the pans well. Butter or ghee will keep the bread from sticking better than oil. When the dough is stretched out (before folding or rolling), you can butter it and add surprises such as nuts, fruit, honey, raisins, etc. Oil the tops of the loaves. You can also sprinkle seeds or finely ground nuts on top of the loaves; but don't put honey on top, as it may burn. Let the bread rise again in the pans. If you allow the bread to more than double in the pans, it will have a coarse texture. Breads with a low gluten content should not be allowed to rise too high or they will fall during baking. At this time preheat the oven.

BAKE your bread at 375° to 400° for the first ten or fifteen minutes, and then lower the temperature 50°. If a large part of the bread is soy flour, or if your baking pans are glass or ceramic, lower all baking temperatures 25° from that stated on the recipe given above. When the bread has risen, put it in the oven and bake it until it is brown and sounds hollow when thumped (thump it as you would shoot a marble). For a crisper crust, remove bread from pans when it is almost done and finish baking without pans. For a soft crust, brush crust with milk when done, or put a small pan of water in the oven while baking. For a butter crust, instead of buttering the bread when it is hot from the oven, slash the uncooked loaf from one end to the other and put thin slices of butter in the slash.

COOL the bread on racks. If no racks are available, take bread out of pans and cool it balanced on the edges of the pans. A note on bread pans: if you don't have bread pans, any dish or pan will work. Round or free-form loaves can be put on cookie sheets. For easy baking, loaves should all be about the same size.

STORE your bread in plastic bags, but make sure it is cool before putting it in them. If you make several loaves at once, it's best to refrigerate or freeze them to keep them fresh. Raw bread dough can be frozen, but shouldn't be kept frozen more than 2 - 3 weeks (the yeast won't be as active). When a standard-size (raw) loaf is taken from the freezer, it will take at least 6 hours to thaw and rise.

Mom's Bread

2 C warm milk (or water)
4 t salt
4 T butter or oil
1/2 C molasses
2 C cold water
2 T active dry yeast
10 - 12 C whole wheat flour

Add salt, butter and molasses to milk. Stir until butter melts. Add cold water and cool to lukewarm. Beat in yeast. Add 6 cups flour. Beat smooth (about 2 minutes). Add remaining flour. Knead 7 - 10 minutes. Let rise one hour or until double. Punch down and let rise until double again. (If you're in a hurry, the second rising can be omitted.) Form loaves. Let rise one hour or until double. Bake at 400° for one hour. Cool on racks. Makes four loaves.

DEXTRINIZING BREAD

Dextrinization is the process of converting starches to easily digestible sugars. Here is the procedure:

Slice bread thin. Lay on oven racks, a single layer thick and bake in as slow an oven as possible — no higher than 250° — until thoroughly dry. A cookie sheet may be used instead of the racks, but then the bread must be turned over several times.

Dextrinized breads made without oil will store indefinitely if kept dry. A bread made with oil may become rancid after a time.

Digger Bread

2 two-pound coffee cans (for measurements and baking)
1/2 C luke warm water
large spoonful flour
1 t - 1 T salt
1/8 can powdered milk
1 T dry yeast
large spoonful honey
1 level can whole wheat flour
2 handfuls raisins (etc.)

Mix the water, yeast, salt, honey and spoonful of flour in one coffee can. Let stand while you combine the other ingredients in a large pan. Add the wet mixture and blend until it reaches a uniform consistency. Cover. Let rise in a warm place until it increases to 1-1/2 times original size. This may take an hour or two. Wash, dry and oil the cans (be careful to cover edges and bottom). Knead the dough (you may need more flour). Divide the dough and knead the halves into balls. Put all rough edges under and pop into cans. Grease the tops of the loaves. Let rise until even with the tops of the cans. Put the cans upright in an oven preheated to 400° and bake for 1 hour and 5 minutes. After baking, let the cans cool 5 - 10 minutes, then with potholders give the bread a twirl in the can to dump it out on the counter.

Light Rye Bread

1 quart hot water
1 C dark molasses
1 T salt
1 T oil
2 T yeast
3 C rye flour
6 - 9 C whole wheat flour
1 to 1-1/2 T caraway seed

Dissolve together water, molasses, salt and oil. Let sit until lukewarm. Stir in yeast. Let sit 5 or 10 minutes until yeast is foamy. Mix in all of the rye flour and enough of the wheat flour to make a stiff batter; let sit 15 minutes. Mix in more wheat flour to make a stiff dough. Knead very well to develop a strong gluten. Finally, knead in caraway seed. Form into small round loaves, cover with a damp cloth, and let rise till double in bulk. Bake at 350° about an hour.

All-Rye Yeast Bread

2 T dry yeast
2 C lukewarm water
2 T honey
2 t salt
2 T oil
5 C unsifted rye flour

Dissolve yeast in lukewarm water. Add honey, salt and oil. Add the flour slowly, beating well. Knead thoroughly. Shape into loaf and place in well-oiled baking pan. Oil top lightly and cover. Let rise in warm place until half again the original size. If you let it rise too high, you will produce a crumbly bread which may fall during baking. Bake at 375° for 50 - 60 minutes. Remove from pan and let cool on rack.   Yields: 1 large loaf.

Triticale Bread

Substitute 5 C triticale flour for rye flour in **All-Rye Yeast Bread** recipe.

Barley Bread

1 T yeast
2 t honey
1 C lukewarm water
3 C barley flour
1 t salt
2 t oil
1/4 C soy flour
a little more barley flour

Dissolve the yeast in the lukewarm water with the honey. Add half of the flour and beat vigorously until air is mixed into the batter and the gluten is developed (batter follows the spoon around without falling off). Stir in salt, oil and soy flour. Add more of the barley flour until you have a compact enough dough to put out on a floured board and knead. Knead until smooth and elastic. Shape into a loaf and place on cookie sheet. Cut a slash across the top and let rise until it is double in size. Bake for 1 hour at 350°. Yields: One loaf.

Batter Bread
(very quick yeast bread)

1-1/2 C lukewarm water
3 T barley malt, molasses or honey
1-1/2 T **Butter Oil Spread** (or melted butter)
1-1/2 t salt
1-1/2 T yeast
3 C wholewheat flour

Mix first five ingredients well and then mix in whole wheat flour. Let rise until tripled, about 45 minutes. Pour into loaf pan. Bake at 350° for 1 hour. Do not let rise after putting into pan. Makes 1 loaf.

Variations: **Herbed Batter Bread** - Add 1/2 C minced fresh parsley, and 1 t dried dill weed or 1 t dried rubbed thyme. **Sweet Batter Bread** - Add 1/2 to 3/4 C raisins and 1 t cinnamon. Sweetener may be doubled.

Sprout Bread

Sprout triticale (or rye or wheat) groats until 1/4 inch long (directions under SPROUTS). Put through a food grinder, medium blade. Mix with the "remaining flour" in **Mom's Bread** recipe and proceed as usual.

Sweet Rolls

Any bread dough
soft butter
honey
ground nuts
raisins
grated apple
dried lemon or orange peel
cinnamon

Make any basic bread dough. Roll out 1/4 inch thick on a floured board. Butter as you would toast, then spread honey on top. Sprinkle with a thick covering of ground nuts, raisins, and grated apple. Then top with lemon or orange peel (don't use too much, it's strong) and cinnamon. Roll up and slice one inch thick. Place on side, close together in pan. Sweetness can be cut by thinning honey with orange or lemon juice. For variety add other fruits besides apples, such as canned apricots, or substitute jam or jelly for the honey. Bake at 350° for 40 minutes, or until done.

Doughnuts

1-1/2 C warm water
1 T dry yeast or cake yeast
1/4 C honey
4-1/2 - 5 C whole wheat flour (regular
　or pastry)
1-1/2 t salt
3 T oil
2 t grated orange rind (optional)
1 t grated lemon rind (optional)
1 quart frying oil

Dissolve yeast in warm water, add honey, salt and oil. Stir in as much of the whole wheat flour as can easily be stirred in. Turn out onto floured board and knead until smooth (about 5 minutes). Let rise until double in bulk in oiled bowl. Split in half and roll out about 1/2 inch thick. Cut into doughnut shapes with doughnut cutter, or cut into circles with the top of a glass and form the hole with your fingers. Set on cookie sheet and set in a warm place to rise for 30 - 45 minutes until almost double in size. Deep fry in a good frying oil, drain on paper towels afterwards. If the oil is the right temperature the doughnuts should not be oily after they are drained. Frost with **Carob Frosting** or any other glaze or frosting.

Variation: try adding 1/4 t nutmeg, 1 C raisins, and 1 grated peel from 1 orange or lemon.

Bagels

1 C warm milk or water
2 t salt
2 T butter or oil
1/4 C molasses or honey
1 C cold water
2 T dry yeast
5 - 6 C whole wheat flour

Mix together liquid ingredients. Add yeast and let sit until softened (a couple minutes), mix well and add flour gradually while stirring until a ball forms in bowl. Turn out onto floured board and knead, adding more flour if necessary until it's a smooth, heavy dough that will keep its shape. Put in an oiled bowl and let rise once. Cut dough into 16 pieces and form each piece into a smooth ball. Make a hole in the ball with your finger and shape it into a doughnut shape. Cover and let rise for 20 minutes. In a large pan, combine a gallon of water and 1 T honey (or, alternately, 1 T salt) and bring to a boil. Cook bagels in the water a few at a time (depending on the size of your pan) for seven minutes, flipping half-way through. Add sesame seeds or poppy seeds to the top when they come out of the water if you want. Set on cookie sheets and bake at 375° for 30 - 35 minutes or until done. Can be served with cream cheese.

Pocket Bread

1 T dry yeast
1-1/4 C tepid water
1/2 t honey
3-1/2 C flour
1/2 t salt

Dissolve yeast in water. Add honey and leave in warm place until bubbly.

Mix salt and flour thoroughly and add to yeast mixture. A bit of additional water may be necessary, but dough should be very firm. Knead thoroughly for fifteen minutes (very necessary). Oil and cover with a cloth in a bowl and let rise in a warm place until double in bulk (1 - 2 hours).

Punch down and knead briefly. Roll into a log shape and cut into 8 equal pieces. Roll each piece out on a lightly floured board into rounds slightly less than 1/4 inch thick. Place on well floured cookie sheets and cover with a floured towel. Let rise about 45 minutes until slightly puffy (they should look like they are going to "pocket": be higher in the middle). Sprinkle breads with water on both sides and place on the racks in a 500° preheated oven. Cook as near the source of heat as possible without overbrowning. In an electric oven with a pre-heat adjustment which puts on both the top and bottom elements, place breads in the middle of the oven and turn preheat on right after putting them in (use preheated oven still). Bake about 10 minutes. The strong yeasty smell will have changed to the smell of baked bread. Immediately after removing from oven, enclose completely in foil, to keep them from drying out.

SOURDOUGH

Sourdough is a yeast culture that is used to make bread rise. It usually will have a sour taste. Originally it was "caught" from wild yeast in the air. Starters can be bought, gotten from a friend, or made from ordinary yeast. You can buy one from:

Sourdough Jack's Country Kitchen
603 Tennessee Street
San Francisco, CA 94107

Toklat Sourdough Starter
Toklat Lodge
Box 239
Aspen, CO 81611

The Toklat strain is over 70 years old; Sourdough Jack's is over 65 years old.

CARE AND FEEDING

OF SOURDOUGH

Always store your starter in a glass or ceramic container. If the container has a metal lid, cover first with plastic wrap and then put the lid on. Always use a wooden or stainless steel spoon or rubber spatula to stir it (never use aluminum). Some people say it should be stirred or beaten every day, but if used at least once a week, this is unnecessary. If you do not use it once a week, it should be fed in the same way you would if you were going to use it (see below). Starters will separate when they are through fermenting. This is a sign that they need to be fed again. In hot weather, don't leave your starter out of the refrigerator too long. If the starter smells like wine, it is happy and healthy.

Bread must be baked and tasted to determine the sourness of the starter. Letting the starter ferment longer outside the refrigerator will make it sourer.

FEEDING: Put the starter in a pottery or stainless bowl (never aluminum). For every cup of starter, beat in 2 C lukewarm water and 2 - 2-1/2 C flour. Leave it out overnight in a warm place. In the morning put at least 1 C back in the refrigerator to save for next time. Don't forget. This mixture is called BASIC BATTER below.

Sourdough Starter
(making your own)

1 T active dry yeast
1 T honey
2 C warm water
1/2 C warm water
2-1/2 C flour

Combine the yeast and warm water. Add honey. Beat in the flour and water. Place in a large pottery or stainless bowl. Cover with a damp cloth (keep it damp) tied over the top of the bowl. Allow to ferment for five days. Each day stir it down. On the fifth day, add 1/4 C flour and 1/4 C warm water. Beat. Cover as before and leave one more day. Then it may be used or refrigerated.

Simple Sourdough Bread

3 C BASIC BATTER
1-1/2 T barley malt or honey
1 t sea salt
1-1/2 T oil
3 T water
4-3/4 C flour (this can be part whole wheat flour, and part rye, triticale, rice, barley or whatever)

Mix ingredients in order given adding flour until the bread pulls away from the edges of the bowl. Knead until it is no longer sticky and feels elastic. Oil and let rise until doubled. Shape into a loaf and let rise until doubled again. (This may take all day for both risings.) Bake at 350° for 1 - 1-1/2 hours. Makes one large loaf.

Sourdough Pancakes

3 C BASIC BATTER
3 C powdered milk
3/4 t soda
1-1/2 t oil
3/4 t salt
1-1/2 T honey

Mix ingredients together. Let rise five minutes. Bake on a hot griddle in dollar-sized cakes (they cook better). For sourdough waffles, use an extra T oil and a hot waffle iron.

Michael's Pancakes

1. Preheat griddle 1 or 2 minutes, or until so hot a drop of water will sizzle and dance.

2. If the pancake batter contains enough added oil, it can be cooked on a dry or lightly greased griddle or skillet. Where there is little or no added fat (as in bona fide crepes or french pancakes), the batter must be cooked in oil. Do not use too much or the pancakes will be greasy. It is generally best to put in just enough for one batch, and add more if necessary between batches.

3. Drop 1 rounded tablespoon full of batter at a time onto griddle, leaving 2 - 3 inches between each to allow for spreading.

4. Turn only once. To check to see if the underside is done, lift edge of cake and see if it is golden brown. Usually when it is ready to turn the top side will be full of bubbles and no longer runny.

5. Do not cook too quickly or the outside will burn and the inside will be moist. Do not cook too slowly or the cakes will be tough.

6. Syrups for pancakes can be straight maple syrup, butter, honey or the like. Thick honey can be diluted with juice and warmed. For a low calorie, less sweet topping, blend a banana with juice in the blender and pour on like syrup. Any kind of berry and many kinds of fruit can be chopped and heated to boiling with honey to make a flavored syrup (try blackberries, peaches, blueberries). For a dinner or heavy breakfast the **White Sauce** recipe with steamed vegetables added or any other recipe from the **SAUCES AND GRAVIES** section would be good.

1-1/2 C flour
1 t baking powder
1/2 t salt
1 C yogurt
1 T honey
1 C milk (more or less according
   to desired thickness)

Combine dry ingredients in one container and wet ingredients in another. Just before cooking, put the two together and mix well. Drop onto a hot griddle, making small pancakes (so they cook all the way through).

Yogurt Pancakes

1 C **Yogurt**
1-1/2 C whole wheat flour
salt to taste

Beat flour into yogurt until consistency of thick pancake batter. Season to taste with salt. Drop by spoonfuls on well-greased griddle. Serve topped with yogurt and honey. If necessary, milk can be added to thin batter.

Buckwheat Pancakes

1/2 cake yeast (or 1/2 T dry yeast)
1 C warm milk
1 C buttermilk or thin yogurt
2 T oil
1-1/2 C buckwheat flour
1 t soda
1 t salt

Soak yeast in warm water. Add buttermilk and oil. Add flour and beat until smooth. Let stand in warm place overnight. In the morning add salt and soda, and bake on hot greased griddle.

Buckwheat-Corn Cakes

1/3 C corn meal
2 C scalded milk
2/3 t salt
1-1/4 C buckwheat flour
1 t yeast
1/3 C lukewarm water
2 T honey
2 T oil
1/4 t soda

Soak meal in milk until it's cool. Add salt and flour. Soften yeast and honey in luke-warm water. Add oil and mix into other ingredients. Put in a pitcher or covered bowl and let rise all night. In the morning add the soda and bake on a hot griddle. Makes about six large cakes.

Sesame Grain Pancakes

1 C unhulled sesame seed
3-1/2 C water
1-1/2 C rolled grain (rye, oat, wheat, etc.)
1-1/2 C cornmeal (or millet meal,
   rice meal, etc.)
1 t salt
2 T oil

Blend water and sesame seeds until smooth in blender. Add all other ingredients. Drop by spoonfuls on well-greased griddle. They take several minutes to cook.

WAFFLES

Waffles can be made with a sturdy pancake batter such as **Michael's Pancakes** batter. A waffle batter generally needs more oil in it than pancakes do, so we suggest adding about 1 T oil per cup of liquid if there is no oil in the recipe, and less if there is some. A waffle batter needs a certain amount of finely ground flour in it to be of the consistency needed in order to keep from sticking. Whole wheat or whole wheat pastry flour work best because they stick together well. My experience is that I can add up to 1/4 the total amount of dry ingredients in high protein and nutrient ingredients such as wheat germ, soy flour, bran or protein powder. Any more than that and they brown too easily and stick. But this amount sure makes for a better break-fast. Sometimes using water for a portion of the liquid in the batter keeps them from browning too fast (leaving the inside raw). Try this variation in **Yogurt Pancakes**.

Preheat the waffle iron before adding the batter. Oil all over it, especially on the edges. A pastry brush works great for this if heat doesn't bother it. You may need to oil between each waffle if your iron tends to stick, or less often if it is a new one or a well-seasoned older model. You may have to adjust the timer on the iron with different types of batter. If the steam that comes out the edges seems to slow down, it could be done. Open up the lid a bit and check to see. Information on syrups is under PANCAKES.

French Toast

4 pieces of bread
1/2 C milk
3 T cashew butter
dash of cinnamon

Blend milk, cashew butter and cinnamon together until smooth (preferably in blender). Dip pieces of bread in mixture. The more the bread soaks, the "eggier" it will be. You may prefer it dipped quickly. Brown in butter until golden. Serve with maple syrup or honey. If you don't have cashew butter, raw cashews and a small amount of oil can be substituted if you blend it with the other ingredients until smooth in a blender.

ALSO REFER TO . . .

SANDWICHES AND SPREADS section for
   things to put on and do with breads
Pizza
Burritos
Enchilados

sandwiches
and spreads

SANDWICHES

A sandwich can be made from just about anything. (You don't even have to use bread!) Whether it's in a bag lunch or in the place of honor at a buffet dinner, the sandwich is an everpresent item in the average American diet. Through habit, or perhaps following the path of least resistance, many people end up eating the same kind of sandwiches day after day. Since we've eaten, prepared, and heard about so many wild and wonderful (and downright strange) sandwiches in our sojourn as cooks, we thought we'd pass along some of the most popular ideas. In most cases, we haven't suggested any particular type of bread, but the bread can really make a big difference in some cases. **Banana-Honey Spread** tastes a lot better (to most people) served on a sweet or neutrally flavored bread, rather than on dark rye or similar breads. Likewise, a lot of folks prefer their cheese sandwiches on something other than apple bread. Aside from these common sense guidelines, the choice of bread is really determined more by availability and individual preference than anything else. For a real change of pace, try using romaine lettuce leaves, red cabbage leaves, or broiled eggplant (or oversize zucchini) slices in place of bread. The realization that sandwiches can be made without bread is especially pleasing to those whose intake of carbohydrates is restricted by their physiology or ideology.

Many of the sandwich suggestions listed below could also include **Margii Mayo**, or any of the spread recipes which follow the suggestions. Likewise, most sandwiches can be served either open face or with two slices of bread. Toast is a nice touch.

COLD SANDWICHES

VARIATIONS on the old standby, peanut butter and jelly, include: substitute another kind of nut butter (almond, cashew, or ?): use honey instead of jam; **Banana-Honey Spread** instead of jam. Or, mix the nut butter with honey, and store in the refrigerator for an instant spread.

SWEET AND STICKY: Spread peanut butter and honey on bread or toast (apple or banana bread is particularly good). Top with sliced bananas and another piece of bread. (This one's a real gut-buster if you're into food combining rules.)

BANANA-HONEY SPREAD is great as an open faced snack for kids.

SAFFRON SPREAD can be served on one of the "bread substitutes" discussed above for an all-vegetable sandwich. Because it is so squishy, it's better served open-face. Try mixing diced celery or other chopped vegetables into the spread.

LEFTOVER LOAF — all of the loaf and burger recipes can be sliced and served cold on a sandwich.

AVOCADO AND ANYTHING — mashed avocado can be used as the base for a sandwich, a spread, incorporating whatever's handy, or combined with sprouts (raw alfalfa and/or cooked lentil).

CREAM CHEESE AND DATE BUTTER served on a sweet bread (banana, apple, or pumpkin) is almost like dessert (also lots of calories).

SOY SPREAD and grated or very thinly sliced carrots makes a delightful taste and texture combination. Try them on an unleavened bread for a real stick-to-your ribs meal.

HOT SANDWICHES

CHEESE SANDWICHES — Many folks like 'em toasted. Grating the cheese results in faster melting. Toasting the bread beforehand simplifies digestion. Cheddars are the most reliable — "regular fat" jack gets greasy. Mozzarella and parmesan are good. Two common methods: 1) Butter one side of each of two pieces of bread. Put cheese in between unbuttered sides of bread, grill until cheese melts. 2) Put cheese on bread or toast. Broil open faced until cheese melts. Garnish with anything listed under cold sandwiches, or add chopped bell pepper or celery.

OLIVE-CHEESE ON RYE — Layer cheese, chopped ripe olives, tomato, and more cheese on rye bread. Broil till cheese melts.

PB and CHEESE — Make open face toasted cheese sandwich, spread peanut butter on a piece of toast, assemble and chew well.

EGGPLANT SPECIAL — Peel eggplant and slice 1/4 - 1/2 inch thick. Roll in wheat germ or corn meal and brown thoroughly on both sides in a skillet. Toast bread, top with a 1/4 inch slice of cheese, and eggplant slice. Broil till almost done, add a tomato slice, finish cooking, garnish with alfalfa sprouts.

GRILLED TOFU — Saute slices of hard Tofu till well browned, serve on bread or whole wheat hamburger buns with whatever trimmings you like.

TOSTADOS — Heat tortilla in dry skillet until limp. Wrap around grated cheese, lettuce and whatever.

MOUNTAIN BURGER — Pile, in this order, on a large piece of toast: grilled zucchini slices, a hot bulgur burger with cheese, and a mound of alfalfa sprouts. Another piece of toast can be placed on the top.

SLOPPY JOYS — Smother a piece of bread with **Spaghetti Sauce**. Variation: put **Soy-burger** under the **Spaghetti Sauce**.

For more ideas, see the recipes that follow and the burger recipes in the **MAIN DISH** sections.

Butter-Oil Spread

1 pound butter
1 quart corn, safflower or other mild
    flavored oil (not soy)
1 - 2 t lecithin (optional, helps emulsify)
1 - 2 t salt (optional)

Let butter sit at room temperature until it is very soft. Add lecithin and salt. Beat in oil, put in containers, and refrigerate immediately. Stir well (occasionally) during cooling. Freezes well, and is soft when cold. This spread can be used in place of butter, and is a nice treat for the body, since it provides the unsaturated fatty acids (and other good things from the oil) in addition to the saturated fatty acids in the butter. Store in refrigerator.

Honey Butter

1 C honey
1/2 C butter

Be sure both ingredients are at room temperature. Add honey slowly to softened butter and beat with a fork. When well blended, pour into a jar and cover. Makes 1-1/2 cups.

Use cold for breads, gingerbread, etc.; hot as a topping for waffles, pancakes.

Orange Honey Butter

1/2 C (1 stick) butter
2 T honey
2 T frozen concentrated orange juice

In a small mixing bowl, cream butter until softened; gradually add honey and beat until light and fluffy. Continue beating while slowly adding orange juice concentrate. Serve on pancakes, waffles, French toast or toasted English muffins. Makes about 3/4 cup.

Banana Honey Spread

1 T honey
1 pureed banana
pinch mace or dash of lemon peel

Combine. Great on bread for snack time, or to sweeten yogurt.

Saffron Spread
(for sandwiches, or as a dip)

5-1/2 - 6 C cooked, sliced carrots
   (approximately 7 medium carrots,
   7 C raw)
1-1/2 - 2 C cooked corn kernels
   (approximately 3 - 4 ears)
optional: sprinkle thyme or other herbs on vegetables before steaming them.

Liquify corn in a blender. Add carrots 1 C at a time, blending thoroughly. Makes an excellent sandwich spread or a dip for raw vegetables. Store in refrigerator. Yields about 4 cups.

Soyspread

2 C dry soybeans
3/4 C oil
4 t salt
1 lemon, juiced
1 C parsley
1 t paprika
1/4 t ground cumin

Wash and soak soybeans overnight (in left-over vegetable steaming water if available). Simmer beans in soaking water until tender (for more complete bean cooking information see **Basic Bean Cooking Recipe** in **MAIN DISH** section). Drain and puree in a blender adding oil, salt and lemon juice for blending liquid. Add as little possible additional cooking liquid as it is very easy to get the spread too thin. Stir in herbs and spices. This freezes well.

Curried Cheese Dip

3 ounces cream cheese
3 T yogurt
1/4 t curry powder
1/2 t lemon juice
1 t finely minced parsley or bell pepper
1/4 C pistachio nuts, almonds or
   sunflower seeds

Combine cream cheese and yogurt and add remaining ingredients. Serve in bowl surrounded with crisp celery and carrot sticks, raw cauliflowerettes and cucumber strips for dipping. Makes about 3/4 cups.

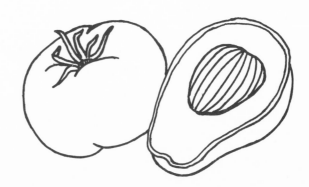

Sage Cheese Crock

1/2 pound grated Cheddar cheese
3 ounce package cream cheese
2 T **Tofu Mayonnaise** or heavy cream
1 t dried sage, crumbled
1/2 t dry mustard
1 T lemon juice

Blend cheese with **Tofu Mayonnaise** or cream until smooth. Add sage, mustard, and lemon; continue mixing until well blended. Put in crock or jar and cover with foil or a snug lid. Store in refrigerator; remove about a half-hour before serving. Serve as a spread for sandwiches, crackers, biscuits or toast rounds. Makes about 1-1/2 cups.

Tofu Mayonnaise

1 pound hard Tofu (Chinese style)
1/2 C lemon juice
1 C safflower oil
1 t sesame salt
herbs to taste

Blend all together in blender. Store in refrigerator.

Sesame Seed Sauce

1 C sesame tahini (or sesame butter)
3/4 - 1 C cold water
1/4 - 1/2 C fresh lemon juice
1 t salt

Beat into the tahini (with a whisk or spoon) 1/2 C of the cold water, the lemon juice and the salt. Still beating, add up to 1/2 C more of water, 1 T at a time, until the sauce has the consistency of thick mayonnaise and holds its shape almost solidly in a spoon. Season to taste. Makes about 1-1/2 C.

Eggplant Spread

1 medium eggplant
1/4 C lemon juice
2 T **Sesame Seed Sauce**
1/2 bell pepper minced
1 t salt
1 T olive oil (or substitute corn
   or safflower oil)
1 T finely chopped fresh parsley

First roast eggplant: prick it in 3 - 4 places, then impale it on a long tined fork and turn it over a gas flame until the skin chars and begins to crack. Or roast in the oven. When eggplant is cool enough to handle, peel it, cutting away all charred parts.

Mash it to a smooth puree; beat in the lemon juice, **Sesame Seed Sauce**, bell pepper and salt. Taste for seasoning. Mound on a plate and sprinkle with parsley and olive oil. Makes about 2 cups.

Humus Tahini

1-1/3 C dried chick peas (garbanzo beans) —
   cook and reserve liquid. Or 2 C cooked
   beans plus 1/2 to 1 C of cooking water.
2 t salt
1 bell pepper, minced
1/4 C fresh lemon juice
1 C **Sesame Seed Sauce**

Puree bell pepper and cooked chick peas. With a large spoon beat in the lemon juice a little at a time. Beating constantly, pour in the **Sesame Seed Sauce** in a slow thin stream and continue to beat until the mixture is smooth. Humus should be thin enough to spread easily. If necessary, add more chick pea cooking liquid. Makes about 2-1/2 cups.

main dishes

182

MAIN DISHES

These are the stick-to-your-ribs recipes, for those who live in cold climates and work hard, newcomers to vegetarian fare, or anyone else who likes the feeling of a really substantial meal. All of these dishes are excellent served alone or with a raw vegetable salad. Many of them freeze well, and can be made in advance and kept on hand to rescue those occasions when unexpected company arrives hungry.

People who prefer a lighter diet will find many other simpler main dishes in the vegetable and grain sections. References to these can be found at the end of the chapter.

Food of Intuition

2 C brown rice
1/8 lb. butter or 1/4 C oil
2 C vegetables cut in bite-sized pieces
4-1/4 - 4-1/2 C water
lemon salt to taste

Combine water, salt and rice in a pan. Bring to a boil. Stir with a fork. Add vegies and butter. Cover tightly and steam for 40 minutes or until rice is tender. Before serving squeeze one fresh lemon over rice and vegies. Serves 8.

1 large firm cabbage (6 - 7" in diameter)
1/4 C oil
1 C minced celery
1/2 C minced green pepper
2 - 4 C cooked brown rice (2/3 - 1-1/3 C raw)
   (amount depends on size of cabbage)
1 t to 1 T mixed herbs (**Italian Seasoning**
   or **Vegetable Herbs** in herb section)
1 - 2 t salt
1/2 C finely ground walnuts or almonds
2 C **Tomato Sauce** seasoned to taste
   with basil

Steam cabbage whole on a rack in a large kettle until firm but not mushy. (May take as long as an hour for a big one). Meanwhile heat oil and saute celery and green pepper until celery is translucent. Add rice, herbs and nuts. If mixture is too dry, add a little warm water. When cabbage is done, remove core and pull out inner leaves until shell is about 1" thick (be careful doing this so as not to make a hole in the top). Finely shred 1 C of cooked cabbage and add to stuffing mixture. Stuff cabbage firmly. Turn cabbage over, core hole down, in a casserole. Coat with a little oil and bake at 350° for 40 minutes or so. Serve with tomato sauce poured over top. Cut in wedges. A large cabbage will serve about 6 people.

Stuffed Zucchini

1 oversize zucchini, 1 - 2 ft. long; slit
   lengthwise, lightly steamed
2 medium potatoes, chopped in 1/2 inch cubes
3 medium carrots, sliced finely
2 C chopped green beans
1 C chopped tomatoes (optional)
2 T oil
1/2 - 1 C grated cheese (preferably cheddar)
1/4 t each: thyme, marjoram, oregano
   and basil (or **Italian Seasoning**)
salt to taste
paprika

Steam potatoes, carrots and green beans
until almost tender. Carefully hollow out
zucchini. Mix steamed vegies, tomatoes
(optional) and enough of insides of zucchini
(if the seeds aren't too big) to make enough
filling to fill zucchini. Dump vegies, zucchini
insides, oil and herbs into a saucepan and
simmer 5 minutes or so. Add salt to taste and
fill zucchini halves with filling, top with
grated cheese and sprinkle with paprika. Bake
at 350° until cheese is bubbly (5 - 10 minutes).
Serves about 4 - 8 (depending on size
of zucchini).

Corn Stuffed Zucchini

6 medium zucchini
1-1/2 C fresh corn
1 bell pepper, minced
1 stalk celery, minced
1 t salt
2 T oil
1/4 C chopped fresh parsley
1/2 C grated cheddar cheese

Wash and cut off ends of zucchini but do not
peel. Steam whole zucchini about 5 minutes
(or bake at 350° until barely tender if too big
for steaming). Cut in half lengthwise and carefully remove pulp, leaving shell about 1/4 inch
thick (good luck). Place shells in shallow
baking dish. Finely chop pulp and combine
with corn, bell pepper, celery and salt in hot
oil in skillet. Cook, stirring now and then
until thick, about 10 minutes. Add parsley and
remove from heat. Fill shells with corn mixture. Sprinkle with cheese. Bake uncovered
at 350° for 30 minutes. Serves 6.

Basic Stuffed Bell Peppers

Pick bell peppers that are reasonably
cylindrical and have a flat bottom. Figure on
1 - 2 stuffed peppers per person. Wash peppers
thoroughly (remember that most commercially
grown peppers are waxed. The wax can be
partially removed by hard scrubbing under
very hot water). Cut out top and remove seeds
and inner partitions from peppers. Boil
peppers 3 minutes in salted water, or
steam briefly.

Stuff peppers with any of the following
fillings or invent your own. Each pepper
will need about 1 - 1-1/2 C stuffing. If
there is nothing in the stuffing for moisture,
a bit of water may be added and peppers can
be baked covered. Also remember color
when stuffing: a bright green pepper stuffed
with yellow corn, red tomatoes and orange
carrots is a delight to the eyes as well as the
stomach. Place peppers in a greased pan and
bake at 400° for 25 - 30 minutes (until
peppers are soft).

Soybean Bell Pepper Stuffing
(enough for 6 small peppers)

1 t salt
1/4 C minced steamed celery
1/2 - 3/4 C buttered bread crumbs
1/2 C tomatoes
2 C soybean pulp (ground or pureed
   cooked soybeans)

Mix above ingredients except bread crumbs
and stuff peppers. Cover tops with buttered
bread crumbs. Bake as directed above.

To make buttered bread crumbs, mix bread
crumbs and melted butter, or toast buttered
bread and then crumble it.

Additional Bell Pepper Stuffings

1) sauteed celery
    brown rice
    topped with cheese and tomato sauce

2) 1 part each:
    steamed minced celery
    tomatoes
    cooked brown rice

3) 2 parts steamed vegies
    1 part cooked brown rice, bulgur,
       or other grain.

4) 1 part steamed corn
    1 part steamed carrots
    1 part chopped tomatoes
    topped with alfalfa sprouts after serving

Chestnut Stuffing

2 C dry chestnuts, peeled (inside and outside),
   boiled and chopped
3 large carrots, sliced thin and steamed
2 stalks celery, minced
3 - 4 C cooked rice (dry)
2 T dry parsley
1/2 t marjoram
1/2 t thyme

Combine ingredients and stuff whatever is
empty with the mixture. Yields 8 - 9 cups
of stuffing.

Vegetable Pie

1 **Pie crust** and top crust (see **DESSERTS**)
4 to 5 C assorted chopped vegetables (such
   as corn, zucchini, tomatoes, broccoli,
   cauliflower, peas, etc.)
2 C grated cheeses
season to taste (a dash sage, 1/4 t turmeric,
   1/4 t oregano, dash curry, 1/2 t salt;
   or **Bouquet Garni**, and salt)
1 to 2 C **White Sauce** (see **SAUCES**)

Mix vegetables, white sauce and cheese.
Place in crust and cover with top crust. Poke
holes in top and bake at 350° for about one
hour. Yields one 9 inch pie.

Macaroni and Cheese

2-1/2 C uncooked macaroni

Sauce:
1/4 C oil
1/4 C whole wheat pastry flour
1 t salt
1/2 t dry mustard
2-1/4 C milk
2 C grated cheese

Topping:
3 T oil
3/4 C dry bread crumbs

In a large kettle, bring approximately 4 quarts of water to boil. Add macaroni. Boil rapidly, uncovered, stirring occasionally, until tender (about 10 minutes). Drain. While noodles are cooking, make sauce. Mix 1/4 C oil and flour, salt and mustard. When smooth, heat while gradually stirring in the milk. Cook over a medium heat, stirring constantly, until mixture begins to boil. Turn down heat immediately and stir in cheese. When cheese is melted, mix sauce with macaroni in a greased 2 quart casserole. Toss bread crumbs in 3 T oil; sprinkle over top of casserole. Bake uncovered at 350° until cheese is golden (about 30 - 45 minutes). Serves 4 - 6.

Good Karma Casserole

3 C very thick **Cheese Sauce**
1-1/2 C **Tomato Paste**
1/2 pound (about 2-1/2 C dry noodles), cooked
1/2 C sliced ripe olives
1/3 head cooked cauliflower
2 C grated carrots
1 C chopped green pepper
1 C cooked broccoli
1/3 pound cheddar cheese, grated
1/3 pound jack cheese, grated
1 C finely chopped walnuts
3 large tomatoes, sliced

Mix cheese sauce and **Tomato Paste**. In a separate bowl, mix noodles, vegetables (except tomatoes), nuts and 1/2 of the sauce. Pour half of the second mixture into casserole. Sprinkle jack cheese on top. Pour in rest of second mixture and then cover with remaining sauce. Sprinkle on cheddar cheese. Garnish with tomato slices. Bake at 350° for 40 minutes until cheese is bubbly. Reheats well. Serves 4 - 6.

Tofu

Ingredients:

2 C soybeans
water
2 t epsom salts

Equipment:

large pan (about 8 - 10 quart capacity)
blender
large bowl
candy thermometer (cheap, costs about $1)
an old sheet (or parts of one)
colander or big strainer

Soak soybeans overnight in a very large jar full of water. In the morning, drain and use water for watering your favorite plant or one that needs some fertilizer.

Blend (liquify) 1 C soybeans with 2 C water until completely smooth. Pour into a large pot. Repeat this process about five times until soybeans are all liquified.

Place a 2 - 2-1/2 foot square piece of muslin over the bowl and pour the liquified soybeans into it. Gather up the edges and squeeze the milk out of the pulp (don't get any pulp in the milk!).

Rinse a large pan and measure soy milk from bowl into it. Add water to make 6 quarts. Heat to a rolling boil and boil 6 minutes. Stir very frequently as it tends to stick. It also tends to boil over quickly.

Remove from heat and let sit until the soy milk cools down to 180°. While it cools, dissolve 2 t epsom salts (you can get it at a drugstore) in 1/2 C hot water. (You use 1 t epsom salts for each cup of dry soybeans that you started with). Stir into soymilk and let sit without disturbing it for 15 - 20 minutes. The curd and whey will separate, and the whey will get straw colored. While it sits, wash the muslin well to remove all soy pulp,

then place it over a colander in the sink. Pour the tofu into it — slowly as the curd is apt to come in a big lump. Pull up edges of muslin as you did before. Put a plate or flat bowl on top and a weight — like a big container of water. Leave it alone for an hour or so. Then remove from press.

The firmness depends on the amount of weight used.

Try seasoning it — add 2 T dried parsley and 1 t thyme to the soymilk before adding the epsom salts or minced bell pepper and 1 t salt.

To store it — keeps about a week to 10 days, although the flavor will change — keep covered with water in the refrigerator. Change water every couple days, and it will keep longer. Also tofu can be frozen in water. Makes 1-1/2 pounds of tofu. May be eaten as is, browned in oil or butter, or used in recipes calling for tofu.

Nama-Age
(deep fried tofu)

1 recipe **Tofu** (or 1-1/2 lbs. store-bought)

Cut tofu into 3 X 1 X 1 inch slices. Drain tofu and dry between paper towels while oil heats so that water will not make oil splatter. Heat 1 - 2 inches of oil (preferably sesame) in a heavy pan until a chunk of tofu browns quickly and evenly, but doesn't cook so quickly that it becomes all crusty. Fry, turning once. When done, remove from oil and put into cold water to dispel oil. Remove when cool and drain on paper towels. Serve in sandwiches, with vegetables, alone as a snack or in other recipes calling for tofu.

Tofu Curry

Prepare **Curried Vegies** substituting chopped **Tofu** for one-quarter of the vegetables. This is nice served with a green salad and rice.

Chinese Vegies Supreme

2 T oil
1 - 1-1/2 pound **Tofu** cut into 1/2 inch squares
1/4 C slivered almonds or whole cashews
3 stalks celery, finely sliced
1 bell pepper, finely chopped
2 C finely cut chinese cabbage
3 C mung bean sprouts
3 T arrowroot diluted with
  1 - 2 T water
1 t vegetable salt or 1/2 t salt or
  1 t **Vegie-herb Sauce**

Heat oil in a wok (or a heavy pan). Brown tofu well on all sides. Add nuts and brown them also. Remove from wok. Stir fry celery in wok until almost done. Add other vegies. Add a sprinkle of water. When all vegies are crispy tender, add diluted arrowroot and **Vegie-Herb Sauce**. Add **Tofu** and nuts and serve immediately. Serves 3 - 4 as a main dish.

Variations: add sliced jicama or water chestnuts.

BEANS

Dried beans, especially soybeans, are a valuable and inexpensive source of dietary protein. Beans are more useful protein sources if they are combined with other foods, such as grains or seeds, to make complete proteins. (See discussion of proteins in **NOURISHMENT** section.) Sprouting increases the nutritive value of beans.

For cooking purposes, beans can be divided into four groups. Those within any of the first three groups can be substituted for others in the same group; the fourth group is made up of beans with distinctive characteristics, which cannot be substituted for one another.

• Group 1: pink, black, cranberry, pinto, red and kidney beans

• Group 2: white beans (great northern, small whites, navy, and pea beans)

• Group 3: lentils, Indian dal, split or whole (dried) green or yellow peas

COOKED BEANS
(Basic Recipe)

Beans are generally washed and then soaked before they are cooked. Allow approximately 1/4 to 1/3 C of dry beans per serving. Soy beans increase 2-1/2 to 3 times in volume during cooking; other beans approximately double their bulk. Wash the beans carefully and take out any rocks or broken beans; then soak the beans using one of the following methods (NOTE: Group 3 beans cook fairly rapidly and need not be soaked ahead of time).

SOAK OVERNIGHT in three to four times as much water as beans. In warm weather, some beans (especially soy beans) may ferment while soaking, unless they are refrigerated.

QUICK SOAK by boiling the beans (4 C water for every 1 C beans) for two minutes and then letting them sit for an hour.

Soak the beans for an hour or two. FREEZE until time to use them. You can have soaked beans ready for cooking at all times this way. The freezing helps soften the structure so they cook faster.

COOK THE BEANS IN THE SOAKING WATER TO PRESERVE THE WATER SOLUBLE NUTRIENTS.

AFTER SOAKING the beans, add enough additional water (to the soaking water) to make four times as much water as beans. Use leftover vegetable cooking water when-ever possible — it enhances both flavor and nutrition. Do not add acids (tomatoes, lemon juice, vinegar) or salt until the beans are completely cooked, or they may never get tender.

Beans should be simmered, as a full boil will break them up. (However, to start un-soaked beans, drop them slowly into four times their volume of boiling water; when all the beans are in the pot, stir and reduce heat.) Cooking with a lid on the pot reduces the amount of time necessary for cooking and conserves energy. Stir the beans enough to keep them from sticking to the bottom and burning (don't scrape them up after they've burned, though). Avoid over-stirring, as this also tends to break up the beans.

Adding 1 T of oil per 1 C of dry beans will help reduce foaming (except with limas). Herbs, or vegetables may be added while the beans are still cooking.

Soybeans which are going to be eaten alone may be flavored with herbs, molasses, or **Yogurt**. Add salt during the last half hour of cooking, when the beans are soft. Beans are done when they are tender — usually 3 - 5 hours if they were soaked. (High protein beans take the most time to cook.) Beans which are to be pureed should be cooked until very soft.

When added to the cooking water, fenugreek, fennel and dill (alone or in combination) seem to help reduce the gas-producing effect of beans. Longer cooking (12 - 14 hours) helps also. One reason that beans cause gas is that carbohydrates require an alkaline digestive medium and proteins require an acid medium. Beans are high in both carbohydrates and protein. The acid and alkaline juices neutralize each other, producing CO_2 gas (just like mixing baking soda and vinegar. For the same reason, it may be advisable to avoid eating beans with very starchy foods such as potatoes or grains. Unfortunately, one can't get the benefits of combining proteins if this advice is followed. Our experience is that drinking tea made from coriander, fenugreek, or fennel helps reduce intestinal gas once it is present.

USING SOY BEANS

To increase the protein content of a dish, soybeans can be substituted for other beans.

(They will change the flavor somewhat.) Soy or soya flour can be purchased or ground at home. It will be easier to digest if roasted slightly. Soya grits can be used like nuts in cookies and other recipes (but should be soaked and probably cooked a while first). They cook a lot faster than whole beans.

BEAN COOKING HINTS

Taste soaking water before putting on to cook. If it tastes bitter, discard. Legumes are tender when soft enough to crush easily between fingers.

Beans can be cooked and then frozen in plastic bags or containers, for use later when a quick meal is needed.

Boston Baked Beans

2 C dried small white beans, washed
   and sorted
water
1/2 C oil
1/2 C molasses or honey
1 t salt
1 t ginger
1 t dry mustard

Soak beans overnight in enough water to cover generously. The next day, simmer beans adding more water as needed until the beans are tender and the skins burst (about 1 - 1-1/2 hours). When done, drain the beans, saving the liquid.

Mix oil, molasses, salt, ginger, and dry mustard and pour over beans in an oiled,

oven-proof pot. Cover and bake at 250 - 300° for 6 - 8 hour, adding reserved bean liquid as necessary to keep beans moist. Remove cover the last hour to brown and crisp top of beans. (Take care not to let it dry out.) Serves 6 - 8.

Spanish Lentils

3 C cooked lentils (approx 1-1/2 C raw)
2 C chopped tomatoes
1 chopped green pepper
1 t **Italian Seasoning**
3/4 C grated cheese
2 - 3 T oil
2 - 3 T soy flour
2 t salt
1 t ground celery seed
1 t basil
2 crushed bay leaves

Combine above ingredients and bake 40 minutes at 325°. Serves 4 - 6.

Spanish Rice: Use 3 C cooked (but not mushy) brown rice instead of lentils.

Lentil Loaf

2 C cooked lentils (approx. 1 C raw)
3 T butter or oil
1 C grated cheese
1-1/2 C chopped mixed vegetables
bread crumbs to thicken
1 T **Italian Seasoning**

Mix the above ingredients and place in greased loaf pan. Bake at 400° for 20 - 30 minutes. Serves 6 - 8.

Nut and Lentil Loaf

2 C lentils, washed
1 quart water
1/4 C oil
12 stalks celery, minced
1 T salt
1 t thyme
1 t oregano
1 C rolled oats, toasted
1 C almonds, finely chopped
1 C walnuts, finely chopped

Bring water to a boil. Add washed lentils and simmer until tender (about 40 minutes). Mix oil, celery and seasonings and simmer over low heat for 15 - 30 minutes being careful not to scorch. Mix all ingredients together and pat into two greased loaf pans. Bake at 375° at least one hour. This loaf is excellent cold in sandwiches. It can be cut into thick slices, wrapped in foil and frozen. It reheats well and provides a quick, easy meal. Excellent with **Loaf and Burger Sauce**.

Falafels

1/2 C finely chopped green pepper
2 C well-cooked garbanzo beans, mashed
　　(approx. 1 C raw)
2 C whole wheat bread crumbs
1 t cumin
wheat germ

Saute green pepper until tender. Add to mashed garbanzo beans and mix in crumbs and cumin. Mixture should be of a consistency that can be formed into balls. Form into one inch balls and rol in wheat germ. Set aside for about an hour so the outside can dry off. Deep fry in very hot oil (not smoking, though). If the oil is not hot enough, they will disintegrate. If they splatter when put in the oil, roll in wheat germ again. These can be eaten as they are or used to fill **Pocket Bread**. Double this recipe to make enough filling for one recipe of **Pocket Bread**.

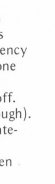

Macroburgers

2-1/2 C cooked soybeans, drained
   (approximately 1 C raw)
4 t vegetable salt, 2 t salt
   or 2 t **Vegie-Herb Sauce**
1/2 t dry mustard
3/4 t dill seed, crushed
3/4 t ground thyme
1-1/2 C steamed millet (approximately
   3/4 C raw)
1 small finely grated carrot
scant 1/2 t ground cumin
3/4 t celery seed
3/4 t sage
1 stalk celery, minced
1/2 C raw wheat germ
grated cheddar cheese
3/4 C rolled oats (optional)
1 bunch finely chopped spinach (optional)

Toast rolled oats in cast iron skillet. Cook millet according to directions in **GRAINS AND CEREALS**. Chop soybeans or grind on a medium to large blade of a food grinder. Mix above ingredients. Form into patties and fry. (If patties are to be broiled add 3 T oil to above mixture). When brown, top with grated cheese and continue cooking until cheese melts. Serve on toasted buns with tomato slices and alfalfa sprouts. Makes about 1 dozen patties.

Variations: substitute left over pulp from **Soy Milk**, or aduki or pinto beans for soybeans.

Bulgur Burgers

2 C raw brown rice or 5 - 6 C cooked rice
1 C raw bulgur or 3 C cooked
1 - 2 C raw chopped cabbage
1 C wheat germ
1 C toasted soy flour
1 T oregano
1 T thyme
2 t salt (or to taste)
1 t basil
1/2 t savory
1/2 t parsley
1 t celery flakes
1/4 - 1/2 C oil

Cook the rice in 3 C water and the bulgur in 4 C water. Steam the cabbage. When done, remove from pan and let cool. Blend together wheat germ, herbs, steamed cabbage and oil. Stir this mixture into the cooked grain. (It will stick to your hands but be manageable.) Fry or broil until brown and done all the way through. May be served with cheese, tomato, and sprouts on bread or not. Makes about 1-1/2 dozen medium burgers.

Green Burgers

2-1/2 C cooked brown rice (1 C raw cooked in 1-1/2 C water)
1 C cooked wheatberries (1/2 C raw cooked in 1 C water)
1 bunch chard, washed and chopped (4 C raw and chopped)
2 t thyme
2 t oregano
2 t basil
1 t salt
2 - 4 T oil (unless burgers are to be fried, in which case oil can be omitted)
grated cheese (optional)

Steam the chopped chard and cool. Puree chard, cooked wheatberries, rice, and herbs in a blender. Add oil and salt. Mix well. Form into 12 burgers. Broil or fry until brown and not gooey inside. Melt grated cheese on top. Serves 4 - 6.

Pretty Potato Patties

3-1/2 C steamed potatoes (4 C chopped raw potatoes)
1-1/2 C steamed carrots (about 2 C raw chopped carrots)
1 C cooked rice (fairly dry, approx. 1/3 C raw)
1 C finely chopped fresh parsley
3/4 C toasted whole wheat flour
2 - 3 t turmeric
1-1/2 t salt
1/4 C oil

Mash thoroughly cooked potatoes and carrots. Add other ingredients and mix well. Form into 1 - 1-1/2 inch balls and then flatten out. Brown in a slow heavy frying pan (lightly greased if necessary). May be reheated in a 250° oven for 10 or 15 minutes. The batter freezes well. Makes 2-1/2 dozen 2 - 3 inch patties.

Basic Soyburger

1 C soybeans
4 C water
1/2 t ground cumin
1 t dry parsley
1/4 t sage
1/2 t thyme
1/2 t ground oregano
1 t salt

Soak and cook the soybeans according to the directions in this chapter. Grind in a meat grinder, blend in a blender (you may have to add liquid to do this, resulting in a thinner burger) or mash with a potato masher. Add the herbs and salt and mix well. Fry in a small amount of oil in a frying pan, breaking into pieces to fit your needs, or shape into patties and fry. If the burger is not thick enough to shape, fry it until it is dry enough to make forms out of.

Basic Soyburger is called for in recipes such as **Tacos**, **Pizza**, and **Spaghetti Sauce**.

Pizza

Dough:

4 C whole wheat bread flour
1 T yeast dissolved in 1-1/3 C lukewarm water
2 T oil
1 t salt

Combine above ingredients and knead 10 minutes. Cover and let rise once until double (about 2 hours). Pat and roll out until very, very thin. Make a "collar" rolled edge to hold in filling. Prick dough with a fork in a few places. (This is enough dough to make two 12-inch pizzas.)

Topping:

3 pints **Spaghetti Sauce**
4 C shredded cheese (combination of
   mozzarella, cheddar, and jack, or
   all mozzarella)

Optional Ingredients:

sliced tomatoes
sliced ripe olives
minced bell pepper
1 - 2 C **Basic Soyburger**
steamed vegies (broccoli is excellent)

Spread dough with **Spaghetti Sauce**. Sprinkle with your choice or all of optional ingredients. Top with shredded cheese. Bake in greased pan at 400° for about 25 - 35 minutes until cheese is bubbly and crust brown. To freeze pizza, cut baked pizzas into convenient sized pieces. Slide the pieces onto cardboard and cover with foil. Freeze. After initial freezing, can be stacked on each other. Reheat in 300° oven for approximately 30 - 40 minutes. Makes two 12-inch pizzas.

Spaghetti

This is a good "company" dinner traditionally served with a large vegetable salad and thick slices of homemade wheat bread.

Make **Spaghetti Sauce**, with or without **Soyburger** — if you're serving non-vegetarians, make it with soyburger. Allow 1 - 1-1/2 C sauce per person.

Boil water in your largest kettle. Add your choice of one or more kinds of spaghetti **Noodles** (most natural foods stores carry whole wheat, soya, buckwheat, artichoke, spinach, and sesame or make your own). Allow a bundle 3/4 inches in diameter of raw spaghetti noodles per person. Drop noodles slowly into boiling water. Cook noodles, stirring occasionally, for 10 minutes or until done. (When a noodle is bitten in two, there should not be any white or light core visible.) Serve sauce on top of spaghetti. Can be topped with grated cheese and/or raw alfalfa sprouts.

Baked Tomato Eggplant Casserole

1 medium eggplant (about 1 pound)
1/2 C minced green pepper
3 T oil
1/3 C wheat germ, toasted
1 t salt
1 t basil
1 t oregano
2 medium tomatoes, sliced
3/4 C grated cheese (romano, parmesan,
     mozzarella and/or cheddar)

Wash eggplant and dice into 1 inch squares. Saute with the green pepper in oil for a couple of minutes. Cover and let cook a few minutes more until tender, but not mushy. Stir in toasted wheat germ, salt and herbs. Remove from heat and put half of the mixture in the bottom of a small casserole. Layer half of the tomato slices on top and sprinkle on half of the cheese. Repeat the whole process with the rest of the ingredients. Bake uncovered for 30 - 40 minutes at 375° until mixture is bubbly and cheese is melted. Serves 4.

Eggplant Parmesan

1 eggplant (dark in color, light in weight)
1/2 pound mozzarella or jack cheese, grated
1 - 2 pints **Spaghetti Sauce** (see **SAUCE** section)
1/2 pound ricotta cheese or 2 C shredded
     shredded **Tofu**
raw wheat germ
grated parmesan cheese

Eggplant may be peeled or not (if eggplant is green, it should be peeled, sliced, and put out on paper towels for 30 - 40 minutes). Cut eggplant as thin as possible — thinner than 1/4 inch. Moisten eggplant slices slightly in water or milk and dip in raw wheat germ. Fry in as little oil as possible until wheat germ browns and eggplant is limp. Continue until all eggplant is done. Then put a thin layer of **Spaghetti Sauce** in the bottom of a casserole. Arrange one layer of eggplant slices on top. Then a layer of **Tofu** or ricotta cheese topped with **Spaghetti Sauce** and grated mozzarella cheese. Continue layering in this manner ending with a layer of sauce and grated parmesan cheese. Bake until bubbly (about 40 minutes) at 350°. Serves 4 - 6.

Lasagne

3/4 - 1 pound dry lasagne **Noodles**,
     cooked and drained
2 C ricotta or cottage cheese or shredded
     shredded **Tofu**
1/2 pound grated mozzarella cheese
1-1/2 pint **Spaghetti Sauce**

Layer ingredients in casserole, starting with **Spaghetti Sauce**, then **Tofu**, then mozzarella, etc., ending with a layer of sauce and a sprinkling of grated cheese. Bake at 350° for 35 - 40 minutes or until cheese bubbles.

Variation: try including layers of spinach or chard, and seasoning with nutmeg.

Tacos

12 **Tortillas**
1 - 2 C **Basic Soyburger**
cumin
oregano
salt
green chilies, chopped very small
1/2 C chopped ripe olives (optional)
1 C shredded lettuce
1 C thinly quartered tomatoes
1 C grated cheese
1 avocado, mashed (optional)
oil

Warm soyburger and season to taste with seasonings above. Heat a little oil in a heavy skillet and toast one side of tortillas. Flip and fold in half, toasted side in. Toast outside and drain on paper. (These may also be just heated in an oven or warmed over an open flame.) Fill with soyburger, olives, green peppers and cheese; top with lettuce, tomatoes and avocado.

Mexican Beans

3 C dry pinto beans, washed and sorted
8 - 10 C water
2 C tomatoes, chopped
3 stalks celery, minced
1 green pepper, minced
1/8 C oil (optional)
1/2 T salt
2 t ground or crushed cumin
2 t oregano
1 t ginger
1 small bunch parsley, chopped fine
    (1/3 C dry parsley or 1-1/2 C fresh
    chopped parsley)

Heat water to boiling. Slowly add washed pintos. Cook at a low boil in a covered pan for 2 - 3 hours until beans are very soft. At this point add vegies, oil and salt. Cover. When vegies are tender, add last 4 ingredients. Cook 1/2 hour more. Serve with tortillas, chapatis, on toast, or as a soup with a tossed green salad. Guaranteed to make a pinto bean lover out of almost anyone. Serves 4 - 6.

Refried Beans

2 C dry pinto beans, washed and sorted
6 C water
1/2 C oil
1/2 C grated cheese
1 t. salt

Simmer pinto beans in the water in a covered pan for 2 - 3 hours until beans are very soft and thick. Mash beans thoroughly. Stir in oil and salt. Place mashed beans in a large frying pan and fry, stirring constantly, until beans are dry enough to shake loose from the pan. Sprinkle cheese on top and serve as soon as cheese melts. Serves 6 - 8.

Burritos

12 large **Tortillas**
1 recipe **Refried Beans**
1/2 - 1 pound shredded cheddar cheese or
    2 C shredded **Tofu**
oil
any kind of chopped vegetables (optional)

Spread a thin layer of refried beans on each tortilla. Cover with a thin layer of cheese or **Tofu**. Roll up. Brush outsides lightly with oil. Place in pan and bake 30 minutes at 350°.

Enchiladas

12 **Tortillas**

filling: (mix well)

2 C grated cheddar cheese
1/2 t salt

Sauce:

1/2 C minced celery
2 T oil
2 C chopped ripe tomatoes
2 small minced green chili peppers
1/2 C minced green pepper
1 t cumin
1 t salt
dash oregano
1 T flour (optional)

Saute celery and peppers in oil. Stir in other sauce ingredients and let simmer until thick. Dip **Tortillas** into oil or melted butter and then into the sauce to soften. Place large spoonful of filling on each and roll up. Arrange in baking dish. Cover with sauce and sprinkle with any remaining filling. Bake at 375° until cheese is melted and bubbly (20 - 40 minutes) Serves 6.

Muth

Very hearty - a little bit goes a long way

3/4 C shelled raw Spanish peanuts
1 C muth beans or mung beans, sprouted
1/2 t cumin
1 t black mustard seeds
1/2 t paprika
1 T honey
salt to taste
2 C fresh or frozen lima beans
3 - 4 T oil
1/2 t fenugreek
2 t turmeric
1 t **Garam Marsala**
1-1/2 T lemon juice (juice of 1/2
    medium lemon)

Sprout beans until 3/4" long. (See discussion of SPROUTS in **VEGETABLE** section for specific instructions.) Heat oil with cumin, fenugreek, mustard seeds until mustard seeds dance. Add other ingredients except lemon juice. Simmer until tender, add lemon juice and serve. Makes about 5 cups (serves 4 - 5 people). This dish is excellent served with a green salad and fresh corn or corn bread. We never serve it with other heavy dishes.

Split Pea and Potato Stew

1 C yellow split peas, washed
2 t salt
2 large potatoes, scrubbed and chopped
2 large tomatoes, chopped
1 t honey
4 C vegetable water
4 t oil
1/4 t turmeric
2 t **Garam Marsala**

Simmer split peas in water until tender and mushy. In another pan, heat oil and add potatoes, salt and turmeric. Stir until potatoes are well coated. Add split peas, **Garam Marsala** and honey. Simmer until potatoes are tender. Add tomatoes and simmer a few more minutes. May need to be thinned with a bit of water. Serves 4.

SOUPS

Vegetable Broth

vegetable scraps (ends, outer leaves, old
   vegetables, etc. can be very bad-looking,
   but not rotten) and parsley or green
   pepper if you have some. Or use the pulp
   from making carrot or vegetable juice.
enough water to cover
salt
herbs: try sweet basil, whole oregano,
   whole thyme, etc.

Chop vegetables scraps small enough to get the most flavor and nutrition out of them into the water in the shortest amount of cooking time. Adding salt helps break down the cells of the vegetables faster. Add the herbs for more flavor. Cover with water and bring to boil, turn down and simmer until vegetables are soft and the broth dark. Drain out vegetables and throw away. Broth can be used immediately, or frozen. The flavor will be fairly strong so it can be watered down for use.

Tomato Soup

5 quarts chopped tomatoes (about 10 pounds)
2 large stalks celery, minced
2 medium bell peppers, chopped
1/4 C minced fresh parsley
1 T dried basil
3 bay leaves
2 t salt
1/4 t ground cloves (optional)
2 - 3 scant T honey
7 T flour
7 T **Butter Oil Spread** or butter or oil
1 T lemon juice

Combine all ingredients except flour, **Butter Oil Spread**, and lemon juice. Simmer until soft. Cool slightly and puree through a food mill or sieve.

Return puree to pan and bring to a boil. Blend together butter and flour. Stir in slowly to tomato puree. Stir in lemon juice. May be thinned with cream or milk. Makes 3-1/2 quarts.

This is excellent for canning. Process pints for 15 minutes in a boiling water bath. See CANNING AND PRESERVING.

Borsch

2 C finely shredded beets
1 C finely shredded carrots
1 C minced celery
1 C minced green pepper
1 C finely shredded cabbage
4 C (approx) vegetable stock
1 C minced fresh parsley
1 t cumin

Shred carrots and beets and put in a pan with just enough water to cover them. Cover tightly and bring to a boil, stirring occasionally. Add other vegies, cover and simmer until thick. Season with parsley, basil and salt. Serve topped with a spoonful of thick yogurt or sour cream. Yield: Makes about 1-1/2 quarts.

Variations: Add tomato puree along with beets or 1/2 C tomato puree may be substituted for 1 C shredded beets.

Minestrone

1 C garbanzo beans
2 stalks celery, chopped
1 carrot, sliced thin
4 - 5 chopped medium tomatoes
  or about 2 C canned
1 T oil
Soup Herbs
lemon juice
salt
4 C water
2 medium zucchini, chopped thin
1/2 green pepper, chopped

Wash garbanzo beans and soak overnight. Cook next day in soaking water. (More water may be needed — use vegetable steaming water if available.) When beans are tender, add other ingredients and simmer until vegetables are tender. Serve plain with grated parmesan, with a salad, or with broiled cheese sandwiches. Our favorite soup. We've never served it to anyone who didn't like it. Serves 6 - 8.

Curry Soup

1 C yogurt
3 C water
1 T garbanzo flour
4 T ghee (clarified butter) or oil
1/2 t black mustard seed
1/2 t cumin seed
3 - 4 whole cloves
1 inch cinnamon stick
1 t salt
1 t turmeric
1 t ground coriander
2 T honey
1 C fresh or frozen peas
1 C fresh or frozen corn
1 C chopped ripe tomatoes

Beat yogurt, water and garbanzo flour together well. Heat the ghee and add to it the mustard seed, cumin seed, fenugreek, cloves, and cinnamon. Stir rapidly. When mustard seed dances, add yogurt mixture and stir well. Lower heat and add the salt, turmeric, coriander, and honey. Let simmer 20 minutes and then add the vegetables. When vegetables are heated through, serve. Excellent as a sauce over grains. Yields: about 1-1/2 quarts soup.

Cream of Bean Soup

3 C great northern beans
1 quart canned tomatoes
6 stalks celery
6 small zucchini
6 large carrots
1/4 C **Soup Herbs**
3 - 4 T salt
juice of 1 lemon

Wash beans and soak overnight. Cover with almost double amount of water and cook until beans are very very soft. (More water may need to be added.) Squish beans with the back of a wooden spoon. Add tomatoes and juice, chopped vegies, salt and cook until vegies are tender. Add soup herbs and cook 20 - 30 minutes more, then add juice of 1 lemon. Serves 6 - 8.

Parvati's Zucchini Cheese Soup

4 C water
5 small zucchinis (sliced)
1 pound sharp cheddar cheese

Boil squash till tender. While boiling, grate cheese. Let cool slightly. Add grated cheese and salt to taste. (If water is too hot, cheese will get stringy.)

Lentil Soup

3 C lentils
3 large tomatoes, chopped
3 grated carrots
1-1/2 C chopped fresh parsley
1-1/2 C shredded cabbage
4 quarts vegetable water
6 stalks celery and tops, chopped
2 T **Soup Herbs**
3 bay leaves
juice of 2 lemons
salt to taste

Cook lentils in vegetable water until tender. Add other ingredients and simmer until vegies are tender and flavors mingled. Serves 6 - 8.

Split Pea Soup

2C split peas
2 carrots, diced
2 stalks celery, diced
1 t vegetable salt or celery salt

Cook above ingredients in water (3 C if you're using a pressure cooker, 4 C if not) until everything is tender and creamy. Add 2 T oil at the end if desired. Run through a sieve or blender for a smooth soup or serve as is. Serves 4. This should take about 15 minutes in a pressure cooker, 45 min. - 1 hr. otherwise.

ALSO REFER TO . . .

The **VEGETABLES** section
The **SANDWICHES AND SPREADS** section
SAUCES AND GRAVIES
Soyspread
Humus Tahini

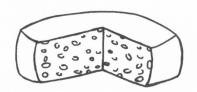

INFORMATION ON MILK PRODUCTS

Milk is a valuable food for human beings. In some form, it is almost indispensable for infants, and in many areas of the world it is used as a source of protein, vitamins and minerals all through life. Although some feel that the use of milk should stop after childhood, others say that it is one of the most sentient foods (good for both the mind and body: see **Food and Consciousness** section) and that it is vital for certain kinds of spiritual practices. Certainly it contains many of the important nutrients required for growing and preserving our human forms.

Calcium and protein are the two best known nutrients readily available in all kinds of milk and their products. These are two important nutrients which an infant or animal baby needs to grow. The protein in milk is high quality, containing all of the 8 essential amino acids. Two cups of milk or their equivalent in milk products provides about 16 grams protein. They provide 65.5% of the recommended daily requirement of calcium, and about 50% of the riboflavin reportedly needed daily by the adult human body. Riboflavin is essential in carbohydrate, fat and protein metabolism, but is easily destroyed by sunlight. For this reason, milk and milk products should be kept out of sunlight and flourescent light during storage, or kept in cartons or brown bottles. Milk and its products are low in iron and ascorbic acid. After six months of age when a child's birth supply of iron has run out, it is recommended that foods high in iron are given as a supplement to milk. Human milk is slightly higher in iron than cow's milk.

Lactose is the major carbohydrate in milk.

It is about 1/6 as sweet as glucose (table sugar) and is absorbed much slower. The ability to digest lactose depends on certain enzymes in the intestines. Some people, especially some third world people and old people have problems digesting the lactose in milk and get gas, diarrhea and indigestion as a result. Lactase, the enzyme which breaks down lactose lactose, may become less available with lack of use. A person who has not eaten any milk products for a long period may have problems digesting the lactose.

Milk or its parts are available in many forms: liquid, evaporated, cultured, dried, as butter and as cheese. The following brief explanations of the major forms available should help you choose the forms most useful to you.

LIQUID MILK

Liquid milk comes in many forms. The simplest form is raw milk. This is milk straight from the animal with no processing or heating. CERTIFIED RAW MILK is milk that is guaranteed to have been produced and distributed under conditions that conform with the standards for cleanliness set up by the American Medical Commissions. PASTEURIZED MILK has been heated to at least 145° F and held at or above this temperature continuously for at least 30 minutes, or to at least 161° F for at least 15 seconds in approved and properly operated equipment. Slight losses of vitamin B 12, K, and pantothenic acid may occur. Losses of thiamin and ascorbic acid are also clear. In HOMOGENIZATION the milk is mechanically treated to break up the fat into smaller globules, which are permanently dispersed in a fine emulsion throughout the milk. The heated milk is forced through very tiny

openings under high pressure. Nothing is added or removed. Afterwards there is no cream separation, and the milk is uniform throughout. Small differences in viscosity and color may be noticed. Homogenization lowers the curd tension which is said to result in a softer curd formation during digestion.

203

FORTIFICATION is the addition of a something not normally in a food. The most common nutrient added to milk is Vitamin D. Vitamin D aids in the absorption of calcium. This fortification has done much to reduce the number of cases of rickets in the U.S. This used to be a very common childhood disease caused by lack of calcium. Some people feel that the 400 International Units (I.U.) of Vitamin D added to a quart of milk can be detrimental to people's health; others disagree. In particular, there may be problems with impaired magnesium absorption. Milk can also be obtained that is fortified with Vitamin A, multivitamin preparations, minerals, lactose, and/or non-fat dried milk. TWO-PERCENT milk is milk with all but 2% of the fat removed. It is usually homogenized and pasteurized. SKIM MILK usually has a fat content of about 0.1%, though it may be lower or higher. The fat is removed by centrifuge. Vitamin A and D are often added (2000 I.U. of A and 400 I.U. of D per quart). However, they cannot be absorbed unless some fat is present in the intestine. CANNED WHOLE MILK has been sterilized and canned for shipping and export. It can be stored at room temperature until opened. FROZEN WHOLE MILK is homogenized, pasteurized whole milk that is quickly frozen. It keeps 1-1/2 to 3 months at temperatures below 10° F, and must be used shortly after defrosting. It is used on ships and overseas military installations.

CONCENTRATED MILK

Milk is also stored and distributed in concentrated form. The most common is EVAPORATED MILK. Slightly more than half of the water is removed in this milk product by heating up to 122 - 131° F. It is homogenized, Vitamin D added (usually), sealed in cans and sterilized at about 239° F for 15 minutes. It requires no refrigeration until opened. CARAGEENAN, a derivative of Irish Moss is generally added to evaporated milk. SWEETENED CONDENSED MILK was developed nearly a century ago as a way to preserve milk. The sugar acts as a preservative. The usual commercial ratio is 18 lbs. sugar to 100 lbs. milk, concentrated to 70% or more milk solids (40-45% sugar in the end product). Blend the following together for a sweetened condensed milk substitute: 1-1/2 C non-instant powdered milk (or 1-2/3 C instant), 2/3 C fresh milk, and 1/3 C honey. One 15 oz. can condensed milk contains 1-1/3 cups. CONCENTRATED FRESH MILK has been pasteurized, homogenized, and 2/3 of the water removed under vacuum, been rehomogenized, re-pasteurized, and packaged. It can retain its freshness for up to six weeks stored near freezing. It is available in only a few areas.

CULTURED MILKS

Cultured milk products such as buttermilk, yogurt, sour cream, kefir, and acidophilus milk are made by adding a "culture" of bacteria to some form of milk, and creating the right environment for those particular bacteria to grow.

In cultured milk products changes are caused by bacterial growth. These include for-mation of lactic acid from lactose, and coagulation of the milk protein, casein. The bacterial enzyme action on protein and fat, plus the effect of the increased concentration of acid changes the physical properties and chemical structure of the milk, resulting in the firm, curdled, and thick products we are used to. These products are said to promote biological synthesis of vitamins within the small intestine.

SOUR MILK can be made by letting raw sweet milk sit out until it sours. A quick way to sour milk is to add 2 t lemon juice or vinegar to fresh raw or pasteurized milk and stir and warm until it thickens and curdles.

BUTTERMILK can be made in two ways. Churned buttermilk is the product of butter-making, It contains about 8.5% or more of the non-fat solids and a small part of the fat lost in the churning process. Cultured buttermilk is generally prepared from fresh skim milk by adding a bacteria which will produce the desired flavor and quantity of lactic acid. It can be made in the same way as yogurt if it is incubated at a lower temperature, for a longer time.

YOGURT is generally made commercially with skimmed milk and enriched with non-fat milk solids. Yogging is accomplished by adding one or more of the following organisms: Streptococcus thermophius, Bacterium Bulgaricum, or Plocamobacterium yoghourtii. Yogurt is incubated at about 112° - 115°F. The quality of commercial yogurts varies greatly. Many brands use preservatives to hold off yeast and mold, artificial flavoring, artificial coloring, and almost all brands use some kind of stabilizer, ranging from agar to gelatin to vegetable gum. Others have additions such as Potassium Sorbate and Sorbic Acid. To be really safe, you can make your own (see **Yogurt** recipe in this section).

KEFIR is made with a bacteria that grows at room temperature. It can be made with raw milk, unlike yogurt. There are two possible ways of culturing kefir. One can use a small amount of plain commercial kefir in much the same way as yogurt is cultured, or one can obtain kefir grains from a friend or in dried form at a natural foods store. Follow the directions on the package if you buy dried grains. Grains which are being used will sit in the bottom of the jar of kefir. The kefir is strained off through a strainer, leaving the lumps called grains in the strainer. After all the liquid has strained through, the strainer is held under running water until the grains have been washed clean. Place them in the bottom of a jar, cover with milk (raw, reconstituted dry, or pasteurized) to fill the jar (or however much you want to make). Cover with a screen or cheese cloth so that air can pass through but bugs can't get in. Let sit for 1 - 3 days at room temperature, depending on how strong you want the kefir to be and the amount of kefir grains you have. The kefir grains grow with every use, and must be in constant use to stay alive.

ACIDOPHILUS MILK is pasteurized skim milk which has been cultured with lactobacillus acidophilus and incubated at 100° F. It is sometimes used to combat excessive putrefaction by changing the bacterial flora of the intestines.

Milk is DRIED in either drum or spray driers. The sequence in both methods is: preheating, clarification, condensing, standardizing and drying. Low heat spray drying is preferred because the dried milk has a better color and flavor due to low temperatures. Also, the protein may suffer less damage at the lower temperature. In NONFAT DRIED MILK, skim milk is pasteurized and 2/3 of the water removed under vacuum. This concentrated skim milk is then dried by spraying into a chamber of hot filtered air. The result is a fine textured product of very low moisture content. It is further instantized for INSTANT DRY MILK. One method of doing this is to moisten the dried milk with steam, then redry. Non-fat dry milk can be stored at room temperature in a moisture proof container. WHOLE DRY MILK is made by the same process, but special packaging is required to prevent oxidation during storage.

MILK FATS

When the Milk Fat is separated from the liquid in the milk, the result is called CREAM. In raw milk, cream can be skimmed off the top after the milk has sat for a while. WHIPPING CREAM is in a concentrated enough form to be whipped with beaters or vigorously by hand. One cup whipping cream makes two cups whipped. It will whip better when it and the bowl and beaters are cold. HALF AND HALF, sold commercially, is half cream and half milk. It is generally used on cereals and desserts, in coffee and tea, and for cooking.

The violent agitation (churning) of milk yields BUTTER. The fat in small globules strike one another and coalesce. There is a change from tiny fat globules in water (cream or milk) to tiny water globules in fat, which is called butter. SALTED BUTTER has salt in it as a flavoring and as a preservative. SWEET BUTTER has no salt in it and should be kept frozen if it is not going to be used immediately. Salted butter also keeps better frozen, but should at least be refrigerated. GHEE is an Indian form of butter, which is CLARIFIED. To prepare, boil sweet butter over medium heat. Remove from heat. Let sit one or two minutes. Skim off the solids on top. Repeat the whole operation two more times. Finally let it sit for ten minutes and pour slowly through cheesecloth, letting the sediment in the bottom remain in the pan. **Butter Oil Spread** is a combination of oil and butter. The recipe for making this can be found in the **SANDWICHES AND SPREADS** section.

CHEESES

CHEESE became an important food because it was an excellent method of preserving milk. It is theorized that cheese was first discovered when milk was carried in animal stomach bags and the rennet in the bag material caused the milk to curdle. People in each area developed their own methods of making cheese, varying the aging process, temperature, types of milk, rennet and the like according to their environment. Today cheese is made by innoculating milk with various suitable organisms to produce cheese. Through the controlling of these microorganisms, the temperature, and the substrate (what is available to feed on), hundreds of different flavored cheeses can be prepared. The final yield of cheese is approximately 10% of the weight of the original milk.

There is quite a variety of things added to the original milk to produce cheeses of various types. Here is a list of some of them. LACTIC ACID producing bacteria are used to sour milk. RENNET is used to coagulate the protein. Commercial rennet is obtained from the stomachs of young calves. Three to 3-1/2 ounces are used to 1000 pounds of milk. A vegetable coagulant (MARZYME) has recently been developed which is becoming increasingly popular because it is relatively inexpensive. In time it may replace animal rennet in all mass produced cheese. It you want to eat only vegetable coagulated cheeses, avoid imported cheeses (made with traditional recipes), and check the labels and contact the manufacturers of your favorite brands. Natural foods stores and co-ops will often know this information. Propionibacterium shermanii is added to SWISS CHEESE to produce the holes. Orange CHEDDAR CHEESE is generally colored with a yellow coloring obtained from the seed pods of a Central American tree. SALT is added to most cheeses. In cheddar cheese, the ratio is 2-1/2 pounds salt to 1000 pounds milk. Some cheeses are salted by soaking in brine. RINDS are produced through exposure to air; addition of edible oil; a black or brown protective coating of oil, lampblack and Fuller's earth; or a covering of cloth and parafin. Some cheeses such as PARMESAN are heated in copper vats. The slight amounts of copper in the cheese is responsible for its brittle texture. BLUE CHEESE is inoculated with spores of Penicillium roqueforti or a similar mold that causes a blue-green mottling in the cheese.

Cheese can be separated into two main classes: unripened and ripened. Unripened

Variety	Water	Protein	Fat	Calcium	Sodium
Cheddar	37.0	25.0	32.2	750	700
Pasteurized process cheese food	43.2	19.8	24.0	570	-
Brick	41.0	22.2	30.5	730	-
Cottage, skim	79.0	17.0	0.3	90	290
Cottage, creamed	78.3	13.6	4.2	94	229
Limburger	45.0	21.2	28.0	590	-
Swiss	39.0	27.5	28.0	925	710

cheeses include COTTAGE CHEESE, CREAM CHEESE, and NEUFCHATEL. Ripened cheeses can be further divided into "bacteria ripened" and "mold-ripened." Bacteria ripened cheeses are those like PARMESAN and AMERICAN CHEDDAR. Mold-ripened includes BLUE CHEESE, ROQUEFORT, etc. Though there are 10 distinct types of cheese, and more than 2000 names, a common classifying system is to group them into four groups according to their consistency: HARD GRATING (Parmesan, Romano), HARD (Gouda. Edam, Cheddar, Colby, Provolone, Swiss), SEMI-SOFT (Brick, Muenster, Roquefort, Blue, Monterey Jack, Mozzarela, etc.), SOFT (Limburger, Cottage, Cream, Ricotta, Teleme, Neufchatel, etc.)

CREAM CHEESE contains 10 - 12% milkfat. Sometimes a small amount of rennet is used in it. NEUFCHATEL is similar to cream cheese but has a lower fat content. COTTAGE CHEESE is made from fresh pasteurized milk and/or reconstituted non-fat dry milk. A lactic acid starter and usually a small amount of rennet is used. CREAMED COTTAGE CHEESE has cream added to yield not less than 4% milkfat. ROQUEFORT CHEESE is an imported sheep's milk product. MYSOST and PRIMOST are made from whey and have a brown, caramel flavor from cooking down.

PROCESSED CHEESE goes through more processing than regular cheese. It is generally prepared by mixing together several kinds of natural cheese with the aid of heat and an emulsifying agent such as sodium citrate, disodium phosphate, monosodium phosphate, etc. These may be added in large enough proportions to make up 3% of the final product. Artificial coloring is added and sometimes an acidifying agent. Alginic acid may be used as a stabilizer to give uniformity of color and flavor. Mythyl cellulose may be used as a thickening agent.

Generally, cheeses should be stored in the refrigerator in airtight containers or covered with plastic film or aluminum foil to keep the cheese moist and retard the growth of mold. When you have a large piece of cheese which is wax coated, cut off a piece for immediate use and cover the end of the large piece with a moisture-proof wrap. Never re-use a piece of wrapping that has previously been around a moldy piece of cheese on a new piece. Even washing fails to remove the mold spores.

Harder types of cheese such as Cheddar, Swiss, Edam and Gouda can be stored in the freezer or frozen rapidly in small (1/2 pound pound) packages. They should be tightly wrapped in moisture proof material, or wrapped in waxed paper and sealed in a plastic container. Thaw in the refrigerator. After freezing, the cheese may be slightly discolored, but the color will improve with thawing. Dehydration is due to poor wrapping. Slow freezing causes the cheese to be crumbly. Parmesan cheese does not mold if grated and stored in a covered jar in the refrigerator. It is good this way on vegies, in sauces, etc.

Cheeses other than cottage cheese generally taste best when served at room temperature. The amount of cheese needed for serving can be removed from the refrigerator and allowed to warm at room temperature for about 30 minutes prior to serving.

OTHER MILKS

This section has focused on cow's milk, because it is the most common milk in North American countries. Other kinds of milk are available in some areas.

HUMAN MILK is of course great for babies. Nutritionally it varies a great deal from cow's milk. One would guess that these variations are profitable for the human child, that the balance of nutrients is naturally the best one for the growing human baby, while a cow's are the best for a growing calf. For this reason some people feel that milk, with all its growing nutrients, is not a good food for human beings beyond early childhood. Milk has, however, traditionally been considered one of the most sentient foods (good for the body, mind and meditation) by yogis.

Human milk differs from cow's milk in the length of fatty acid chains. Fatty acid chains in human milk are less saturated and have longer carbon chains and are utilized more effectively than the short-chain, more saturated fatty acids in cow's milk. An unidentified factor in human milk has been designated as the Lactobacillus bifidus factor since it creates a medium in the gastointestinal tract conducive to that microorganism's growth. This microorganism depresses the growth of pathogenic organisms and decreases the infant's susceptibility to infection. This reduces problems with diarrhea and the like. Colostrum, the mammary secretion which flows from the breast immediately after birth, gives the infant consumer a high degree of passive immunity to diseases because antibodies from the mother flow through it intact during the first few days of life.

GOAT'S MILK is said to be more easily digestible than cow's milk. In appearance and flavor goat's milk is comparable to other kinds of milk. Its fat globules are smaller and by nature remain in emulsion, so mechanical homogenization is unnecessary. In circumstances where human milk is not available to an infant, goat's milk is often considered the best substitute. A nutritional comparison of human, goat, and cow's milk is included in this section. For more information, contact the American Dairy Goat Assn., P.O. Box 186, Spindale, North Carolina 28160.

Nutritional Comparison between Cow, Goat and Human milk, measured per cup of milk.

	Cow	Goat	Human
Calories	160.0	165.0	163.0
Fat (grams)	9.0	10.0	9.0
Protein (grams)	9.0	8.0	3.3
Calcium (mg)	288.0	315.0	72.0
Iron (mg)	0.1	.2	1.5
Vitamin A (units)	350.0	390.0	542.0
Vitamin C (mg)	2.0	2.0	4.9

Yogurt

3 to 4 C powdered milk
2 quarts water
2 T yogurt (see below)
one 16 ounce can evaporated milk
    (makes yogurt much thicker)

209

The yogurt is a "starter": the culture will grow and turn your milk into yogurt. The mixture is said to "yog." You can use 1/2 gallon whole milk instead of the water, powdered milk, and evaporated milk. Don't use "plastic" yogurt from grocery stores for starter: it has so many additives that it doesn't work as well. However, it is not necessary to buy a Bulgarian yogurt culture (these are expensive). Buy some good yogurt at a natural foods store. It must be fresh. If you do not make yogurt at least every four or five days then you will have to use store-bought yogurt for a starter each time. Otherwise, your old batch can be used to start the new one. The more often you make yogurt, the sweeter it will be. Also, cooler milk makes the yogurt sweeter; hotter milk makes it sourer.

METHOD 1: Blend the powdered milk, water, and canned milk. Strain through a sieve to remove lumps. Heat slowly and stir frequently so milk doesn't burn or stick to the bottom of the pan. When milk starts to boil (as bubbles rise to the surface) remove from heat and let it cool. When you can hold your finger in it to a slow count of ten, it is time to add the starter: first add a little warm milk to the starter and then add this mixture to the pot, stirring it in one direction only until starter is blended in. (One direction may be only superstition, but it's easy enough.) Place a cardboard lid, several thicknesses of paper, or paper towels over the top of the pan (to absorb extra moisture) and cover with the pan lid. Wrap the pan up in a heavy coat or several thick towels. Place it on top of the pilot light on your gas stove and forget it for 6 - 8 hours. Do not move it.

METHOD 2: If you don't have a pilot light or suitable warm nook in your house, make the yogurt as for method 1, but after the starter has been stirred in, pour the yogurt into clear, wide-mouth Mason jars. Have ready a hot 115° water bath in a big kettle with a rack on the bottom. Place jars of yogurt on rack and maintain temperature of water bath until yogurt is formed.

HINTS: sometimes a yogurt culture will go bad by picking up some yeast or bacteria from the air. In this case, you have to begin again with a fresh culture. Don't make bread on the same day, because the yogurt will pick up the yeast from the air, and smell and taste like yeast.

If your yogurt doesn't yog, maybe it's because: (1) your milk was too cold or too hot when starter was added; (2) the room wasn't warm enough; (3) your culture was no longer good.

If your yogurt separates while yogging, it has over-yogged. Don't let the next batch yog as long. If it separates after it has been in the refrigerator a few days, it is too old, and you should get a new culture. Some people say you should get a new culture every month or so, because (even though it yogs) it may not have all the bacteria in a new culture which are an aid to digestion. To make thicker yogurt, add more milk powder.

YOGURT TIPS

When you are adding yogurt to other foods you should always fold it in rather than beat it in. Cook it at low heat if that is required so that it doesn't separate. Beating in a little flour

called for in a recipe will help smooth it out before adding, making mixing easier, and reducing separation. Equal parts of yogurt can be substituted for sour cream in most recipes.

Yogurt Cheese

This is similar to cream cheese. Hang a half-batch of **Yogurt** in a couple of thicknesses of cheesecloth. Let the bag hang for 12 - 24 hours, depending on the consistency you want. If the whey that drains from the cheese at first is thick, it may be used instead of buttermilk or sour milk in baking.

Panir

1 quart whole milk
juice of 1 lemon

Bring milk to a boil and add lemon juice. Stir well. Turn off heat and let milk sit a few minutes. (It will curdle). Bring to a boil once again and then let it cool. When lukewarm, put it in a muslin bag and strain the whey from the curds. Hang the bag up and let it drip. Do not squeeze the bag or your cheese will be tacky. This cheese can be fried in deep fat or eaten plain. Keeps only two or three days.

Cottage Cheese

Raw whole milk (1 quart for every 3/4 C
  end product, approximately)
Cloth (preferably cheese cloth) to hang
  cheese in
Butter
cream
salt to taste (optional)

Leave milk out in covered bowl until clabbered (usually a few days) or use milk that has clabbered in the refrigerator (do not use pasteurized milk, as it rots rather than sours). When solidly clabbered, place bowl over a pan of hot water. Slowly heat on stove until the curd and whey separate. Do not boil as this will make the curd tough. Strain through cheese cloth. Hang for a while and then squeeze out extra whey. Squeeze well for a dry cheese.

Use as a dry cheese in casseroles and cheese cakes; form into little cakes with some additional butter, cream and salt; or add more cream for creamed cottage cheese.

Orange Jubilee

1 C fresh orange juice
1/2 C powdered milk powder
1-1/2 T honey or to taste
a few drops vanilla extract
1/2 C shaved ice

Whirl in a blender until frothy.

Spiffy Carob Cooler

5 - 6 regular size ice cubes
1 C cold milk
4 - 6 T carob powder
1/4 C dry powdered milk
1/2 t vanilla
1 - 2 T honey

Blend together in blender. Yields: slightly less than 4 C or 3 servings.

Date Milk

Simmer 6 dates in 2 C milk for about 15 minutes (until dates are sort of dissolved). Serve plain or garnished with cinnamon. Serves 2.

Hot Date Milk

2 T date sugar
1 C hot milk

Combine and enjoy.

Ginger Milk

1 C milk
honey to taste
1/4 t ground ginger or less, no more

Heat to drinking temperature. Because of ginger, dried milk tastes just about as good.

Ginger Buttermilk

For each serving, combine 1 C chilled buttermilk, 1/4 C orange juice, 1 t lemon juice, 2 T honey and a dash of ground ginger. Beat until well blended. Chill.

Krsna Drink

1 C yogurt
1 C buttermilk
1 small banana
6 dates, pitted

Combine ingredients in blender until smooth. Serve cool.

Spiced Nut Milk

2 C milk
2 T honey
pinch saffron, crushed
12 pistachios, shelled
6 cashews
6 blanched almonds
few raisins
pinch ground nutmeg

Gently warm above ingredients. Do not scald. Serve warm. Serves 2.

Golden Milk

3 C milk
3 spoonfuls honey
1 t turmeric
1/4 t American saffron, crumbled
1/2 t nutmeg
2 T cashews (optional)
1 T raisins (optional)

Combine ingredients and serve warm.

Date Milk Shake

2 T date sugar
3 scoops ice cream
1 C milk

Blend together in a blender until smooth.

ALSO REFER TO . . .

The **MAIN DISHES** and **VEGETABLES** sections for recipes using cheese and small amounts of milk and milk products

Pudding recipes in the **DESSERTS** section
Good Karma Casserole
Parvati's Zucchini Cheese Soup
White Sauce
Cheese Sauce
Cream Cheese Frosting
Raw Cheese Cake Filling
Baked Cheese Cake
Almond Yogurt Coffee Cake
Pumpkin Pie

SAUCES
AND GRAVIES

To make a good gravy or any sauce with flour and a butter or oil base, the roux (as the basic mixture is called) must be cooked to rid it of any raw flour taste and to make it more digestible.

To increase the flavor, give it a brown color and increase digestibility, the flour can be browned. Stir whole-wheat pastry flour in a dry, heavy cast iron pan over low heat until evenly golden brown, or brown it in the oven at 350° for about 30 minutes, stirring frequently. Do not let it get too brown or it will be bitter. Remember that it will continue browning after being taken off the burner if left in the pan.

To make the roux, mix oil or melted butter and flour gently over low heat for at least five minutes, stirring. It will get browner and have a delicious baked aroma. (For a white sauce, stop cooking before it turns brown.) Stir the roux frequently so the starch in the flour will cook evenly, making the end sauce more evenly thickened.

When the roux is ready, remove from heat and quickly stir in the liquid, adding only part of it at first if you are making large amounts. A wire whip makes this very easy. When you are sure all the roux is dissolved, return to heat and bring to a boil. If, due to the coldness of the milk, water or broth, the butter in the roux lumps, you may have to heat it very slightly and then stir it in. Bring it all to a boil, stirring constantly all the way down to the bottom, and boil for a minute or two. If the right balance of ingredients were used, it should be just right. Salt to taste.

Some hints: White sauce is made with un-browned flour, the roux is just cooked for a short time, and the liquid is milk. Brown gravies are generally made with browned flour, long-cooked roux, and water or vegetable broth. Spices are sometimes added. The usual ratios in gravies are: equal amounts of butter or oil and flour. 1 tablespoon flour to a cup of liquid makes a medium thick sauce, 2 tablespoons a thick sauce, and 1/2 table-spoon makes a soup-like sauce. Butter makes a more delicately flavored sauce. If your sauce is too thin, toasted or raw flour can be mixed in with water or milk until there are no lumps and this can quickly be stirred into the gravy, and then all of it brought to a boil again. If the gravy does happen to lump, it can be blended in the blender or put through a strainer.

Whole Wheat Gravy

2 T sesame seeds
2 T whole wheat flour
1-1/2 C water
1/4-1/2 t salt

Brown sesame seeds and flour in iron skillet. Combine with 1/2 C of the water in a blender. Blend until sesame seeds are fairly small. Pour back into the skillet, add the other cup of water after using it to rinse out the blender. Add salt and heat to boiling. Stir while it boils for 2 minutes. More water can be added at this point if you want a thinner gravy, or it can be cooked longer for a thicker gravy.

White Sauce

(cream sauce or bechamel)

2 T butter (or oil)
2 T flour
1 C milk or cream or 1/2 milk, 1/2 cream

Season with one or more:

1/2 t salt
1/2 t curry (optional)
1/2 t celery salt
2 T chopped parsley (optional)
1/2 t thyme (optional)

Slowly melt butter. Add flour, stir until well blended. Simmer for 3 - 5 minutes. Slowly stir in the milk. Season. Simmer sauce while stirring frequently with a wire whisk until it is smooth and comes to a low boil. If desired it can be thickened in the oven at 350° for about 20 minutes, but then the sauce will need to be strained.

Variations: for thin sauce: 2 t flour and butter for 1 C milk. For thick sauce: 3 T flour and butter for 1 C milk.

Cheese Sauce

This sauce is good for using up all the little tidbits of various cheeses in your refrigerator. Serve it over steamed vegetables. Broccoli and cauliflower are superb.

2 T oil
2 T wholewheat pastry flour
1-1/2 C milk
1 - 1-1/2 C grated cheese (1-1/2 C will make a thick sauce — cheddar cheese is best but almost anything will do. Combinations are often excellent.)
1/2 t salt
1/4 t paprika
1/2 t thyme or 1/2 t dry mustard or both for a spicy sauce

Mix oil and flour in a saucepan until smooth. Stir in milk and bring to a boil. When smooth and boiling, reduce heat to a simmer and stir in cheese and seasonings. Yield: about 2 C.

Loaf and Burger Sauce

(good on vegies too)

4 T oil
2 T flour
2 T arrowroot dissolved in 1/4 C water
2-3/4 C water
2 T tomato paste
salt to taste

Brown flour in oil in a heavy skillet. Gradually add arrowroot paste and then rest of water and tomato paste. Season to taste with salt. Cook very slowly for at least 30 minutes. Serves 2 people.

Easy Tomato Sauce

4 C chopped tomatoes (4 pounds or 6 medium)
1/2 C minced bell pepper
1 stalk celery, minced
1/4 t basil
1/4 t oregano
1/4 t thyme
1/2 t salt
1 T flour
1 T oil

Simmer the tomatoes, bell pepper, celery, herbs, and salt until soft. Puree through a food mill or sieve. Thoroughly blend flour and oil. Return tomato puree to saucepan and bring to a boil. Slowly stir in oil and flour mixture. Simmer until thick, about 15 - 20 minutes. This may be used in any recipes calling for spaghetti sauce, and can be canned in the same way as **Spaghetti Sauce** (See **CANNING AND PRESERVING**.) Yields about 1 quart.

Tomato Paste

8 C very ripe tomatoes, chopped

Simmer tomatoes until very soft and thick. Remove from heat and cool slightly. Put through a food mill to remove seeds and skin. Simmer slowly until thick. This will take almost all day. Makes approximately 1-1/2 C. This recipe can be canned in the same way as **Spaghetti Sauce** (See CANNING AND PRESERVING.)

Spaghetti Sauce

4 large stalks celery, minced
3 bell peppers, minced
1 large bunch parsley, finely minced
4 C eggplant, cubed or chinese cabbage, finely shredded
12 - 16 chopped fresh tomatoes or 9-1/2 C chopped or 2 - 3 quarts canned
1/4 C oil
18 - 24 oz. tomato paste
4 C basic **Soyburger** (optional)
1 T basil
1 T thyme
3 pinches tarragon
1/2 T sage
1 T oregano
1/2 C tamari, or salt to taste

Wash and cut up vegetables. Heat oil and saute green pepper and celery. When limp and transparent, add cabbage and parsley. Saute until cabbage is limp. Add tomatoes and tomato paste. Stir and cover to steam liquid out of tomatoes. If desired, add **Soyburger**. Simmer until a homogenous mixture results. The longer it simmers, the better it is. Add herbs and tamari and simmer another hour. Serve over spaghetti **Noodles** and garnish with alfalfa sprouts. Or use in recipes calling for **Spaghetti Sauce** (**Eggplant Parmesan**, **Lasagne**, **Pizza**, etc.). Remember when tasting this spaghetti sauce that it will be served over noodles or in casseroles and thus is slightly over-seasoned when eaten plain. Yields: one gallon.

Soybean Curry Sauce

Curry concentrate:

2 C pureed cooked soybeans (in a blender)
1 T **Curry Powder**

Mix **Curry Powder** and beans. Simmer 1/2 hour. This mixture will be too highly seasoned to eat. Freeze in small containers.

To serve:

1 C curry concentrate
1/2 - 1 C yogurt
1 C chopped ripe tomatoes

Mix, heat and serve over brown rice.

Variations: add 1/4 C raisins, 1/4 C cashews or almonds, vegetables, coconut, etc.

Indian Gravy

1 C Indian dal or yellow split peas
4 to 8 C water
2 T oil
1 T chopped hot green peppers
4 whole cloves
1 t salt
1 t turmeric
1 t cumin seeds
1/2 t black mustard seed

Cook dal in water until mushy. In a separate pan heat oil and seasonings. When mustard seed pops, add dal and water. Bring to a boil again and serve. Reheats well.

Sunseed Sauce

1-1/2 C sunflower seeds
water
1/2 - 1 t sesame seeds

Blend 2 C of water with sunflower seeds in blender until smooth and creamy, to make a very thick (just pourable) sauce. To get a pudding consistency add 1/2 C more water.

Suncheese Sauce: 1 C grated cheese added to above, heat until cheese melts.

Buttered Almond Sauce
(other nuts too)

Use over vegies — ummmm . . .

1/4 C butter
1/4 C blanched, finely chopped almonds
   or cashew, pumpkin, sesame seeds, etc.

Saute butter over low heat until lightly browned. Add almonds, stirring until hot. Season with salt to taste, but don't overdo it.

Lemon Herb Butter

1/2 C butter or oil
pinch tarragon
1 t herb salt
1/2 t basil
1/2 t thyme
1 lemon, juiced

Warm butter or oil. Add herbs and simmer a few minutes to release the flavor of the herbs into the butter. Remove from heat and stir in lemon juice. Serve on steamed artichokes, broccoli and other steamed vegetables. The herbs will settle out so stir just before serving.

desserts

DESSERTS

DESSERTS

Making desserts without eggs can be a real challenge for a natural foods cook. This section is provided to alleviate the feeling that cakes and cookies can't be made without eggs, that candy can't be made without refined sugar, and that white flour is the pastry cook's best friend.

The many delicious recipes in this section are all made from pure, wholesome, natural ingredients. They are the result of countless hours of experimentation, criticism, intuitive searching and just plain luck. Like other recipes in this book, they have undergone multiple tests in their final form. We're confident that they'll all be delicious if they're made according to the directions.

Whether you want a wedding cake, cookies for the kids, Christmas candy, or a genuine pumpkin pie, you'll find (in the pages that follow), a recipe that's as nutritious, reliable, and delicious as can be.

EGG SUBSTITUTES

The following information is to help you to convert your favorite recipe from eggful to eggless.

Eggs serve two purposes: they act as a leavening agent and as a binder. The white is primarily a leavening agent, the yolk primarily a binder. Before choosing one of the following substitutes, try to determine whether you need a leavening agent or a binder.

BINDERS: (to hold patties, cookies, etc. together)
• nut butters
• oat and soy flours mixed with a little water
• one part soy flour to two parts water, mixed in blender till very thick. Simmer in double boiler one hour. Beat in 2 T oil and 1/4 t salt for each C soy flour. Store in refrigerator. Use 2 T to replace one egg as binder.

LEAVENING AGENTS: (to replace white of egg or slightly beaten egg)
• Increase baking powder by 1 t for each egg omitted. Commercial baking powder may contain powdered egg whites (as well as aluminum salts — aluminum is a cumulative poison, like lead).
• garbanzo flour mixed wth flour in recipe will cause slight leavening — experiment with 2 T per C of flour.

TO REPLACE BEATEN EGG WHITES: (as in meringue)
• Use whipped flax jell: soak 5 T flaxseed in 5 C cold water for an hour. Simmer 20 minutes. Strain. Refrigerate until cold. Beat as you would egg whites. Will not hold shape when heated.

TO REPLACE EGG ACTING BOTH AS BINDER AND LEAVENING AGENT:
• Use 4 T almond or cashew butter plus 2 T lemon juice.

• Synthetic egg replacers are available. If you must eat synthetic food, be sure you know the sources and effects of all the chemical ingredients.

COOKIES

Kate's Oatmeal Cookies

1/2 C oil
1/2 C honey
1-1/4 C oats
1-1/4 C whole wheat pastry flour
3 T milk
1 t baking soda
1/4 t salt
1/2 t nutmeg
1 t cinnamon
1/2 C raisins
3/4 C sesame seeds

Preheat oven. Mix wet ingredients. Mix dry ingredients. Combine the two mixtures. Drop by rounded tablespoonfuls onto a greased cookie sheet and flatten with a fork dipped in cold water. Bake at 350° for 8 - 10 minutes. Makes 3-1/2 dozen.

Oatmeal Cookies

3/4 C oil
1 C honey
1/4 C water
1 t vanilla
1/2 t nutmeg
2 C flour, whole wheat or barley
4 C oatmeal

Combine ingredients in order given. Drop by spoonfuls on a cookie sheet. Bake at 350°, 12 - 15 minutes, or if using barley flour, 15 - 18 minutes. Yields 4 dozen.

Variations: Substitute granola for part or all of the oatmeal. Use barley flour in place of whole wheat flour.

Banana Oatmeal Cookies

2/3 C oil
2 C flour
4 C oatmeal
1/2 - 1 t mace, cinnamon, nutmeg, or allspice
3/4 C honey
3 large bananas, smashed
1/2 t salt (optional)

Combine ingredients. Drop onto cookie sheets. Bake at 350° for 12 - 15 minutes.

Ginger Cookies

1/2 C honey
1 C molasses
1/2 C almond or cashew butter
2 t soda
2/3 C thick yogurt or sourcream
1 t each: cinnamon, cloves, ginger, nutmeg
2/3 C oil
1/3 C soft butter
4 C whole wheat pastry flour

Cream together cashew butter and butter. Add in order, stirring well after each addition: thick yogurt, honey, molasses, and oil. Add soda and spices to flour, stirring together. Add to wet mixture and stir well. Drop onto cookie sheets. Bake 20 minutes at 350°. Makes approximately four dozen 2-inch cookies.

Gingersnaps

4 C barley flour (or whole wheat flour)
2 t soda
1/2 t salt
1/2 C oil
1-1/3 C molasses
1 T ground ginger
1 T ground cinnamon
1/2 t ground cloves
date sugar (optional)

Mix ingredients (except date sugar) in order listed. Roll into one inch balls and roll in date sugar. Bake at 350° for about 15 minutes. When made with barley flour, these will still be soft (slightly gooey) when done. Makes 4 dozen.

Vanilla Cookies

3/4 C honey
1/4 C **Butter-Oil Spread**
2 C pastry flour
1 t cinnamon
1/2 t cloves
1 t soda
1 t.vanilla
1/4 t salt
1/2 t nutmeg
1/2 t allspice

Combine ingredients and mix well. Make 1 inch balls and flatten. Bake for 10 minutes at 350°.

Carob Cookies

1/2 C honey
1/2 C butter or oil
3/4 C carob
1-1/4 C pastry flour
1 t cinnamon
1/2 t allspice
1 t vanilla
1 t soda
1/4 t salt
a little water, if needed, to make the
  dough workable

Mix as in Vanilla Cookies.

Variations: Make marbled cookies by kneading Vanilla Cookies and Carob Cookies together, and then rolling into balls. Make pinwheel cookies by rolling each type into sheets, placing on top of each other, rolling up and slicing the roll.

Almond Raisin Tea Cookies

1 C chopped raisins (or coconut)
1 C butter
1/4 C honey
1 t vanilla or almond extract
1/2 C chopped almonds
2 C whole wheat pastry flour

Cream butter, add honey in a fine stream while continuing to cream butter. Stir in vanilla, raisins and almonds. Stir in flour. Chill 1/2 hour. Form into small balls, put on ungreased baking sheet. Bake 15 - 18 minutes at 350°.

Variation: Any kind of nuts will work. Raisins may be omitted, and nuts increased to one cup.

Sunflower Seed Cookies

1 T vanilla
1 T salt
2 C oil
2 C honey
4 C sunflower seed pieces
2-1/2 - 3-1/2 C pastry flour

Mix, adding flour last until not sticky, but not doughy yet. Bake at 350° until edges are brown. Makes 5 - 6 dozen cookies.

Joy's Raisin-Nut Holders

1-1/2 C date particles
3/4 C oil
2 C whole wheat flour
3 C oatmeal
2 C nuts
2 C raisins
1 t salt
2 t baking powder
1-1/2 C (or more if needed) milk
  or apple juice

Combine ingredients. Drop onto cookie sheets and bake at 350° for 10 - 15 minutes.

Macaroons

1-1/2 C non instant dry milk
2/3 C liquid milk
1/2 C honey
2 t vanilla or almond extract
6 - 8 C shredded coconut (fresh or dried —
  if dried, fine shred works best)

Blend the milks, honey and vanilla in a blender until smooth. Stir in coconut until mixture holds together but is not runny. Let sit for 10 - 20 minutes so that the coconut will absorb the moisture. Spoon tablespoonfuls on a cookie sheet (either lightly oiled or well seasoned). Bake at 350° for 10 - 12 minutes (but not until brown as they will be dry if overdone). Yields about 4 dozen.

To tell whether a cake or bar cookie is done:

- Toothpick test: toothpick inserted in middle should come out clean
- Finger indentation test: indentation should bounce up rather than stay down.
- Should not have glossy surface.

Fruit Bars

Make 1/2 of an **Oatmeal Cookie** recipe.

Mix:

2 C ground figs or other dried fruit
3/4 C water
1 t lemon peel

Cook until soft.

Pat 1/2 of the half **Oatmeal Cookie** recipe on the bottom of a 9 inch pan. Spread the filling over it, then pat on the rest of the cookie recipe.

Variations: try prunes, dates, raisins, apples.

Wheat Germ Bars

8 C raw wheat germ
1-1/2 C honey
1 T butter or oil

Toast the wheat germ by the oven method (see **GRAINS AND CEREALS**). While wheat germ is still hot, add honey until mixture sticks together. Add butter or oil and pack into oiled 8 X 12 (or similar) pan. When cool, cut into squares. Other cereals or dried fruit may be added.

Wheat Germ Brownies

Mix in order listed:

1/2 C oil
1/2 C honey
1/3 C molasses
1 C raisins (optional)
1/2 - 1 C chopped walnuts or sunflower seeds
2 t vanilla
1/3 C water
1/2 t salt

Then sift in:

1 C non-instant milk powder
1-1/2 t cream of tarter
1-1/2 t baking soda
2 C lightly toasted wheatgerm

Stir. Pour into 8 X 12 inch pan. Bake at 350° for 30 minutes. Cut while still hot. Makes 2 dozen brownies.

Carob Brownies

Follow recipe for **Wheat Germ Brownies**. Substitute sifted carob powder for non-instant powdered milk.

Honey Cake

1/4 C butter
1/2 C honey
1/4 t salt
1 t cinnamon
1 t vanilla
2 C pastry flour
1 t cram of tartar
1 t baking soda
2/3 C water or milk

Beat butter, honey and salt together. Combine flour, soda, and cream of tartar. Stir dry ingredients into beaten mixture alternately with hot water or milk. Pour into well-oiled 9 inch square baking pan and bake at 325° for 30 minutes or until done.

Carob Honey Cake

3 T oil or soft butter
6 T carob
1-1/2 C whole wheat pastry flour or
   whole wheat flour
1 t vanilla
1/2 C honey
1 C milk or water
1 t salt
1/2 t baking soda
1/2 t cream of tarter

Beat butter and honey together until almost frothy. Add vanilla, mix dry ingredients well and add alternately with milk to butter and honey mixture. Beat well after each addition. (The more beating, the lighter the cake will be.) Pour into well-greased and floured 8 inch or 9 inch cake pans. Bake at 350° for twenty minutes or more, until done.

Variations: substitute flour for the carob and add 1 t orange peel and a handful of raisins.

Carrot Cake

3/4 C oil
1/2 C almond or cashew butter
2-1/2 C whole wheat flour
1/2 t baking soda
1 C chopped walnuts (optional)
1-1/2 C currants (optional)
2 T vanilla
1 t cinnamon
1/2 t nutmeg
1/2 t cloves
3/4 C honey
1/4 C lemon juice
2 t baking powder
1/2 t salt
2 C raw grated carrots
   (or 2 C pulp from juicer plus
   1-1/2 C milk)

Mix oil, honey, almond butter, and lemon juice. Sift dry ingedients together and add them to the wet mixture. Add the vanilla and cinnamon. Blend well and bake in an oiled and floured 8 X 12 inch baking dish at 350° for 45 minutes. Serve plain, with light cream, or frosted with **Broiled topping** or **Cream Cheese Frosting**.

Aunt Agnes' Applesauce Cake

2 C applesauce (or 1 C applesauce and 1 C
    mashed banana)
3/4 C honey
2-1/2 - 3 C flour
1 t each: cloves, cinnamon, nutmeg, ginger
the grated rind of 1 lemon
3/4 - 1 C butter or oil
4 t baking soda
1/2 t salt
9 - 10 dates (optional)
1-1/2 C raisins or currants

Combine all ingredients and bake in a greased and floured loaf pan at 350° for about an hour.

Brave Heron's Gingerbread

3/4 C honey
3/4 C oil
1 C molasses
4 C whole wheat flour (pastry is best)
1-2/3 C sour milk, yogurt, or kefir
1 t salt
1-1/2 t powdered cloves
1 - 2 t baking soda
1 t ginger
1-1/2 t cinnamon

Mix honey, oil and molasses. Sift dry ingredients together. Add flour mixture alternately with milk to honey and molasses. Pour into greased 8 X 12 inch pan. Bake at 350° for 40 minutes.

Almond Yogurt Coffee Cake

2 C sifted flour
1/2 C butter
1 C date sugar
1 C honey
1/3 C sifted flour
1 t soda
1/3 t salt
1/2 t cinnamon
1/4 t cloves
1/4 t nutmeg
pinch of lemon peel
4 T nut butter
1 t lemon juice
1 t vanilla
1 C yogurt or sour cream
1/2 C chopped nuts

Cut butter into 2 C flour until it is like coarse corn meal. Add date sugar until just combined. Set aside 3/4 C of this mixture for the topping. To the rest add 1/3 C flour, soda, cinnamon, cloves, nutmeg, lemon peel and salt. Mix well, and then add the nut butter, honey, lemon juice and vanilla (which have been combined together) and yogurt. Add the nuts to the mixture reserved for topping and sprinkle onto the mixture after pouring it into a 8 X 12 inch pan. Bake at 350° for 45 - 55 minutes.

Variations: you can use oil instead of butter but it tastes a lot better with butter.

FROSTINGS AND TOPPINGS

Cream Cheese Frosting

1 pound cream cheese (softened at
   room temperature)
1 C butter (softened)
3/4 C honey

Cream together cheese and butter, then add honey. Mix well. Makes a lot. Especially with cream cheese which doesn't contain a vegetable gum, the ingredients must be at room temperature. Whips up best with electric beaters, but can be done by hand if you have plenty of time and warm ingredients.

Broiled Topping
(for cakes)

3 T butter, melted
2 T rich milk (omit for thicker topping)
1/2 C shredded coconut (optional)
1/3 C honey
1/4 C chopped nuts

Mix ingredients and spread over top of warm cake. Make slashes in top of cake for mixture to seep into cake. Broil until it bubbles (about 3 minutes). Watch so that it doesn't burn!

Sweet Nut Topping

Mix chopped nuts with maple syrup or melted honey. Drizzle over ice cream, yogurt, pancakes, regular cakes, or pies.

Carob Frosting

1-1/2 C roasted carob powder
3/4 C honey
1 C milk
1 t vanilla

Follow directions for carob syrup, makes enough for double recipe of **Carob Honey Cake**.

Carob Syrup

1/3 - 1/2 C honey
3/4 - 1 C milk (less for stronger, thicker syrup)
3/4 C roasted carob powder, sifted
1 t vanilla or 1/2 t mint extract

Mix honey and milk in a heavy saucepan or double boiler. Add carob powder. Cook slowly until close to desired thickness, stirring frequently (it will thicken more as it cools). For a syrup to flavor milk, cook about 5 minutes (use 3 - 4 t for a glass of milk). For a topping for ice cream, etc., cook about 15 minutes. Remove from heat and stir in flavoring. Store in a covered jar in the refrigerator.

Honey Hard Sauce

Cream 1/3 C butter and gradually beat in 3/4 C honey. Add 1 t lemon juice. Chill.

Heat honey in saucepan and bring to a hard boil. Remove from the heat and stir in the cream and spices. Return to heat, stirring until the sauce just reaches the boiling point. Remove from heat immediately. Serve on pancakes, waffles or fritters. Makes 1-1/3 C.

Lemon Sauce

Combine over low flame, stirring constantly:

1 C honey
2 T arrowroot
1-3/4 C water

In five minutes or when sauce thickens, remove from heat and add:

2 T butter
1/2 t grated lemon rind
1-1/2 t lemon juice
1/8 t salt

Makes about 2 C.

Spiced Cream and Honey Sauce

2/3 C honey
2/3 C heavy cream
1/4 t cinnamon
1/8 t cloves
1/8 t allspice
1/8 t nutmeg

Steamed Pudding Sauce

Heat 1 C honey, 1/2 C butter, and 1/2 C rich milk or cream in a double boiler. When very hot and thoroughly mixed, add 1 t vanilla.

PUDDINGS

Arrowroot Pudding

2 C milk
3 T arrowroot
1/4 C honey
1 t butter
1 t vanilla

Stir together all ingredients. Heat in a saucepan over medium heat, stirring constantly. When the mixture reaches a full boil, remove from heat and stir in vanilla. This is a very plain pudding, and except for small children, will need some brightening up with fruit, flavorings, or the like.

Tapioca Pudding

2/3 C pearl tapioca (first soak 1 hour in
   1-1/2 C water)
1/2 C honey
1/4 t salt
3-3/4 C milk

Combine ingredients in a double boiler. Cook without stirring over rapidly boiling water for 7 minutes. Stir and cook 5 more minutes. Remove from heat. (Tapioca thickens as it cools.)

After removing from heat, stir in: 1 t lemon or orange peel or vanilla; or 1/2 C coconut or slivered almonds; or 1 C chopped dates; or 1 banana crushed and 1 banana diced. Serves 8.

Tapioca Fruit Pudding

1-3/4 C water
2/3 C pearl tapioca (pre-soaked 1 hour in
   1-1/2 C water)
1/2 C honey
1/4 t salt

Boil water in the top of a double boiler over direct heat. Add tapioca, honey and salt. When ingredients are boiling, place over rapidly boiling water. Cook and stir five to ten minutes (until tapioca is clear). Remove from heat and cool slightly.

Fold in:

2-1/2 C crushed pineapple, cooked with small amount of water for 5 minutes and drained. (approximately 1 whole pineapple)
3 T lemon juice or 1-1/2 - 2 C cooked fruit pulp or crushed berries.
1 T lemon juice.

Chill. Serve with cream. Serves 8 easily.

Hasty Pudding

1/3 C molasses
1/3 C honey
1/3 C water
1 C flour
1-1/2 t baking powder
1/2 t salt
1/4 C honey
1/3 C milk
1 t vanilla
1/4 C oil
1/4 C raisins

Make a syrup by combining the molasses, honey and water in a pan and bringing to a boil. Set aside. Mix dry ingredients together, mix unused wet ingredients together and combine the two mixtures, mixing only until smooth.

Pour into oiled 1 quart casserole pan and sprinkle with raisins. Pour boiling syrup over batter. Bake at 350° for 35 - 40 minutes. Serve warm. Yields 5 - 6 servings.

Carob Pudding

4 C milk
1/3 C honey
1 t pero (instant grain drink)
1/2 t salt
1/4 C roasted carob powder
6 T arrowroot
1 t vanilla

Combine 3 C milk, honey, pero, salt and carob in a heavy saucepan or double boiler. Mix arrowroot thoroughly with 1 C milk. Slowly, while stirring frequently, bring mixture in pan to a slow boil. As pudding heats, stir in arrowroot and milk mixture. Stir frequently to avoid lumping, making sure you get the thick stuff off the bottom. Continue cooking at a slow boil for 20 minutes. Remove from heat and stir in vanilla. Let cool until firm. Makes four large servings.

May be frozen for fudgesicles or poured into graham cracker crust for carob creme pie.

CANDIES

Nut Bars

3/4 C honey
1-1/2 C finely chopped nuts (brazils are good, may be part coconut)
1/4 C oil
1/4 - 1/2 t cinnamon

Combine and press into pan. Chill before cutting. Crumbly.

Carob Candy

1/3 C honey
2/3 C nut butter
2 C carob powder
1 C shredded coconut
2 C mixed nuts, chopped

Heat honey and nut butter in double boiler or over low heat until liquid. Add carob; mix well. Stir often to avoid sticking or burning. (Takes some muscle). Add nuts and mix well. Pat into 9 inch square pan. Makes one pan one inch thick.

Honey Spice Nuts

1-1/2 C honey
1 T cinnamon
3 T water
1/2 t salt
1/2 t nutmeg
1/2 t vanilla
3 C — 4-1/2 C nuts, depending on how
   nutty you want it. (Whole or halves,
   walnuts or almonds.)

Combine all ingredients except vanilla and nuts. Cook over medium heat, stirring occasionally until it reaches soft ball stage — about 243°. (To test for soft ball stage, drop a few drops from a spoon into cold water. If it forms into a soft ball, it is done.) Do not overcook. Remove from heat, add vanilla and nuts. Stir until mixture gets creamy. Turn out on greased glass or ceramic plate or pan. Let dry, cut into squares. Makes about 1-1/4 pounds.

Maple Moksha

Pure maple syrup
Vanilla ice cream or yogurt

Mix and enjoy. The deluxe version comes in the form of a banana split topped with chopped nuts.

PIES AND OTHER GOODIES

Oil Pie Dough

For one 10 inch double crust:

3 C whole wheat pastry flour
1/2 t salt
1/2 C oil
about 6 T cold water

For one 9 inch double crust:

2 C whole wheat pastry flour
1/3 t salt
1/3 C oil
4 T cold water

Follow PIE DOUGH DIRECTIONS.

Grandmother's Pie Dough Revisited

2 C whole wheat pastry flour
1 t salt
1/2 to 3/4 C **Butter-Oil Spread**, butter or
   soybean margarine
2 - 4 T ice cold water (the amount will depend
   on air temperature, altitude, amount of
   Butter-Oil Spread and the mood of the cook.)

Follow PIE DOUGH DIRECTIONS.

PIE DOUGH DIRECTIONS

When you start out, everything should be cold: the bowl, the utensils, and all the ingredients. Put the flour and the salt in the cold bowl and mix. Put a hole in the center and add the butter or oil. Cut in with a pastry cutter, a fork, two knives or your hands (working fast) until the mixture is in pieces the size of peas. Add water 1 T at a time (you can make sure it is cold by taking it table-spoonful by tablespoonful from a bowl of water with ice floating in it), mixing very lightly with a fork. Refrigerate until chilled, but not really cold.

Divide into two balls. Roll out between two opened plastic bags or 2 sheets of wax paper. Peel off the plastic every now and then and replace it so that the dough doesn't stick to it too much. Rolling the dough between the sheets of plastic eliminates the need for additional flour, which makes the dough more tender. It also makes the crust easier to flip into the pan. Roll from the center outwards so it doesn't get too thin on the edges.

When it is the right size, peel off one side of the plastic and flip the dough, plastic side up, into the pie pan. Push into the corners and remove the second piece of plastic. Trim on the outside of the pan edge with a sharp knife. Put in the filling. Put top crust on and make vent holes (either with a fork or pastry wheel). Press edges of bottom and top crust together with a fork or pastry wheel and retrim. Bake at 400° for 10 minutes and then lower to 350° and bake until done (40 minutes for soft fruit, 1 hour for apple, etc. Test by inserting a fork to test for tenderness.) If fruit is done before the crust is browned,

put under the broiler to brown and watch very carefully.

Graham Cracker Crust

2 C graham crackers, finely crushed
1/4 C butter, melted
2 T honey
1 T date sugar
1/2 t cinnamon

Graham crackers may be crushed by placing in a bag and rolling with a rolling pin. Mix all ingredients together adding a bit more honey it if won't hold together. Press into a pie tin. Makes one 9 inch pie crust.

BASIC PIE RECIPES

• Any fresh fruit can be used in a pie.

• Juicy ones need thickeners. 1-1/2 - 3 T arrowroot can be stirred into the fruit or 3 - 6 T of pastry flour.

• 1/2 - 3/4 C honey can be poured over the fruit. Date sugar can be substituted for part of this.

• 1 - 2 T lemon juice should be added to sweet fruit.

• To make a tall pie, heap the fruit very high, as it will shrink in cooking.

- Put a cookie sheet or foil underneath the pie in the oven, to catch drips.

- Pies should be cooked immediately so the bottom doesn't get soggy.

- APRICOTS don't need thickener

- VEGETABLE pies can be made with leftover **Curried Vegetables**

- **Apple Pie**: sprinkle 1/4 inch date sugar on the bottom crust. Add sliced apples and an optional layer of raisins if desired. Dribble 1/4 C honey on top and liberally sprinkle with cinnamon, nutmeg and lemon peel. Top with crust.

Pumpkin Pie

4-1/2 C pumpkin, mashed or pureed smooth
  (see below)
2-2/3 C thick milk (part regular and part
  powdered, or evaporated)
2/3 C arrowroot
1 C honey or 1/2 C honey and 1/2 C molasses
1 t cinnamon
1 t ground dried lemon peel
3/4 t mace (or nutmeg)
3/4 t allspice
3/4 t ginger
1/2 t salt
1 T vanilla

Combine all ingredients, beating until smooth. Pour into 2 unbaked pie shells and bake 15 minutes at 425°. Lower oven temperature to 300° and bake 1 to 1-1/2 hours. You can tell when it is done by: 1) the top will turn from shiny to dull all the way to the center. 2) as it bakes it will crack; when it is done, the cracks will go all the way to the center. 3) a clean, room temperature, dull knife stuck into the center will come out fairly clean (but not perfectly). DO BE PATIENT; the pie is worth waiting for.

Variations: Use cream cheese in place of milk. Bake 15 minutes at 425° and then approximately 1 hour at 300°. Or, use sour cream or yogurt in place of all or part of the other dairy products, adjust time accordingly.

HOW TO TURN A PUMPKIN INTO PUMPKIN PUREE

If possible, bake your pumpkin whole at 350° for an hour or so, until tender. (Put on a pan or foil, it may ooze.) This retains the moisture in the pumpkin. After baking, cool until touchable, peel and remove seeds and puree with a potato masher or fork, in a food mill, or in a blender (blender will take just a little at a time). Freeze unneeded pumpkin for future pies.

If the pumpkin is too big to fit in your oven, it can be cut (with a strong arm and a sharp knife) into sections and baked in a covered pan or steamed (steaming adds moisture). Cover the pumpkin when baking it in pieces so it does not dry out. If you don't have a pumpkin, we suggest pureed cooked pumpkin, rather than pumpkin pie filling that is already flavored. Both come in cans.

Purple Pie

1 9-inch pie crust or graham cracker crust
4 frozen bananas
1 pint fresh blackberries
3 fresh ripe bananas

Peel and mash frozen bananas. When thoroughly pureed, smash in the berries, mixing well. Slice the fresh bananas, fold them into the rest of the fruit, and dump the whole mouth watering mess into the pie shell. Return to freezer for a while, until the filling is fairly firm and will hold its shape when cut. May be garnished with whole blackberries, banana slices or strawberry slices. Serves 6 as a dessert and 3 as a main dish.

Variation: For pink pie replace blackberries with strawberries.

Banana "Pies"

Peel bananas and cut crosswise. Roll them in date sugar and cinnamon. Wrap them in oblongs of pie crust and bake 15 minutes at 450°. Serve with lemon sauce.

Raw Cheese Cake Filling

For 1 9-inch pie:

2-1/2 C cream cheese
1-1/4 C yogurt
3 - 4 T honey
1 t vanilla

For 5 10-inch pies:

5 pounds cream cheese
1 quart yogurt
honey to taste
1 T vanilla

Beat cream cheese and yogurt until smooth. If possible use an electric mixer so that mixture becomes light and airy. Add honey and vanilla. Pour into graham cracker crust and refrigerate until firm. Serve chilled.

Baked Cheese Cake

1/2 recipe **Graham Cracker Crust**
1 pound cream cheese
1/2 C honey
1 T arrowroot mixed with 1/4 C water
1 t vanilla
1 t orange juice
1 t lemon juice
1 T honey
1/2 pint sour cream

Line 9-inch pie pan with **Graham Cracker Crust**. Beat together the cream cheese and honey. Mix in the dissolved arrowroot and the flavorings. Pour into the pie crust and bake for 20 minutes at 350°. Meanwhile, mix 1 T honey with 1 pint sour cream. Pour this over pie and then bake for 5 - 7 minutes more. Chill thoroughly, preferably overnight.

Peach Cobbler

1/2 C melted butter
1 C whole wheat flour
1 C milk
1/2 C honey
1 t salt
1/2 t cinnamon
1/2 t nutmeg
1 T baking powder
6 C sliced peaches

Mix all ingredients together in pyrex or earthenware bowl. Bake at 325° for 45 minutes. Serve with yogurt. Makes six generous portions.

Apple Crisp

1/4 C honey
1/2 t cinnamon
1/4 - 1/3 C lemon juice (optional, for use with sweet apples)
pinch salt
1 C raisins (optional)
2-1/2 C rolled oats or granola
1/2 C whole wheat pastry flour
1 T soy flour (optional)
1/4 t salt
1 C date sugar

1/3 C oil
1/3 C chopped nuts (optional)
1/2 t vanilla
3/4 t cinnamon

Fill a 9 X 12 inch pan with grated or finely sliced apples. Stir in the honey, cinnamon, lemon juice, salt and raisins. Mix together the rest of the ingredients and spread over the top of the apples. Sprinkle with a little water. Bake for about 40 minutes at 375°, until the apples are tender. Good served with ice cream.

Variation: Use other fresh fruits or drained canned fruits. The baking time may vary.

ALSO REFER TO . . .

Sweet breads in the **CRACKERS AND BREADS BREADS** section
The **FRUITS** section
Banana Ice Cream
Jyoti's Banana Bread, Almost
Carrot Molasses Muffins
Vanilla Extract

herbs
and spices

HERBS AND SPICES
(and flavorings)

HERBS, SPICES AND FLAVORINGS

Herbs and spices are the seeds, roots, leaves, flowers, and barks of plants that are used for flavoring, teas, beverages, and folk medicine. Natural flavorings are derivatives of herbs or of other plants and fruits (such as lemon peel, vanilla extract, etc.)

EQUIVALENTS: 1/4 t dry herbs is equal to 1 t fresh herbs. An exception is citrus peel, which loses flavor in drying. Use more dried lemon peel when fresh peel is called for in a recipe to compensate for the loss of flavor.

RELEASING OF FLAVOR: Herbs must be cooked (especially dry ones) before they will release much of their flavor into the food. Be careful when you add herbs that you do not add too much because the flavor has not come out yet. If a dish containing herbs is going to be cooked more than an hour, add the herbs for the last hour only, as the flavors will be lost somewhat with more cooking. Fresh ground spices are more potent than ones that have been sitting around for a while. Most of the flavors in herbs come from their oils. Rubbing a leaf herb between your fingers before adding it to a dish or grinding whole herbs in a mortar will help release the flavors. Certain kinds of dishes (like many curries) will allow you to put seeds and whole spices in oil for a few minutes to release the flavor. Care needs to be taken not to overheat them in this way.

STORAGE: Spices and herbs need to be stored in airtight containers to keep in the flavors. They need to be either kept in a dark place (like a cupboard) to keep the sun from leaching the flavor and developing moisture inside the jars, or in dark jars or containers. Spices and herbs deteriorate when exposed to light and oxygen.

DRYING: You can dry your own herbs by hanging upside down, with the bunch tied together with string. Herb books have more information about this.

BUYING HERBS AND SPICES: The cheapest way to buy herbs is in bulk, from an herb store or a co-op. When you buy packaged brands in stores, you are paying for the display, the fancy container, the advertising, the cost of packaging into a small bottle, etc. (not to mention the perhaps excessive profit). There are also mail order places through which you can order spices and herbs. You will be amazed at the price difference between bulk and packaged herbs.

In this section we have included some herb and spice blends and flavoring recipes which are called for in this cookbook and which you will find helpful in your own recipes.

NOTE ABOUT SPICES: everyone has their favorites. We decided not to repeat the true-but-tired advice which many cookbooks contain in regards to what spice to use with what food. The best way we know to learn about spices is to use them any way you want to. It's really pretty difficult to make a mistake in spicing a dish, and those that can be made aren't particularly vulnerable to rules. Some basic suggestions:

• Grind herbs and spices immediately before use.

• Keep tasting.

• If you don't know which herb to use, try smelling them and see if they smell like they should go into your ingredients

HERB TEAS

Herb teas are often used in medicinal ways. We have decided to refer people to the many excellent herb books which are available for information about the medicinal uses of herbs. It would be difficult to give much useful information here without being in danger of getting into a full-blown herbal manual.

Many herb teas teaste excellent and can be enjoyed without reference to their medicinal properties. There are several different ways to prepare herb teas. Here are some general ideas on that subject.

WARM WATER is necessary in order to extract the flavor from the herbs. Sun tea is made by leaving herbs and water in a clean jar (with a lid on it) in the sun for most of a day. The more common practice is to boil the water on the stove, add the herbs, and then steep in a covered container. BOILING THE WATER AFTER THE HERBS HAVE BEEN ADDED IS NOT RECOMMENDED. It results in a bitter tea.

USE 1 - 3 T herbs per C water depending on how strong a flavor is desired.

STEEP (in a covered container) for 10 - 30 minutes. Medicinal properties are generally not extracted in less than 20 - 30 minutes. Some herbalists recommend letting the herbs soak in the water for hours after the original

STEEP (in a covered container) for 10 - 30 minutes. Medicinal properties are generally not extracted in less than 20 - 30 minutes. Some herbalists recommend letting the herbs soak in the water for hours after the original heating.

STRAIN herbs out of tea.

SERVE WARM OR COLD, with or without honey and/or lemon juice.

FLOWERS should not be steeped at high temperatures or for prolonged periods of time, as they will release their bitter flavor under those conditions.

BARKS generally require more steeping than other types of herbs.

Here are a few of the many popular tea herbs: Alfalfa, Anise, Camomile, Comfrey, Hibiscus, Lavender, Lemon grass, Licorice, Peppermint, Red clover, Red Rasberry, Rosehips, Sassafras, Spearmint.

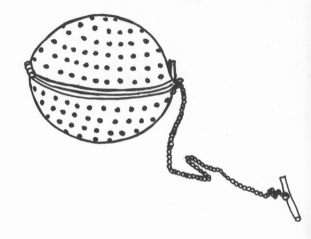

Vanilla Extract

2/3 C warm water
4 - 8 vanilla beans (depending on strength desired)
2 t lecithin (as an emulsifier)

Soak beans for several hours. Blend water and beans in blender. Bring to a boil in a covered pan and immediately turn off. Put in a jar, cover tightly and let stand overnight or longer. Strain into blender, mix in lecithin in blender at low speed. Pour into bottles, cap tightly. Must be refrigerated. May be slightly less potent than alcohol based extracts purchased at the store.

Vegie-Herb Sauce
(To replace Tamari and similar flavorings)

1 carrot, grated
1 sweet potato, peeled and grated
1 parsnip, grated
3 T honey
1/2 C cold water
1/4 t each ground cloves, allspice,
   and cinnamon
3 bay leaves
1 T salt or vegetable salt

Mix vegetables. Spread 1/3 of them on the bottom of an unoiled baking pan. Drizzle with 1 T honey. Repeat with vegetables and honey twice again. Bake at 450° oven until the mixture becomes dark brown. Transfer to top of stove. Add water, spices and salt. Cover. Simmer, stirring occasionally, until mixture forms a rich, brown, thick syrup. Strain. Keep refrigerated and tightly capped in the refrigerator, or reheat and seal in hot, sterilized jars. Use in soup stocks etc. as a substitute for soy sauce (tamari). About 1/2 t is equal to 1 T tamari. Add salt to taste in recipes after adding **Vegie-Herb Sauce.**

Italian Seasoning

1/3 t thyme
1/3 t basil
1/2 t oregano
pinch of tarragon
pinch of cumin (optional)

Simple Salad Herbs

Equal parts:

Oregano
Basil
Thyme
Optional: 1/4 to 1/2 part ground cumin,
   savory, dill, or parsley.

Salad Herbs

1 part each: lemon thyme, summer savory
4 parts each: marjoram, basil, tarragon,
   parsley, dried celery tops, chervil.
1 part each: oregano, basil, thyme.
optional: 1/4 - 1/2 part cumin and/or dill

Vegetable Herbs
(For steamed vegetables or rice)

1 t each: marjoram, basil, chervil, parsley.
Pinch: savory, thyme

Soup Herbs

2 parts each: parsley, chervil, basil, marjoram,
   celery tops
1 part each: thyme, summer savory, sage,
   rosemary, dried ground lemon peel

Garam Marsala
(used in Indian cooking)

2 cardamom pods, seeded
30 whole peppercorns
1 two-inch piece of cinnamon stick
1 t whole cloves
2 t whole cumin seed (optional)

    Grind as finely as possible with mortar and pestle, nut grinder or blender.

Curry Powder

5 cloves
6 cardamom seeds
1 1-inch piece cinnamon (thick)
1/2 t black mustard seed
1/2 t cumin seed
1 t turmeric
1 t salt
1 t coriander powder
1 T finely minced fresh ginger

    Use 5 t to one gallon of vegetables or fruit, or 1 - 1-1/2 t to one quart.

Gomasio

Sea salt
Sesame seeds (5 parts of seeds to 1 part salt, or experiment and make your own ratio)

    Wash seeds to remove dirt: Put in pot and pour cold water over seeds. Agitate and pour into strainer. Do this four or five times; on last washing, pour last of water and seeds out slowly so dirt stays in the pot.

    Toast salt: put in a heavy frying pan over high flame; move salt around with wooden spoon or paddle for five minutes or so. Then put salt in suribachi (a serrated or grooved grinding bowl; you can also use a mortar and pestle, or a bowl and spoon. Don't use a blender; the oils will not be properly released.

    Toast the seeds in frying pan on high heat, moving them around quickly for ten to fifteen minutes. They are done when you can easily crush them between your fingers. Put seeds in suribachi with the salt.

    Grind with wooden pestle until 80% of the seeds have been reduced to a fine powder. Store in tightly covered jar. Make weekly or more frequently (gets rancid). Sesame salt can be purchased in natural food stores, but homemade is different and some folks like it better.

Cleansing Yogi Tea

To make an 8-ounce cup, start with 1-1/4 C water and add:

4 whole cardamom seed pods
6 whole peppercorns
1 slice fresh ginger root
3 whole cloves
1/2 stick cinnamon

    Boil 20 - 30 minutes. Serve hot or cold with milk or honey. (One Margii recommends: Put on all your clothes and drink this tea in front of an open window in the cold air until your sweat smells of ginger. Cleans out your bloodstream and pores! Don't do it more often than once a week or it will lose its effectiveness.)

CANNING AND PRESERVING

CANNING AND PRESERVING

This section contains some basic information about the long-term storage of food. Step-by-step instructions for canning fruit, and making jams and jellies are included, along with briefer discussions of pressure canning, freezing food, storing fresh produce, and drying fruits and vegetables. More information about food storage can be found in the **KITCHEN WAYS** section.

CANNING

Canning (or perhaps it should be called "jarring," since that is what home canners use) is a method by which food and its container are sterilized. The high temperatures involved in the process kill microorganisms which might cause spoilage or disease, and also de-activate all enzymes in the food, thereby arresting the natural processes of decay.

Canned food may be kept at room temperature, allowing for easy storage throughout the year, and eliminating the cost of constant refrigeration which would otherwise be necessary. Canned foods are easy to transport. The quality of the food is reduced by canning: since all the enzymes are killed, it is, in a sense, lifeless food. Fresh food has much more life-energy, but it is, of course, not always available or affordable. Canning is one way to preserve summer's surplus for winter use.

There are two basic ways to can food. The WATER BATH method involves a low temperature process suitable for fruits (including tomatoes) and certain other foods which have a high acid content. Water bath canning doesn't require a lot of fancy equipment or jars, and good results can be realized even by those with little or no experience.

PRESSURE CANNING is a high temperature process which can be used to preserve vegetables and some other foods. Low acid foods require processing at very high temperatures to kill the enzymes and microorganisms in them, so canning jars and a pressure canner are used. Since certain of these microorganisms can be very poisonous to human beings, it is necessary that great care be taken in canning low acid foods. Before they are eaten, foods that are pressure canned at home must be brought to a boil and cooked for 20 minutes or used in a dish that requires cooking at a high temperature for 30 minutes or more (e.g., casseroles).

When deciding to get involved in canning, it is important to understand the expenditure of time, energy and resources that it requires. All produce must be of good quality, and a fair amount of preparation of the produce is required before it can be canned. The canning process itself requires a good amount of energy. It is important not to overwork yourself or try to take short-cuts. If you over-extend yourself, it will show in the results. In hot weather it is good to work in the early morning or late in the evening to avoid over-heating yourself.

CANNING EQUIPMENT

JARS: The most readily available jars are mason jars with a lid (seal) and band. Check even new ones for cracks or flaws in the jars or chipped or cracked lips. The band should be flawless, without dents or deformations. Lids should have no imperfections in the rubber or bashes around the sides. DO NOT REUSE LIDS. Look at the inside of a used one and you will see the mark made by the jar's lip when sealed. If you tried to reseal it the lip would be in a different place and the warping generally caused by opening would keep it from sealing. Discard all jars, lids and bands which are not perfect, as they will most likely cause the jar to not seal. It isn't worth the danger and wasted food to try and make inadequate equipment do the job.

Jars do not need to be sterilized for canning: the water bath or pressure canner does that during the course of canning. When hot packing food, it is wise to have the jar warm. Never pour boiling hot food into a jar on a cold metal surface, as it will crack. Set the jars on a towel or a rack when filling with hot food, and preheat them with warm water first.

When choosing new jars think about what you are going to can, and for whom. Do you eat a lot of fruit at one time or just a little (half-gallon versus pint jars)? If you think you might be using the jars for freezing at some time, get tapered jars that give the frozen food room to expand without breaking the jar. The wide mouth jars are more convenient for cold packing large pieces of fruit, as you can reach further down into the jar, but the lids are substantially more expensive.

By all means check with your friends and relatives to see if you can scrounge any free jars. If you are scrounging jars, choose those with lips that screw into a wide or regular mouth band. Any such jar can be used for water bath canning (it's best to use real mason canning jars for pressure canning because of the greater stress involved).

LIDS: There are a couple different kinds of lids on the market. The ones with enamel inside are less apt to corrode or discolor from the action of acid of the food inside the jar. This is particularly important with tomatoes.

A WATER BATH CANNER or a pot must be large enough to allow jars on a rack to be covered with 1 inch of water, while still leaving room for the water to boil.

A PRESSURE CANNER is needed for canning vegetables and other low-acid foods. Pressure saucepans can be used for canning pint jars, if they are set to maintain 10 pounds pressure. Check the pan carefully to make sure it is functioning properly before investing time and energy in preparing food. Authorities recommend that when you are using a saucepan type pressure cooker that you lengthen the processing time to 1-1/2 times the recommended amount of time. If you use a pressure canner that is old, take it in and have it checked to make sure that it maintains 10 pounds pressure and all seals and rubber parts are in good shape. A dealer can tell you where this can be done. Always follow the manufacturer's instructions carefully.

The kettle or canner needs to have a RACK on the bottom so the jars don't touch the area where the heat is entering the pan. Theoretically, they should not touch the sides or each other either, but usually if they slide together nothing disastrous will happen.

Other utensils you will most likely need are: a SHARP PARING KNIFE for peeling and cutting out bad spots; a BOWL OF WATER for rinsing hands during preparation so you don't drip sticky stuff all across the room; a CONTAINER FOR COMPOST to put all the skins, scraps, etc. in; a LADLE or CUP for putting syrup or hot pack fruit in jars; MEASURING CUPS; A PAN FOR SYRUP; A TABLE KNIFE to remove air bubbles with (see below); and HOT PADS (mitts are best).

Optional utensils include a FUNNEL to control spillage when putting food into jars, TONGS for lifting jars out of hot water if the hot pack method is used, and JAR LIFTERS for lifting jars out of boiling water-bath (these are especially handy if your rack doesn't have handles; if you have neither you will have to ladle or suck the water out with a baster until there is enough room to easily and securely grasp jars).

It is a common fallacy that fruit not good enough for eating fresh is good enough to be preserved. Preserving can maintain flavor and texture but not improve it, so if the fruit isn't excellent, don't bother canning it. Another common fallacy is that fruit to be canned should be slightly green. Slightly green fruit will maintain its shape better so it is prettier to look at; however, it does not have full flavor, and more sweetener will need to be used.

There are two basic methods for packing fruit for canning; hot pack and cold or raw pack. First we will describe the steps in the two methods. Following that will be a chart that shows which method is best to use for different types of fruit.

HOT PACKING FRUIT:

- (1) Prepare a canning syrup of 2 parts liquid (water and/or juice) to 1 part honey.

- (2) Cover fruit with syrup and bring to a boil.

- (3) Using a slotted spoon (one with holes in it), pack fruit into the jars hot.

- (4) Then fill with syrup (1/4 inch from top for pints, 1/2 inch for quarts, 3/4 inch for half-gallons.)

Many authorities say that pricking whole, unpeeled fruit will prevent the fruit from bursting inside the jar, but we haven't found this always to be so. Follow PROCESSING

INSTRUCTIONS FOR HOT OR COLD PACKED FRUIT times given on the QUICK REFERENCE CHART.

COLD PACKING FRUIT:

- (1) Prepare syrup (directions follow) and keep warm.

- (2) Peel fruit if necessary (chart will give guidelines). Some fruits will need to be blanched in order to be peeled. To blanch fruit, bring a pan of water to a boil. Dip fruit in for 30 - 60 seconds; remove, and place in cold water. The fruit can be placed on a fork or in a basket or strainer for easy dipping. The skin will peel right off after the fruit has been blanched. Cut fruit in half and remove pit or core. Some fruits should be cut in smaller pieces (see chart).

- (3) Fill the jar with fruit, putting half of a piece of fruit cut side down in the middle of the bottom and then spiraling fruit around and up, overlapping, cut side down, putting as much fruit as possible into the jar, stopping 3/4 inch from the top.

- (4) Fill with syrup to 1/4 inch from the top in pint jars, 1/2 inch for quart and 3/4 inch for half gallons. (This is "headspace.")

- (5) Take a wide bladed table knife and insert through the middle of the fruit to the bottom of the jar. Twist slightly and tap jar gently. This expells air bubbles. Then put knife down between the jar and the fruit to any air bubbles so they are released up the knife.

- (6) Add more syrup if necessary to be the correct distance from the top.

PROCESSING INSTRUCTIONS FOR HOT OR COLD PACKED FRUIT

- (1) with a moist, clean rag, clean the lips of the the jars. Any food reamining on the lip will prevent the jar from sealing.

- (2) Put on a new clean lid and screw band on firmly.

- (3) Put jars on rack in a canning kettle 2/3 full of water. If you are using jars that are not mason canning jars, start out with warm water at this stage so the quick change in temperature will not break the jars. Otherwise use very hot water. If necessary, add water until it covers the jars by 1 inch. Heat water to boiling and then continue boiling for the time listed in the following chart. Start timing from the point when the water reaches a rolling boil, and the whole top is in bubbles.

- (4) After food has been processed, remove from the water bath. Let cool on a rack, away from drafts.

TESTING FOR SEAL

When cold, test for seal: hear the seal by tapping it with a spoon when the jar is cold. A clear, ringing sound means a seal. You can see the seal. If the lid is curved inward, the jar is sealed. You can feel the seal by pressing the center of the lid. If it is down and will not move, it is sealed. The bands can be removed after 24 hours. It is very important to determine whether the seal has been made. Unsealed jars will eventually result in dangerously contaminated food. If you do not have a seal, either use the food within a few days (store in refrigerator until used) or reprocess with a new lid.

CANNING SYRUPS

A syrup composed of liquid and sweetener is used on fruits that are canned. The liquid is needed for the jar to seal and the sweetening keeps the liquid from leeching out the flavor as plain water does.

One part honey to three parts water makes a nice, light canning syrup sweet enough, yet not too sweet for most fruits. For fruits that pack more densely in jars (such as peaches), a sweeter syrup can be used, as sweet as equal parts water and honey.

Syrups used can also be spiced with orange or lemon peel chunks, cinnamon or other sweet spices. Use about 1 t ground spice per quart of canning syrup. Whole spices may be used by placing them in each jar with the fruit or simmering them in the syrup and removing them before using it. The flavor will be fuller if the spice is in the jar with the fruit. A small stick of cinnamon or 2 - 3 cloves is about right for a quart jar.

Any sweetener can be used. Honey is mentioned most here, but sorghum, molasses or the like can be used, though each results in a different flavor.

The water in a canning syrup can be replaced with fruit juice either from the fruit being canned (e.g., blackberries canned in blackberry juice) or some other fruit (peaches canned in plum juice, cherries canned in apple juice). The syrup is made the same way as with water. Fruit can be canned without sweetener, if you use fruit juice.

Don't throw away left-over canning syrup. It can be refrigerated until you can again, or canned with your last batch for the day, and saved until it is needed.

THE PROCEDURE FOR MAKING SYRUP IS AS FOLLOWS: Combine liquid, honey and spices in a pan large enough for the honey to foam up some. Bring to a simmer and keep hot all the time you are canning with it.

INSTRUCTIONS FOR INDIVIDUAL FRUITS

It is generally advisable (especially with the rising cost and increasing unavailability of canning jars) to get as much food into a jar as possible. Therefore, in the instructions for canning fruit that follow, some fruits are recommended for hot packing and some for raw or cold packing because these are the ways we have found most effective in packing large amounts of that particular fruit in the containers.

250

Fruit	Amount which will fit in quart jar	Pack	Processing Time (minutes)		Recommended Procedures
Apples	2-1/2 - 3 pounds	hot pack in apple	Pints: 15 Qts: 15		Peel, cut into fourths, core, bring to boil in cheap apple juice for 3 mins., add cinnamon and other spices, if desired.
Applesauce	4 C	hot pack	10		
Apricots	2-1/2 pounds	raw (cold) pack	Pints: 25 Qts: 30		Pack unpeeled, but pitted.
Berries (not strawberries)	2 - 4 pints	raw pack	Pints: 10 Qts: 15		
Cherries	2 - 3 pounds	hot pack	15		
Nectarines Peaches	2 - 3 pounds	raw pack	Cling Pints: 25 Qts: 30 Freestone Pints: 20 Qts: 25		Blanch, remove peel, pit; orange peel chunks and cinnamon may be added.
Pears	2 - 3-1/2 pounds	raw pack	Pints: 20 Qts: 25		Peel and core. 1-1/2 t ginger per quart of canning liquid or very strong peppermint tea can be used.
Plums Prunes	2 - 2-1/2 pounds	hot pack	15		
Rhubarb	1 - 2 pounds	hot pack	10		Cut in 1/2 inch lengths, add 1/2 C honey to each quart. Let stand 3 - 4 hours for juice to evaporate. Bring to boil. The best rhubarb is picked in the spring.
Tomatoes	2-1/2 - 3-1/2 pounds	hot pack	15		Blanch, peel, bring to a boil. No syrup. To each quart add 1 t salt and 2 t lemon juice (the lemon juice is important to prevent bocculism)
Tomato sauce or paste		hot pack	15		Prepare according to recipes in this book. Add 1 t salt and 2 t lemon juice per quart.

Tomato Juice

9 pounds tomatoes or 20 cups
   chopped tomatoes
1 T lemon juice
1/4 t salt per pint

Cook tomatoes until soft, stirring frequently
to prevent them from sticking. Put through
food mill. Return 12 C tomatoes to kettle and
bring to a boil. Add 1 T lemon juice. Pour into
jars, leaving 1/2 inch headspace. Add 1/4 t salt
to pints, 1/2 to quarts.

Process pints 10 minutes, quarts 15 minutes
in boiling water bath. Yields 6 pints. Note:
1/2 t lemon juice per pint helps insure that
the low-acid tomatoes which are popular
these days will be acid enough to be safe.

Tomato Mincemeat

3 pounds tomatoes (may be green tomatoes)
1 lime
1 orange
2 cups (packed) date sugar
1-1/2 C raisins
1/4 C lemon juice
1 t salt
1 t cinnamon
1/2 t cloves
1/4 t allspice
1/4 t ginger
1/2 t nutmeg

Grind tomatoes, lime and orange on medium
blade of food grinder. Pour mixture into a

4 quart pan. Stir remaining ingredients in and
heat mixture to boiling. Reduce heat. Simmer
uncovered over low heat stirring occasionally
1-1/2 hours. Can leaving 1 inch at top. Process
10 minutes.

251

Pickled Figs

Fresh figs (about 70)
1 gallon water
small handful salt
2 C vinegar
4 C water
12 C honey
spice bag containing 2 small boxes broken
   stick cinnamon and 2/3 C whole cloves
sterile jars

Wash figs and leave stems on. Make a brine
of one gallon water and the salt. Put as many
figs in as will still be covered. Let stand overnight and wash next morning. Boil together
2 C vinegar, 4 C water, 12 C honey and the
spice bag. Put figs in and boil 15 minutes.
Set aside and repeat boiling for 3 mornings.
Move the spice bag around each morning.
On the 4th morning bring to a boil and can in
hot sterile jars. If you don't have enough syrup
to cover figs, add some boiling water to last
few jars.

PRESSURE CANNING

Canning is not usually the best way to preserve vegetables. Better tasting results can be obtained when the vegetables are dried or frozen (instructions later in this section). Detailed information about canning vegetables can be found in several of the books and pamphlets listed in the bibliography of this section. We have not included that information here, because we weren't certain that it would be of interest to the majority of readers. Here are the basic instructions for canning a few recipes from this book. (Be sure to become familiar with the procedures for water bath canning, because that knowledge is assumed here.)

Spaghetti Sauce: Follow recipe in this cookbook. Fill canning jars 1/2 inch from the top with the hot mixture. Clean lips, put on lids and bands. Set in the pressure canner on the rack. Fill with water 3/4 way up the sides of the jars. When pressure builds up to 10 pounds, maintain the pressure and process for 45 minutes. Let the pressure go down slowly and remove jars when it is gone. Check for seal when cool. Cook for 20 minutes or more at a boil or 30 minutes or more in the oven before using in case of contamination resulting from poor canning procedures, or a lack of a good seal. Be sure to read the information on CANNING EQUIPMENT in this section.

To can **Cranberry Pudding** or **Boston Brown Bread**, fill the jars 1/2 full with raw batter. Process for 1 hour at 10 pounds. Use wide-mouthed, tapered jars.

JAMS AND JELLIES

WHEN USING HONEY IN JAMS and the like, (1) use a large kettle as honey tends to foam; (2) cook slightly longer than called for in sugar recipes to compensate for the extra moisture in honey, if you want the same consistency.

PECTIN is what causes the jelly or jam to jell. There is relatively more pectin in unripe fruit than in ripe fruit. It is concentrated right under the peel. You can test fruit juice to see how much pectin it contains by adding 1 t of cooked fruit juice to 1 T of rubbing alcohol (70% alcohol). Stir slightly to mix, but don't taste. Juices rich in pectin will form a jelly-like mass that can be picked out. Juices low in pectin will form only a few pieces of this material. If the juice is low in pectin, add commercial pectin or mix with another juice high in pectin (see, for example the use of apple peels in **Grape Apple Jelly**.) If you want to guess how much commercial pectin is needed, use a sample cupful of fruit and measure in pectin and mix well until your alcohol test is positive, and add corresponding amounts to the rest of the juice.

BOTTLING THE JAM: Boil your jars to sterilize them. Remove from boiling water when your jam or jelly is bubbling hot and completely cooked. As you remove each bottle, immediately fill with the bubbling jam. Clean around the lid and add a thin layer of melted but not-too-hot paraffin. When cooler add another thin layer. Don't move until really cool. Store the jars in a cool, dark, dry place. If you have to move them during the year, it is best to seal in canning jars instead of using paraffin, as paraffin can melt and allow mold and bacteria to enter. Generally, if mold develops on the top of your jam or jelly, remove it and you can eat the rest of the jam that has not been touched by the mold. The sweetening itself (especially honey) and the acid of the fruit act as preservatives of sorts; however, the paraffin is needed to keep out bacteria.

TO TEST FOR THE JELLING POINT one can either test for consistency, or use a method of cooling which is slow but fairly reliable. You can test by dipping a spoon in the jelly and watching how the liquid runs off. As the liquid reaches the jelling point it will first slide off in two drops, then as it gets just right, the drops will run together and run off in a flake or sheet from the side of the spoon. Remove the jelly from the heat at once. A third way is to put a little of the jelly on a plate and put it in the refrigerator. If it jells in a few minutes it is done. You must remove the jelly from the heat while doing this so you don't overcook it. Perhaps this is best for jellies that the spoon method has been used on, to double check. If it doesn't jell, reheat the jelly until a test is positive.

apple peels and cores
grape juice
honey

Fill a pan with apple peelings and cores, preferably from cooking apples (green transparents or not-very-ripe apples). Add grape juice until you can barely see it through the apples. Cook slowly until apples are very soft. Place in a pillow case or muslin bag and let the juice drip out. Squeeze out the last juice (the more you get out, the higher the jelling ability of the mixture, but it causes cloudiness in the jelly). Measure the juice and add 1 C honey for every 4 C juice. Cook very slowly until it slakes off the spoon (see description immediately above). This may take all day.

Cherry Jam

3-1/2 pounds sweet cherries, pitted (7-1/3
   C pitted cherries)
1-1/2 C honey

Grind the cherries and juice into a large or medium bladed food mill. Add honey (the amount could vary according to sweetness of cherries). Cook at low boil or simmer until thick, stirring occasionally to prevent sticking. Remember it will appear less thick when hot than when cool. Try setting a little saucer of it in the freezer or refrigerator to test (see TO TEST FOR JELLING POINT). When cooked enough, remove from heat and let the foam form. Skim it off. Pour into jars and cap with seals and paraffin (see BOTTLING THE JAM).

Royal Ann cherries are the best for canning and jam. Bings tend to have a tough skin when cooked.

Pear Apple Jam

4 C peeled diced pears
4 C peeled diced apples
4 C honey
5 t lemon juice
grated rind of one lemon

Mix all ingredients thoroughly and bring to a boil. Boil, stirring often for 30 minutes. Remove from heat and let stand a couple hours or overnight to plump fruit. Bring back to a boil, turn down heat to a simmer and simmer until thick — about 1 hour. Pour into hot sterilized jars and seal. Yield: 6 cups.

Orange Marmalade

4 C orange peel, sliced thinly
4 C orange pulp, cut in chunks
1 C lemon, sliced thinly, seeds removed
4-3/4 C water
5 C honey
1/4 t salt

Add water to fruit. Bring to a boil and simmer for 5 minutes. Cover and let stand 12 to 16 hours. Bring to a boil and cook rapidly until peel is tender (about 1 hour). Measure fruit mixture and add salt and 3/4 cup honey for each cup fruit mixture. Cook rapidly until the jelling point is reached (221° F). Stir frequently to prevent sticking. Pour into hot sterilized jars and seal.

Pear Conserve

15 C chunked, peeled and cored pears
  (5 - 8 pounds whole)
4 - 5 C honey (depends on sweetness of
  pears and how sweet you like your jam)
2 - 2-1/2 C raisins
1/4 C dried orange rind or about 1/2 C
  fresh, cut fine
1/2 C orange juice
1/4 C lemon juice

Mix all ingredients. Bring to a boil. Lower heat and simmer until thick and pears are cooked, but not completely mushy. Stir frequently as raisins stick to bottom. Pour into hot sterilized jars and seal with canning lids or paraffin.

Blackberry Jam

8 C blackberries, cooked and smashed
4 C honey
1/4 C pectin

Bring to a boil (which won't stir down) and boil for 4 minutes. Pour into hot sterilized jars and seal.

Spiced Pear Butter

6 pounds firm ripe Anjou or Bosc pears
  (about 12 large)
1/4 C lemon juice
1-1/2 t ground cinnamon
1/4 t ground cloves
3-1/2 C honey

Wash, quarter, and core, but do not peel pears. In a 6-quart or larger pan combine pears, water, and lemon juice; cover and simmer until fruit is soft, 20 to 30 minutes. Whirl mixture in a blender (a small portion at a time) or puree in a food mill. Return to pan and add the cinnamon, cloves, and honey. Simmer, uncovered, stirring more frequently as the mixture thickens, until mixture is very thick and reduced to about 8 cups — it takes about 1-1/2 hours.

Ladle boiling hot butter into hot clean canning jars to within 1/4 inch of top. Slide a spatula between jar and butter, wipe rim; then set on hot lid and screw on ring band.

Place filled jars on a rack in a canning kettle half-filled with hot water. Add boiling water to cover jars with an inch of water. Cover kettle. For half-pints or pints, process 10 minutes after water boils. Remove jars and cool. Makes about 4 pints.

Spiced Apple Butter

Follow the recipe above, using 6 pounds (about 12) apples and add 1/2 cup orange or apple juice.

Cranberry Conserve

1 quart cranberries
1 orange
1 C raisins
1 C honey
1 C chopped nuts
1 t cinnamon
1/2 t cloves
1/2 t allspice

Wash cranberries. Cover with water and cook until tender. Then press through a sieve. Peel orange and put peel through food chopper. Dice peeled orange. Mix cranberries, chopped raisins, orange, orange peel and spices together and cook slowly for 10 minutes. Then add honey and simmer very gently until thick. Add nuts to mixture a few minutes before cooking is complete. Pour into sterilized jars to within 1/2 inch of the tops. Put on caps, screw bands firmly tight. Process in boiling water bath for 10 minutes. Yields 3-1/2 pints.

FREEZING

Frozen fruits and vegetables taste better and are more nutritious than canned food. However, one needs to be aware of the cost of freezing food. First, there is the initial investment in the freezer, and secondly, there is the cost of running it all year round. The food can easily be ruined if the electrical power goes out for any period of time. A small refrigerator-freezer is practical only for freezing small amounts of things for a short time. It is handy to use for prepared casseroles, baked goodies and the like, though.

GENERAL TIPS

• Freeze in amounts that are easy to use. Smaller portions defrost faster, and waste is reduced by thawing only the amount you can use right away.

• Freeze food immediately: don't store in refrigerator first.

• Package food in airtight, moisture-proof packages to prevent flavor and moisture loss and the transference of flavors, but leave room for expansion of food during freezing.

• Date packages and label: freezing will disguise the contents.

• Don't refreeze food, since you will lose nutrients and there is a chance of bacterial infection.

• Plastic bags inside washed milk cartons make good freezing containers if the bags are tightly sealed. Jars must flare towards the top or they will crack when the food expands during freezing.

There are 4 STEPS IN FREEZING VEGETABLES: (1) blanching (peas and corn do not need to be blanched), (2) cooling, (3) drying and packaging, (4) excluding air from the package and freezing.

COOKIES and BREADS can be frozen in plastic bags after they have cooled. Don't keep these things over 6 months in the freezer. All prepared foods (except pies) should be thawed at room temperature in their airtight containers to prevent drying out.

CORN can be frozen on the cob by either husking and putting in sealed plastic bags, or leaving the husk on and freezing.

BLANCHING is sometimes an advisable first step in freezing foods. It can be accomplished by preparing the fruit or vegetables, (cleaning, cutting and the like), setting it in a colander or strainer and dipping it into a pan of rapidly boiling water for 1 - 2 minutes to kill the enzymes and bacteria in it. Remove from water and dip into cold water to cool it off quickly. DRAIN or DRY by dumping on cloths, hanging to drain or the like. Package into plastic bags or containers. Some people with very cold freezers like to spread the food out on cookie sheets so that each piece of vegetable dries individually, and then package them the next day. When packaging get rid of as much air as possible, and SEAL TIGHTLY.

The following chart shows HOW LONG VEGIES CAN BE FROZEN without a great quality change:

30°F	quality will change after		5 days
25°	"	"	10 days
20°	"	"	3 weeks
15°	"	"	6 weeks
10°	"	"	3 months
5°	"	"	6 months
0°	"	"	1 year

HERBS can be frozen to be used in cooking later. Examples are parsley, chopped green pepper and the like. Try others and see how they work.

PREPARED FOODS can be cooked in larger amounts than needed and then frozen for a quick meal or dessert later. It is recommended that prepared foods be used in 2 - 4 months after freezing. After cooking or baking, let food cool to room temperature. Package in airtight containers, leaving headspace for expansion. PIES can be frozen better raw. Bake without thawing for 15-20 minutes in a preheated 450° oven and then at 375° until done. Pack **Pizzas** on cardboard covered with wax paper and put the whole thing in a tightly sealed plastic bag. CASSEROLES such as **Eggplant Parmesan** are best frozen in the container they were baked in and reheated in that container.

STORING FRESH FOOD

The easiest way to store fresh vegetables is to LEAVE THEM IN THE GARDEN. Except in the very coldest areas, things like Jerusalem Artichokes, root vegetables, kale, collards, parsnips, salsify, brussel sprouts, etc. can all easily be left in the ground for winter storage. A thick mulch of straw or other suitable material will protect the vegetables from the cold (put them under a "blanket," in bed for the winter).

A ROOT CELLAR of some sort is the other simple way to store fresh produce. It involves some original investment of time and resources in establishing good conditions and containers for storage, but the preparation of the produce itself is very simple. Vegetables like potatoes, sweet potatoes, yams, beets, turnips, parsnips, rutabagas, salsify, carrots, kohlrabi, etc., can all be stored for long periods in a properly designed basement, cellar or outbuilding storage area, or even pits built to the proper specifications. Even foods such as broccoli, cauliflower, cucumbers, cabbage, squash, apples, winter squash, figs, cranberries, pears, and melons can be stored for limited periods of time. A number of books and pamphlets are available that give good instructions for designing storage areas. One is **Storing Vegetables and Fruits**, another is **Stocking Up** (see BIBLIOGRAPHY, this section). See also **KITCHEN WAYS**.

DRYING FOODS

There are several methods for drying fruits and vegetables which apply themselves best to certain kinds of produce and give varying products afterwards. We will quickly go through different ways to dry foods. You can adjust these to your own produce, climate and needs. More information is available in other resources (books, pamphlets and magazines) which will be of help to you if you really want to get into drying foods.

FRUIT LEATHERS are made by pureeing fruits such as apricots, plums, and peaches and straining the pulp through a fine strainer to remove any pieces of skin. Pour the puree thinly onto cookie sheets with plastic on them and set in a flat place in the sun to dry. Bring in at night. If the sun fails to shine, the leather can be dried in the oven at 150°, leaving the door open at least part of the time to let the moisture escape. It is dry enough when it peels up easily from the plastic. Can be stored rolled up in airtight packaging for a couple of months at room temperature. Will hold about 4 months in the refrigerator, or a year in the freezer. Good for snacks. Sweetener can be added when pureeing.

PIECE DRYING: Fruit and vegetables which are to be dried should be in good condition. The blemishes need to be cut out. Fruit should be ripe, but not over-ripe. Wash the produce and dry it with a towel. Figs, grapes, prunes, plums and very small vegetables can be dried whole; others should be pitted (if applicable) and cut into pieces. Really juicy fruits need to be cut into small pieces; apples, pears and peaches need to be quartered. The fruit or vegetables can be layered one layer deep, not touching, on a double screened drying tray to let air in and keep insects out. Take trays indoors at night. Solar dryers are available and can speed up the process. Make a simple one by elevating a piece of glass over the drying food at an angle to catch the sun. Write to "Organic Gardening and Farming" magazine to get the best angle for this in your area. Stuff can be dried in the oven if it is set at the lowest possible temperature. Turn the oven off occasionally so it cools some, and shift racks around. Temperature should be less than 110°F.

Some fruit and vegetables need to be blanched before they are dried, if you are going to store them for six months or more. The purpose is to destroy enzymes which might otherwise cause the fruit or vegetables to decay. See FREEZING.

Certain foods dry better when HUNG on a string. One example is green peppers which can be cut into circlets and strung up. "Leather britches" are green beans which have been strung up with a needle and thread, looking like a clothesline of britches when you are done. Herbs are best dried when bunches of leaves and stalks are hung upside down (so the flavor doesn't concentrate in the stems, but goes into the leaves). Apples can be sliced in circles and strung up through the hole where you removed the core.

Foods like honey, sugar, salt and vinegar have long been used as preservatives, since bacteria do not grow well in them. The **Dried Honeyed Fig**, **Dried Sweet Corn**, and **Fruit Glace** recipes included in this section can be used with other foods also.

Dried Honeyed Figs

10 pounds firm ripe figs
water
1/4 C salt
7 C honey

Soak figs in water 4 hours with salt. Wash and drain. Lay greenest on bottom of large pan, cover pan and simmer on lowest heat 1 hour or until figs are half covered in their own juice. Add honey and simmer until dissolved. Turn off heat, cool to lukewarm, bring back to simmer about 5 times, cooking in between. Cook at low temperature with a cover until translucent and skin is tender. Drain and put on 2 or 3 large pans (such as cookie sheets) and dry in oven set at lowest possible temperature. Dry until dry on outside (about 2-1/4 hours). The oven door should be left ajar. Do not leave too moist or they will mold later. Put in jars with lids.

Variations: Use other fruits. Bring to simmer only a couple of times.

Fruit Glace
(candied or glazed fruit)

1 C honey
1/2 C water
4 - 5 C fruit

Combine honey and water in a saucepan and bring to a boil. Add fruit and cook in syrup turning frequently until tender. Remove and drain.

The fruit may be cherries, pineapple chunks, orange and lemon peel, or apple chunks. Fruit is used in the same way as commercial candied fruit (example: in fruit cake).

Dried Sweet Corn

8 pints raw sweet corn, cut off cobs
6 T honey
4 t coarse salt
1/2 C sweet cream (optional, can be
   replaced with smaller amount of water)

Boil above ingredients in a heavy pan for 20 minutes, stirring constantly so that mixture doesn't stick. Take from heat and spread in shallow pans in an oven turned to its lowest possible temperature. Stir often. When corn is dry and rather crispy put it in clean brown paper sacks. Tightly close (to keep out bugs) and hang in the driest place in your house. When the corn is finished drying, it will rattle inside the sacks. Then it can be stored in glass jars with tight lids. It doesn't need to be presoaked and is good cooked in milk instead of water.

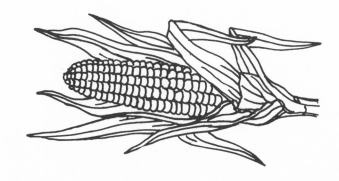

260

USING COMMERCIALLY CANNED FOODS

Canned food has less nutritional value than fresh food, of course, but still, for many of us, it has its place. Here are a few suggestions to help you use it more effectively. Retain the canning water for use in other dishes, as it contains many of the water soluble nutrients. Always clean off the tops of cans before opening to remove dust and perhaps poisonous sprays used in grocery stores and warehouses. Watch for metal slivers as you open can. Start cutting on one side of the seam down the side of the can and stop before you go over it on the other side. Be aware of the metallic flavor that food picks up when stored in already-opened cans. Often it is better to transfer the food to other containers if it has to be stored after the can is opened.

BIBLIOGRAPHY

CANNING AND PRESERVING

BALL BLUE BOOK, Ball Corporation, Dept. PK2A Box 2005, Muncie, Indiana 47302. About canning.

COMPLETE BOOK OF HOME STORAGE OF VEGETABLES AND FRUITS, Evelyn V. Loveday, Garden Way Publishing, Charlotte, Vermont 05445. 1972

FREEZiNG FOODS AT HOME. Circular 500, CA Agricultural Experimental Station, Extension Service, 2200 University, Berkeley, CA

HOME CANNING OF FRUITS. University of CA extension service address above. Publication HXT-32. Very good.

KERR HOME CANNING AND FREEZING BOOK. $1 from Kerr Glass Mfg. Corp., Consumer products division, Sand Springs, OK 74063.

MAKING JELLIES, JAMS AND PRESERVES, Univ. of CA extension, as listed above, HXT-91.

STOCKING UP, Edited by Carol Stoner, Rodale Press (Organic Gardening and Farming staff). $8.95. Doesn't use sugar, by far the best book we've run across. Includes information on meat.

STORING VEGETABLES AND FRUITS. U.S. Department of Agriculture. Write the Superintendent of Documents, U.S. Government Printing Office, Washington, D.C. 20402. $ .15.

NOTE: Many states publish information similar to the extension service pamphlets listed above.

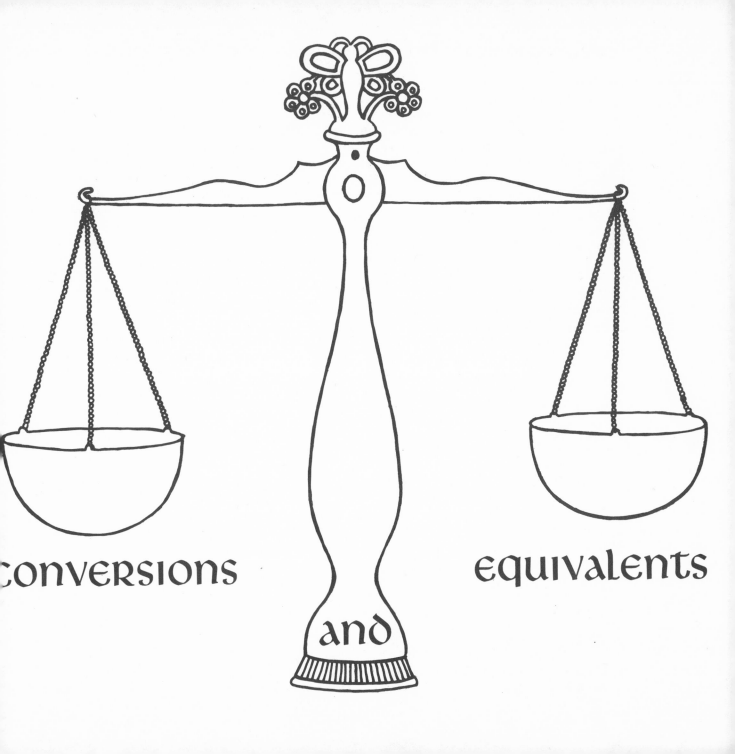

conversions and equivalents

People all around the world will be using this cookbook. Some of the people using these recipes will be in the habit of using cups, tablespoons and pounds. Others will be in the habit of weighing their ingredients in grams and measuring in liters. At one point in the development of this book, we considered listing measurements in both American customary measurements and in the System International (SI) or metric system. We encountered confusion in how to do this in such a way that Europeans would find the conversions easy to use for the weight measurements that they are used to, and Americans who switch from volume measurements in cups to metric liters could also use it. To list American volume measurements, liter measurements, and gram measurements took too much space. For this edition we have decided to include a conversion section, and omit individual listings. This section has been designed in such a way that you can remove the pages, mount them and hang them on your wall, or lay next to your cookbook as you work.

Included in this section are brief explanations of the American customary measurement systems and the System International, as they both relate to the recipes used in this book. Charts are included to make conversions quickly. Sections on temperature and pan size will help you in adjusting those to the SI system. Finally, a list of ingredients and their equivalents will help all readers to buy and measure ingredients easier.

American recipes are generally written in cups, tablespoons and teaspoons. These volume measurements are based on the space that a certain amount of a certain ingredient takes up. Weight does not matter in this system, only volume. If the volume of an item is not measureable, weight is sometimes used. A whole pumpkin might be listed by weight ("a five pound pumpkin") since it is to be cooked whole. In this case the weights are rarely expected to be exact since few American cooks own their own scales. Only when a certain ingredient comes in standard weight packages will an exact weight be expected (butter, for example, comes in 1/4 pound cubes or sticks). American recipes also use liquid measurements such as pints, quarts, and gallons. Equivalents for these are given below.

In American recipes:

1 tablespoon = (is equal to) 3 teaspoons
48 teaspoons = 16 tablespoons = 1 cup = 8 fluid ounces
16 cups = 4 quarts = 1 gallon
1 pound = 16 ounces

As you can see, the customary measurements used in American recipes are rather confusing since they involve a number of different measuring systems. The number of one unit which measures another unit varies from three teaspoons to make a tablespoon, to sixteen ounces to make a pound. The

System International involves a standardized system that makes all unit divisions at increments of 10. An example of this is:

1 KILOGRAM = 1,000 grams
1 hectogram = 100 grams
1 dekogram = 10 grams
1 gram = 1 gram
1 decigram = .1 gram
1 centigram = .01 gram
1 milligram = .001 gram

The metric system uses only two units of measure when working with recipe ingredients: grams measure weight and liters measure volume. Following is a chart that shows the SI units and their relationship to the measurements used in this book:

ABBREVIATIONS

t = teaspoon
T = tablespoon
C = cup
fl. oz. = fluid ounces
lb. = pound
oz. = ounces
ml = milliliter
g = grams

Volume Measurements:

Metric		American Customary
1 milliliter	=	1/5 of a teaspoon
5 ml	=	1 teaspoon
15 ml	=	1 tablespoon
34 ml	=	1 fluid ounce
100 ml	=	3.4 fl. oz. or .4 C
240 ml	=	1 C or 16 T or 8 fl. oz.
1 liter	=	34 fl. oz. or
		4.2 C or
		2.1 pints or
		1.06 quarts or
		.26 gallons
50 ml	=	1/5 C (approximately)
470 ml	=	1 pint (2 C)
.95 liter	=	1 quart (4 C)
3.8 liters	=	1 gallon (4 quarts)

Weight Measurements:

Metric		American Customary
1 gram	=	.035 oz.
100 grams	=	3.5 oz.
500 grams	=	1.10 pounds
1 kilogram (1000 grams)	=	2.205 pounds or 35 oz.
30 ml or 28 grams	=	1 fl. oz.
454 grams	=	1 pound

Food	American Volume (Cups)	American Weight*	S.I. Volume (Millileters)	S.I. Weight†
Agar, flakes	5/8 C	1 ounce	150	28 g
Agar, granulated	1/2 C	1 ounce	120	28 g
Alfalfa seed	2-1/4 C	1 pound	540	454 g
Almonds, raw	3-1/2 C	1	840	
Arrowroot powder	3 C	1	720	
Apricots, unsulfured	3-1/2	1	840	
Barley, whole	2-1/2	1	600	
Berries, fresh	3 - 4 C	1	720-960	
Brazil nuts	3	1	720	
Brown rice, whole	2-2/3		638	
Buckwheat groats	2-3/4		660	
Carob powder	5-1/2	1	1,279	
Cashews	3-1/2	1	840	
Cheese, grated	4	1	940	
Chestnuts, dry dry tree	3	1	720	
Corn flour	4-1/2	1	10810	
Corn meal	3	1	720	
Cottage cheese	2	1	480	
Coconut, dry shredded	5 - 6	1	1200 - 1440	
Date sugar	2-1/4 C	1	540	
Dates, pitted	2 - 2-1/2	1	480-600	
Dried fruit	2	1	480	
Figs, black	2-1/2	1	600	
Filberts	3-1/2	1	840	
Garbanzos	3	1	720	
Graham flour	4	1	940	
Honey	1-1/2	1	360	
Lentils	2-1/2	1	600	
Maple Syrup	2	1	480	

Food	American Volume (Cups)	American Weight*	S.I. Volume (Millileters)	S.I. Weight†
Milk, all kinds	2	1	480	
Millet, whole	2-1/2	1	600	
Molasses	1-1/2	1	360	
Mung beans	2-3/4	1	660	
Nut meats	1	5 oz.	240	142
Oat flour	4-1/2	1	1,080	
Oat meal	6	1	1,440	
Oat groats	2-3/4	1	660	
Oil (varies with type)	2-1/4	1	540	
Peaches, un-sulfured	3	1	720	
Peas, green split	2-1/4	1	540	
Peanuts	3	1	720	
Pecans	4	1	960	
Pinenuts	4	1	960	
Popcorn	2-1/3	1	559	
Prunes, whole	2-1/2	1	650	
Raisins	2-3/4	1	720	
Raw sugar	2-1/4	1	540	
Rice polish	2	1	480	
Rye flakes	5	1	1,200	
Rye flour	6	1	1,440	
Salt	1-1/2	1	360	
Sesame salt	3	1	720	
Soy beans, dry	2-1/2	1	600	
Soy, 1 pound, cooked	6-1/2	2-1/4	1,560	1,021.5
Soy flour or milk powder	4	1	940	
Sunflower seeds	4	1	960	
Unbleached white flour	4	1	940	
Walnuts	4	1	960	
Wheat flakes	4-1/2	1	1,080	
Wheat germ	4	1	960	
Wheat groats	2-1/2	1	600	
Whole Wheat flour	3-1/4	1	840	

* in pounds unless otherwise noted

† these are all 454 grams unless otherwise noted.

Pan Size

Sometimes we have indicated certain pan sizes that a recipe size and its cooking time is based on. You can choose a pan close to this size if you know that:

1 inch = about 2.5 centimeters

This means an 8-inch round pan would have a diameter of about 20 centimeters. A nine-inch square pan would measure about 22.5 centimeters on each side. Other sizes shouldn't be hard to figure out. Multiply the number of inches we give by 2.5 cm and you will have the same size in centimeters.

Temperature

Temperature is another measurement that varies around the world. The two most commo common scales of temperature used in cooking are the Fahrenheit (F) scale and the Celsius (C) scale (formerly referred to as Centigrade). In the Fahrenheit scale water freezes at 32° and boils at 212°. In the Celsius system water freezes at 0° and boils at 100°. To convert from °F to °C this equation is helpful:

$$°C = \frac{5 \times (°F - 32)}{9}$$

To convert °F to °C, substract 32 from the Fahrenheit temperature (°F), multiply the difference by 5 and divide the product by 9. The result is the Celsius temperature (°C).

3-1/2 pounds ALMONDS in shell = 1 pound, shelled

1 pound unpared APPLES = 3 cups pared
and sliced apples

5-1/2 pounds fresh APRICOTS = one pound dried

3 cups DRIED APRICOTS = one pound

2 t ARROWROOT = 1 T CORNSTARCH
or 4 t flour

1 t BAKING POWDER = 1/4 t BAKING SODA
plus 5/8 t cream of tarter

3 - 4 medium sized BANANAS = 1 pound or
1-3/4 C mashed

1 stick BUTTER = 1/4 pound = 4 ounces = 1/2 C

1 C BUTTERMILK = 1 C YOGURT

3 T CAROB POWDER plus 3 T liquid
1 ounce CHOCOLATE

HERBS - see the HERBS AND SPICES section

1 C HONEY = 1-1/4 C SUGAR plus 1/4 C liquid

The juice of 1 LEMON = about 3 T

The grated peel of one LEMON = 1 t

1 pound fresh RHUBARB = 2 C cooked

1 pound (6 cups) raw ROLLED OATS = 8 C cooked

1 C SUGAR = 1 C HONEY with 1/4 C less
liquid in recipe

2 C TOMATO SAUCE = 3/4 C TOMATO PASTE
plus 1 C water

1 pound WALNUTS in the shell - 1-1/2 C shelled

1 cake compressed YEAST can be used to
replace 1 T (or package) dry yeast

1 pound or 2-1/4 C LENTILS = 5 C cooked

1/2 C MAPLE SUGAR = 1 C MAPLE SYRUP

1 C whole MILK = 1/2 C evaporated plus 1/2 C water
= 1 C **Nut Milk** = 1 C other liquid when
called for in baking

SOUR MILK can be made quickly by adding
1 T lemon juice or vinegar to 1 C milk

1 large GREEN PEPPER (about 6 ounces) =
1 C diced

3 medium size POTATOES (about 1 pound) =
2-1/4 C cooked or 1-2/3 C mashed potatoes

index